D0777366

PATHWAYS TO PEACE

PATHWAYS TO PEACE

America and the Arab-Israeli Conflict

Daniel C. Kurtzer

Editor

palgrave
macmillan

PATHWAYS TO PEACE
Copyright © Daniel C. Kurtzer, 2012.

First published in 2012 by
PALGRAVE MACMILLAN®
in the United States—a division of St. Martin's Press LLC,
175 Fifth Avenue, New York, NY 10010.

Where this book is distributed in the UK, Europe and the rest of the world,
this is by Palgrave Macmillan, a division of Macmillan Publishers Limited,
registered in England, company number 785998, of Houndmills,
Basingstoke, Hampshire RG21 6XS.

Palgrave Macmillan is the global academic imprint of the above companies
and has companies and representatives throughout the world.

Palgrave® and Macmillan® are registered trademarks in the United States,
the United Kingdom, Europe and other countries.

ISBN: 978–1–137–30479–7

Library of Congress Cataloging-in-Publication Data is available from the
Library of Congress.

A catalogue record of the book is available from the British Library.

Design by Newgen Imaging Systems (P) Ltd., Chennai, India.

First edition: November 2012

10 9 8 7 6 5 4 3 2 1

Printed in the United States of America.

CONTENTS

FOREWORD

James A. Baker III and Samuel Berger

We served in two different governmental positions—secretary of state and national security advisor. We served two different presidents—George H. W. Bush and Bill Clinton. One of us is a Republican; the other is a Democrat. We have, on occasion, found ourselves on opposite sides in political campaigns and policy debates.

But we share two bedrock convictions. First, US engagement in the international arena is critical if our nation is to protect its interests and promote its values. Second, American leadership is nowhere more critical than in the Arab-Israeli dispute.

We both have scars to show from our involvement in advancing Middle East peace. There is perhaps no more intractable, yet vital, issue in US foreign policy—one made all the more daunting by its political contentiousness here at home. But however strong the temptation may be, we simply cannot walk away from our traditional leadership role in the region.

Every American administration since 1967 has faced a crisis associated with the Arab-Israeli conflict. These crises, in most cases involving terrorism or the outbreak of war, have required the investment of significant time and political capital by the United States. They have pushed other American priorities to the back burner and have resulted in substantial casualties and destruction on all sides. The conflict itself has persisted and worsened.

Significantly, every administration has also been given opportunities to advance the prospects of peace and reconciliation. Sometimes the wars or the violence have catalyzed American diplomacy; at other times, the United States has created an opportunity through creative diplomacy. Not all administrations have been successful in their peace efforts, but persistent efforts by the United States have helped the parties take some important steps in the right direction. With American help, Israelis and Arabs have negotiated and implemented two peace treaties, an Israeli-Syrian disengagement agreement that has lasted for almost forty years, a peace conference that changed forty years of Arab unwillingness to acknowledge Israel's right to exist and that launched bilateral and multilateral negotiations, and several agreements as part of the Oslo Accords. United States efforts have helped the parties negotiate to a point where the shape and content of a final settlement can be envisaged and are no longer a mystery.

There should be no illusions. Progress may be more difficult now than ever. Trust between the parties has eroded. While most Israelis and Palestinians agree on the general outline of a final agreement, few think it is possible. Extremists on both sides are being empowered and emboldened, creating their own cycle of violence and terror.

The calculations of the parties have changed. For the Israelis, risk taking has been compounded by the uncertainties and upheavals around them. Israel's traditional peace partners are either gone, like Egypt's Hosni Mubarak, or under greater pressure, like Jordan's King Abdullah. The rise of the Islamists and the Muslim Brotherhood in Egypt will only increase the pressure on Israel. Syria is not only imploding; it is on the verge of exploding into the region. Arab politics have also become more complicated for Palestinians. With public opinion and Islamists playing a larger role, there is no guarantee that other Arabs will support the concessions that President Mahmoud Abbas and Fatah will have to make to reach a negotiated settlement with Israel. And Egypt under President Mohamed Morsi may be inclined to support Hamas in a way it never would have under Mubarak.

Moreover, the internal politics on both sides of the conflict are challenging. Israel's concern over the deteriorating regional security situation, not only on its immediate border but, even more seriously, from Iran, is understandable. It is our firm view that Israel would have a stronger hand in any confrontation with Iran if it took the Palestinian issue off the table. Palestinians, too, will be constrained by the absence of one gun, one authority, and one negotiating position due to the differences between Fatah and Hamas. Indeed, the greatest obstacle to a serious negotiating process on the Palestinian side is that division which exists within the Palestinian national movement.

The next US administration's inclination and ability to try to create an opportunity for peacemaking is further hampered by the extraordinary array of other American priorities that cry out for attention—reigniting the American economy, still the world's powerhouse; addressing the debt crisis that threatens our future prosperity; and upgrading our physical and human capital in ways that will ensure our competitiveness in an increasingly global marketplace. The foreign policy agenda for the next four years will be no less daunting. It will include stabilizing relations with emerging powers in Asia, especially China, while adjusting traditional alliance structures to meet challenges that are quite different from those that prompted their creation; strengthening international efforts against terrorism and proliferation of weapons of mass destruction; and negotiating a broad array of bilateral and regional trade agreements.

Against these domestic and international backdrops, is it reasonable or wise for the next administration to try to create an opportunity for Arab-Israeli peace? Our considered answer and advice is "Yes."

None of these challenges means that Israeli-Palestinian peace is less important now. Indeed, it is more important. Unresolved, it is a catalyst for radicalism across the Arab world at a time when its heart and soul are in play. It strengthens the hand of Iran in its confrontation with Israel and the West. The Palestinian territories are not immune from the currents of dissatisfaction roiling the Arab world. And the demographic clock that erodes the chance for a two-state solution will not stop and wait for the region to sort itself out.

The administration in office after the November 2012 election can be certain to face the prospect of renewed crisis in the Israeli-Palestinian arena at some point during the next four years. The uneasy calm on the surface today masks roiling waters underneath, born of the frustrations created by the occupation and the Israeli settlement enterprise on one side and unending rocket fire on Israel from radical groups in Gaza on the other.

Not only is this conflict not self-correcting, but the political space and substantive basis on which to build an agreement are shrinking. The window for negotiating a just and enduring two-state solution is rapidly closing. At what point will the growth of Israeli settlements foreclose the possibility of creating a viable and contiguous Palestinian state? At what point will Palestinian terrorism and rocket assaults persuade the people of Israel to give up on a negotiated peace with their neighbors? At what point will both populations tire of the rhetoric that promises a two-state solution while they endure a reality that seems to lead only to despair? At what point will the word "peace" become a relic of an earlier time, as the center of gravity on both sides moves toward a de facto "one-state" solution—a winner-take-all outcome that can only be decided by a constant resorting to power and force?

Clearly, it is not within the power of the United States to impose peace between Israelis and Palestinians. If it were, there would have been a comprehensive agreement years, if not decades, ago. But there is, just as clearly, no alternative to a leadership role for the United States in peace talks. No other country or group of countries possesses our long and deep involvement in every facet of the dispute. No one else can aspire to gain the confidence of both parties. No one else can mobilize the international community in support of any future settlement. In other words, if the United States disengages from peace talks, there will be no one to take our place. The Arab-Israeli conflict will not fix itself, and the current leadership in the region appears unprepared to take risks for peace. Hoping for calm and stability is no substitute for sound policy. Nor is waiting until the time is ripe for a comprehensive settlement. Timing is, of course, critically important in terms of moving peace talks forward. But waiting for the perfect moment will likely mean waiting forever. In the meantime, settlements will grow no matter which Israeli party is in power; groups even more radical than Hamas will find traction among Palestinians; and mistrust will grow among the most moderate on both sides.

In short, the Arab-Israeli conflict will not take a vacation during the next four years. Whether the United States plans for it or not, this conflict will end up diverting the president's attention and absorbing more energy in crisis stabilization than what might have been needed for crisis aversion. We are not prophets of doom and gloom. We are simply looking at realities that have confronted every administration that has tried to wish away its involvement in Arab-Israeli peacemaking.

There is an alternative, and it will require the kind of determined leadership, diplomatic strength, and bipartisan solidarity that our country has shown itself capable of producing in the past. Our two great political parties differ far less on Arab-Israeli issues than political campaigns would have us believe. We are a people united when it comes to supporting Israel, preserving Israel's ability to secure itself, and expanding Israel's economic well-being and diplomatic recognition. We are of one mind in support of a peaceful settlement that is just, fair, and secure—a settlement that will result in a state of Palestine and the State of Israel living side by side in peace and security. We are united in a determination to condemn and to try to end the terrorism and the hateful incitement that perpetuate this conflict. And we are one in understanding that occupation is a dead-end street.

Agreeing as Americans do on these essential principles, it is imperative that our elected representatives—Democrats and Republicans—provide bipartisan support to the president as he develops a strong, creative, comprehensive peace strategy and begins on the arduous but necessary path to peace. This volume of essays by some of the smartest and most experienced American, Israeli, Palestinian, and Jordanian diplomats offers a vibrant and creative menu of options and ideas for our leadership to absorb and choose from. We know the authors, for many of them worked for us during our own tenure in government, or with us as they represented their respective governments. Do we agree with all of their analysis and every element of their proposals? Of course not. But we know them to be individuals of goodwill, whose commitment to Arab-Israeli peace is unimpeachable. And we believe it critical that policy makers listen carefully to their advice.

Our own advice can be laid out succinctly: To serve our most important national strategic interests, our president should make a concerted and sustained effort to advance the prospects of Arab-Israeli peace. To help him do so, Congress and the American people should be united and speak with one bipartisan voice of support. Helping Israel and the Palestinians achieve peace will respond to our highest moral values and principles as a people, and to our most significant and urgent national interests.

INTRODUCTION

Daniel C. Kurtzer

"The era of procrastination, of half-measures, of soothing and baffling expedients, of delays, is coming to its close. In its place we are entering a period of consequences." —Winston Churchill, "The Locust Years," speech in the House of Commons, November 12, 1936

Middle East upheavals are challenging long-held assumptions about politics and governance. Authoritarianism is on the defensive as forces of change—potentially democratic change—assert themselves in ways unimaginable just a few years ago. These upheavals have created a Churchillian moment, when the half-measures, short-sighted expedients, and delays of the past can no longer sustain an untenable status quo. This is as true in the Arab-Israeli peace process as it is being proved true in the politics of the Arab uprisings.

The United States can make a difference in advancing the prospects for Israeli-Palestinian peace. The issues in dispute between Israel and the Palestinians are well-known, thoroughly debated, and resolvable. Mutually reinforcing decisions by Israeli and Palestinian leaders can bring about solutions that meet the essential political, national, and even religious requirements of both peoples. Intense, smart, determined, creative, and sustained American leadership can help these leaders make the right decisions. The attainment of peace between Israelis and Palestinians will serve important American national security interests.

No one is oblivious to the skepticism, cynicism, and real problems standing in the way of progress toward peace. Indeed, a dispassionate assessment of the readiness of the parties and the region for a serious peace effort would conclude that the chances of actually making peace, or even making serious progress toward peace, are minimal at best under present circumstances. The regional situation is also more complicated, with massive change under way in Arab countries and the ongoing threat posed by Iran's nuclear weapons ambitions. These issues cannot be ignored, and they are surely related in regional leaders' minds to the question of moving ahead in the peace process.

The argument for US diplomatic activity does not rest, however, on naïve optimism or assurance of success, but rather on a realistic assessment of the consequences of continuing in the same mode as before: the two-state solution is losing ground fast; the status quo in the West Bank is deceptively calm, not stable; and progress on the Palestinian issue could actually help stabilize Israel's relations with its neighbors and help the region focus better on Iran. In this larger context, the United States needs a sound, durable policy that represents something more than a desire to return to negotiations.

There is no shortage of analyses or prescriptions for dealing with the conflict; peace plans fill the shelves of libraries. Around the time of every American presidential election, a plethora of books, monographs, and articles appears assessing whether the time is right to get involved in the peace process. This is not one of those standard Washington products.

This volume brings together smart, experienced experts who analyze the options and elements and lay out the essential building blocks and ingredients for helping the president think through a serious, active, energetic, integrated, and sustained policy to end the Palestinian-Israeli conflict. These essays will help the president, the Congress, and the American public to understand what's at stake. Whether this is the last chance for Israeli-Palestinian peace is an arguable proposition. But there is no doubt that time is not an ally if the goal is a durable and equitable solution.

The authors in this volume are concerned that the prospects for a two-state solution are diminishing, and they understand the urgency of achieving that outcome. They do not necessarily agree on a strategy, and there are several alternative perspectives and approaches laid out in these chapters. The book focuses on what to do and why, the consequences of inaction or weak policy, and the risks of action as well. This volume does not presume to deliver a full-blown American initiative, but rather a menu of critical issues, analyses, and recommendations for US policy. The contributors speak for their own views.

William Quandt assesses the implications for American policy of the dynamic, dramatic changes under way in the Middle East and concludes that progress in the peace process will advance American interests substantially. Quandt confronts opponents of the "linkage" argument—who argue in favor of delinking US policy in the peace process from other pressing issues in the region—with the reality that Arab populations perceive and American officials should understand the intimate connection between what the United States does or fails to do in the peace process and how successfully America can pursue its other regional interests.

Marwan Muasher reminds us that the Arab states have lent their support to peacemaking in the Arab Peace Initiative, and advocates means for bringing the Arabs more directly into the peace process. Such involvement would provide a critical safety net and stimulus for Palestinians, and it would help persuade the Israeli public that peace will yield tangible benefits including Arab recognition. This requires, however, active and timely US involvement from the day the next American president is elected. Muasher suggests one possible scenario for how this can be achieved and how to operationalize the Arab Peace Initiative before it is too late.

Avi Gil looks at the changes in the region through the prism of Israeli interests and politics, and he weighs the arguments in favor of hunkering down or of being proactive while the region is in flux. Gil concludes that a proactive Israeli policy will help cement Israeli relations with Egypt and Jordan, Israel's traditional partners in the region, and will also help to invigorate the reality and perception of American power and influence.

Samih Al-Abid and Samir Hileleh answer critical questions often raised regarding Palestinian participation in peace negotiations: Is there a Palestinian partner for peace, and can the Palestinians reach and implement an agreement with Israel? They answer these questions with a categorical "Yes," and at the same time ask Israel to turn a mirror on itself and ask itself the same questions. The authors acknowledge the reality that Palestinians have the most to gain from peace and the most to lose from the absence of an agreement.

Yossi Alpher and Ghassan Khatib, in separate chapters, analyze how Israelis and Palestinians look at the American role in peacemaking. After forty years of American involvement, the parties continue to pay lip service to the idea of the indispensability of the American role; these essays explain what they mean and don't mean in saying this, and suggest ways to move forward.

Gershom Gorenberg analyzes the spectrum of Israeli public opinion on peacemaking, particularly the ambivalent center and the settlement-based Right. To produce Israeli political support for a new peace initiative, he writes, the US administration must not only negotiate with the Israeli government but also interact with the public. The growth and radicalization of the Israeli Right is not a reason to postpone Israeli-Palestinian negotiations, but rather to regard them as urgent.

Robert Malley assesses the politics in Palestine, with special emphasis on the potential political problems that may ensue if the peace process gets relaunched. He assesses the interests and activities of opponents of peace and the degree to which the Palestinian Authority, as well as the United States, can deal with those who have not been part of the peace process or are likely to oppose it.

Aaron David Miller identifies ten core elements relating to both the process and the substance of peacemaking that are likely to determine the success or failure of any American initiative. That an American president is committed to serious peacemaking and that an agreement is in the American interest are necessary but not sufficient for success. Many of these elements must be in place too.

Robert Danin analyzes the "bottom-up" approach to peacemaking, focusing on Palestinian state-building and institution-building. Danin suggests that rather than concentrate exclusively on negotiations, future American peacemaking must integrate "top-down" diplomacy with "bottom-up" support to develop and enhance the economic, security, and governing institutions of a Palestinian state. He notes the integral, mutually reinforcing connection between ground-up and top-down approaches to the peace process—one cannot succeed without the other.

P. J. Dermer and Steven White tackle the all-important and complex security conundrum. Drawing in part on their own work in the field, they assess the spectrum of security requirements of both sides and how the United States can help shape outcomes that satisfy the interests of all parties. They argue that American leadership is essential to foster the necessary security conditions for advancement on the political front.

Daniel Kurtzer argues for the United States to act strategically and boldly and to develop a comprehensive policy and smart, flexible tactics. He urges the president and the American people to ignore the naysayers, the procrastinators, the purveyors of half-measures, and the ideologically motivated. Act now as the United States has done in the past when vital interests were at stake: confidently, creatively, and persistently, even in the face of obstacles abroad or at home. Kurtzer lays out the arguments for and the content of a comprehensive US policy and suggests a way to activate it. A draft set of substantive parameters that can act as terms of reference for negotiations is found in the appendix.

Numerous arguments will be mounted against the policy recommendations in this volume—that now is neither the right time for a US initiative nor the right time to expect the parties to take risks for peace; that the peace process is too hard and promises too little gain; that the United States cannot want peace more than the parties; that leadership in the region is weak or beset by internal political problems that tie their hands; that the narratives of the parties are too far apart; that constituent politics in both Israel and Palestine militate against the possibility of compromise; that politics in the United States are too partisan; and that there are higher priorities for the administration to pursue. None of the authors in this volume subscribe to the notion of American defeatism that underlies some of these arguments—nor to the equally invalid notion of American triumphalism. There is also no support for lame excuses for inaction. The United States can continue to lead and others will follow—abroad and at home. This volume lays out a menu of considerations involved in formulating a serious, comprehensive, and sustainable American approach.

The authors are also mindful of the complex and overloaded agenda that the United States faces at home and abroad. But continued inaction on the peace process promises to damage American interests, while the possibility of success can be transformative. After forty years of American support for an Israeli-Palestinian peace agreement, it is time to try for success.

I

THE REGIONAL DIMENSION

1

ISRAELI-PALESTINIAN PEACE PROSPECTS IN REGIONAL CONTEXT

William B. Quandt

Like a massive earthquake followed by many aftershocks, the Arab Spring has weakened the foundations of the old order in the Middle East and has raised many questions about the future. From the perspective of the United States, the old order, with its many flaws and fault lines, had the advantage of a certain degree of predictability and stability. That is now largely gone, and the new circumstances will require policy makers in Washington to assess national interests in this strategically important region with a degree of seriousness that is generally absent in public discourse. Central to any such reassessment should be an effort to figure out where the Israeli-Palestinian conflict and its resolution figure in the new calculus of national interest.

While many in American policy circles, including recent presidents, have treated the Israeli-Palestinian conflict as politically toxic, and probably beyond the reach of diplomacy in any case, it is striking that two recent commanders of CENTCOM (US Central Command), the military command that includes the sensitive Persian Gulf region, have stated that Israeli-Palestinian peace would significantly serve US strategic interests. In prepared testimony before the Senate Armed Services Committee, General David Petraeus stated on March 16, 2010, that

> The enduring hostilities between Israel and some of its neighbors present distinct challenges to our ability to advance our interests in the AOR [Area of Responsibility]. Israeli-Palestinian tensions often flare into violence and large-scale armed confrontations. The conflict foments anti-American sentiment, due to a perception of U.S. favoritism for Israel. Arab anger over the Palestinian question limits the strength and depth of U.S. partnerships with governments and peoples in the AOR and weakens the legitimacy of moderate regimes in the Arab world. Meanwhile, al-Qaeda and other militant groups exploit that anger to mobilize support. The conflict also gives Iran influence in the Arab world through its clients, Lebanese Hezbollah and Hamas.[1]

A year later, his successor, General James Mattis, stated before the same committee:

> Lack of progress toward a comprehensive Middle East peace affects U.S. and CENTCOM security interests in the region. I believe the only reliable path to lasting peace in this region is a viable two-state solution between Israel and Palestine. This issue is one of many that is exploited by our adversaries in the region, and it is used as a recruiting tool for extremist groups. The lack of progress also creates friction with regional partners and creates political challenges for advancing our interests by marginalizing moderate voices in the region. By contrast, substantive progress on the peace process would improve CENTCOM's opportunity to work with our regional partners and to support multilateral security efforts.[2]

The occupant of the White House in January 2013 should weigh seriously the views of these senior military officers. Their perception of a close "linkage" between regional trends and the Israeli-Palestinian conflict is certainly correct, albeit controversial in some circles. The question in the aftermath of the Arab Spring is not whether we would be better off if Israeli-Palestinian peace could be achieved. We would be. But is such a peace still possible, or has it been made even more unlikely because of the upheavals of recent years?

This chapter will argue that Israeli-Palestinian peace is more central than ever to a coherent and effective American strategy in the region; it has been and remains a difficult but not impossible challenge for American diplomacy, and success in the future will require a much more clear-sighted and determined effort than the incrementalist and tentative approaches of the past.

No president in recent memory has been able to ignore the continuing conflict between Israelis and Palestinians. After previous "earthquakes," such as the October 1973 Yom Kippur War, the Iranian revolution of 1979, and Saddam Hussein's invasion of Kuwait in 1990, American presidents embarked on energetic, and partially successful, peacemaking efforts as part of a strategy to shape the post-earthquake terrain in ways that would advance American interests. The Egyptian-Israeli peace treaty of 1979 and the Madrid Conference of late 1991 stand as impressive testimony to what American leadership in the peace process has been able to achieve in the past.

Is there an analogue for the Arab Spring upheavals that could persuade the president and his foreign policy team to try again in 2013? This chapter will argue that important American interests are affected by the ongoing tensions and that in the absence of a negotiated peace agreement, we are likely to witness some form of violence that will have dangerous consequences for the region and for the United States. Therefore, a renewed effort at Israeli-Palestinian peace should be attempted. Before settling on this conclusion, however, it is important to assess the various dimensions of the changes in the Middle East in recent years to judge their impact on the realities surrounding the Arab-Israeli conflict.

RECENT WARNING SIGNS—AND SOME LESSONS

In the past dozen years, we have seen the outbreak of the Second Intifada in 2000, the Israeli-Hezbollah War in 2006, Hamas's rocket barrages and the Israeli offensive against Hamas in Gaza from late 2008 to early 2009, and the *Mavi Marmara* incident in May 2010. The last of these disrupted Turkish-Israeli relations and put the United States in an awkward position as its two closest partners in the Middle East clashed over the rights and wrongs of Israel's blockade of Gaza. To prevent more such dangerous clashes, a serious Israeli-Palestinian peace effort is needed. But there is also a strong case to be made that the chances for a successful negotiation are very limited.

It will soon be twenty years since the seemingly hopeful breakthrough of the Oslo Accords. With the advantage of hindsight, we can see the flaws in the Oslo design, and it is probably fair to conclude that the chance of transforming Oslo into a platform for peace began to diminish rapidly after the assassination of Yitzhak Rabin in November 1995. True, there were flickers of hope in later years—Clinton at Camp David II with his parameters outlining the terms of a settlement in 2000, and the seemingly promising talks between Ehud Olmert and Mahmoud Abbas late in 2008. But the simple truth is that despite many diplomatic initiatives aimed at finding a basis for Israeli-Palestinian peace, the parties are essentially stuck where they were in the mid-1990s, albeit confronting much more tangled demographic realities in East Jerusalem and the West Bank.

American presidents have tried, some more energetically than others, to break the deadlock, but the basic facts of the conflict remain: Israel continues to occupy most of the territory taken from Jordan in 1967; some half-million Israeli Jewish citizens, with encouragement from their government, have moved into that area and established themselves in sizable towns such as Maale Adumim and Ariel, the Gush Etzion bloc, and many smaller settlements; Palestinian refugees from the 1948 conflict and their descendents continue to live in precarious circumstances and help keep alive a keen sense of injustice among Palestinians and many other Arabs and Muslims; Israel surrounds much of Gaza, although it has withdrawn its military and civilian presence there; and many Israelis still feel that Palestinians will never accept the legitimacy of a Jewish state in any part of Palestine and that concessions of territory or on refugee claims will never be enough to win peace and recognition.

So, looking at these bleak facts on the ground, why should an American president decide to pay much attention to this apparently intractable regional conflict? The answer, in broad outline, is fairly obvious. Peace between Israel and Palestine, as noted by the generals cited above, would be good for US interests in the Middle East. This is not to say it would be a panacea, but it would certainly be a plus. It would reduce risks of violence, strengthen moderate forces in the region, isolate extremists, and make life for most Israelis and Palestinians much better than the alternative of continued occupation and hostility. In fact, very few analysts make the case that US interests would not be well served by Israeli-Palestinian peace. The debate is about its feasibility, not its desirability.

Skeptics will say that Israeli-Palestinian peace is no longer within reach, if it ever was, and that it is, in any event, not as central as was once believed to the broad developments in the Middle East region. One can argue endlessly—and probably pointlessly—about how much benefit would flow and to whom it would flow from a successfully negotiated Israeli-Palestinian peace, but it is hard to make the case that there is a big risk in trying. True, failure of any US diplomatic initiative may entail some reputational costs. But the same is true of doing nothing.

So, if the case for the benefits of Israeli-Palestinian peace seems strong, what about its feasibility? Isn't it too late for the two-state solution? Perhaps, but it has never really been given a serious chance. The Clinton efforts in 2000 were too little and too late. The Israeli and Palestinian leaders were embattled and spent too much time looking over their shoulders at domestic opponents, and the US role was conducted by a core group that was wedded to an incrementalist approach to diplomacy that had little chance of closing the deal. President George W. Bush never made much of an effort because of his conviction that it would be better to turn attention to other matters such as Iraq and the war on terrorism. President Barack Obama launched his presidency with the intention of advancing the peace process but largely abandoned the effort after several years of failed tactics because he realized that the domestic political costs of trying to push hard for Israeli-Palestinian peace were becoming too great.

It is, however, not true that the Israeli-Palestinian conflict is uniquely complex, too difficult to resolve, or too rooted in ancient animosities or religious zealotry. In fact, the general outlines of a two-state solution that might be acceptable to majorities of Israelis and Palestinians are pretty familiar.

What has been missing is courageous leadership—in Israel, Palestine, and the United States.

Left to their own devices, Israelis and Palestinians are very unlikely to close the deal. The power imbalance is so great between the two parties that there is little chance of a "normal" give-and-take style of negotiation. It is often said that confidence-building steps must be taken to create the needed atmosphere of trust, but this has been the mantra of negotiators for the past thirty years, and there is less trust now than there was previously. In the absence of trust and some degree of parity between the parties, a strong mediator, or mediators, will be needed.

The United States, despite its privileged relationship with Israel, is seen by many Arabs as an important party precisely because Washington has the potential to both pressure and reassure Israel in a way that no other power can. But there are other possible mediators who can also help, including Europeans, the UN, key Arab and Muslim states, and even Russia and China. At a minimum, all of these players could be counted on to support a serious diplomatic effort, as occurred with the Madrid initiative in 1991, to solve a conflict that most of them believe has gone on for far too long. A strong group of mediators, with a supportive international climate, could help the parties with the problems of closure and commitment that have bedeviled previous negotiating efforts, and they could also make concrete contributions to security and to a fair resolution of refugee claims.

COULD 2013 BE THE YEAR?

The United States has an interest in Israeli-Palestinian peace that is important enough to warrant another try at negotiations. At the same time, it is imperative to avoid the dead-end approaches of the recent past and to carefully assess the new strategic environment for peacemaking. The upheavals of recent years in the Middle East have made Israeli-Palestinian peace even more important for the protection of American national interests, and it is not intuitively obvious that it is any less feasible. We need to look carefully at a number of cross-cutting currents in the area. The period of 2013–2014 could be a time for a resumption of serious peace diplomacy.

What makes the coming years propitious ones for peacemaking? After all, much conventional wisdom in Washington seems to argue precisely the opposite. But conventional wisdom is often wrong. First, we have considerable empirical evidence that the Palestine issue remains a key concern for many Arabs and Muslims, and the Arab Spring has made leaders even more sensitive than before to populist currents in their countries. Second, public opinion among Israelis and Palestinians is skeptical about peace, but not hostile in principle to the idea of a negotiated settlement. Third, most Americans, if not necessarily the most vocal, would support an engaged and fair-minded US-led effort to push for Israeli-Palestinian peace (and even for a more comprehensive Arab-Israeli peace if Syria emerges from its present trauma with a government that is willing to negotiate with Israel).

It is true that the Middle East landscape has changed significantly since the last promising foray into Israeli-Palestinian and Israeli-Syrian negotiations in 2008. Let us look at how some of those changes might affect a prospective peace effort.

THE ARAB SPRING: EGYPT

What effect might the dramatic changes in Egypt since January 2011 have on Israeli-Palestinian peace prospects? Many observers seem to believe that Hosni Mubarak's downfall represents not only a reduced chance for expanding the circle of peace around Israel, but might even call into question the centerpiece of the peace process, the Egyptian-Israeli treaty. While Egypt's future is impossible to forecast with great confidence, several points should be kept in mind:

1. Egypt's military establishment and civilian president have indicated that Egypt has no intention of tearing up the peace treaty with Israel.
2. While Egypt is showing growing signs of support for Hamas, it is still dealing with the leader of the PLO as the primary spokesman for the Palestinians. President Mohamed Morsi has met with the leaders of both Fatah and Hamas and seems to support the project of bringing the two parties closer together.
3. The Egyptians are easing some of the restrictions on movement in and out of Gaza, which will give them considerable influence with

Hamas, unlike the Mubarak regime, which sought to isolate Gaza and undermine the Islamist movement. Now that Hamas does not enjoy Syrian patronage, growing Egyptian influence could have a moderating influence on the militant wing of the Palestinian movement.

4. US-Egyptian relations remain normal, and Secretary of State Hillary Clinton has met with the new Islamist president and with the military leaders of the country. For the moment, the substantial military aid relationship remains intact.

In short, there is no reason to conclude that Egypt's role vis-à-vis Israeli-Palestinian peace is likely to change for the worse. In fact, one might argue that Egypt's support for reconciliation between Fatah and Hamas could be a positive development, and Hamas's growing relationship with Egypt could reinforce trends toward pragmatism that have been apparent for some time. Egypt, like Turkey, wants to see a resolution of the conflict between Palestinians and Israelis and believes that bringing Hamas into the process, or at least blunting its opposition to peace talks, is an essential step. While this is not a popular idea in Washington, it has considerable merit and should not be rejected out of hand. On balance, changes in Egypt do not seem to make future peace efforts less promising and might even be advantageous.

THE ARAB SPRING: SYRIA

The impact of developments in Syria on Israeli-Palestinian peace prospects is extremely hard to assess, in large part because the range of possible outcomes of the Syrian crisis is so wide. While the regime of Bashar al-Asad is certainly under unprecedented pressure from both within and without, it could still hold out in some form for a considerable period of time. It does seem unlikely, however, that Asad will reassert his authority over the country, that calm will return any time soon, and that Syria will go on much as before.

A change of regime in Syria would raise a host of questions. Who among the many contending factions would be able to consolidate power? Most speculation assumes that power would flow toward a Sunni-led coalition that would include a significant role for Islamists of various stripes. There is no reason to expect that such a government would subscribe to positions on Arab-Israeli issues that would be much different from those of the Asad regime. In short, any new regime will want to recover the Golan Heights from Israel and will offer at least verbal support to the Palestinian cause, although Damascus will most likely be less inclined to support Hamas, which was patronized for so long by the Asad regime, and will be more favorable to the mainstream PLO.

A new regime, probably supported by the Saudis and Qatar, would not necessarily be particularly pro-American, but it would be less aligned with Iran and would not support Hezbollah, a long-standing Asad ally, in Lebanon. This could, in time, mean that Syria might resemble Turkey and Egypt in reflecting a moderate Sunni political outlook that would resist Iran's regional influence while trying to promote a peaceful resolution of the Arab-Israeli conflict. The rather optimistic scenario of a soft transition to a Sunni-majority regime would not seem to radically change the odds of, or the need for, Israeli-Palestinian peace.

A more pessimistic future for Syria is, of course, possible to imagine and is perhaps more likely. A prolonged civil war, accompanied by external intervention, is an outcome that could call into question many aspects of Middle East politics. Iraqi politics could be affected by the growth of Sunni militancy, including Al-Qaeda, in Syria. Israel has mused about the possible need for its own military intervention in the event of regime collapse and the prospect of chemical weapons falling into the hands of radical groups. Some Americans imagine that the United States should actively intervene to protect safe havens or to establish no-fly zones. In short, Syria could become, for a period of time, a focal point for a very deep regional crisis with wide ramifications. Were this to happen, the chances of reviving Israeli-Palestinian peace talks would be much more complicated.

One final note is needed regarding Syria and its own peace talks with Israel. On several occasions—in 2000, in 2008, and again in 2011, just before the onset of Syria's domestic crisis—Israeli and Syrian leaders, working through mediators, came quite close to resolving the key issues in their bilateral dispute. For a variety of reasons, one could imagine such talks resuming if and when the current crisis subsides. A new Syrian regime will want the legitimacy that would come from recovering its lost territory. Americans and many Israelis might see the strategic logic of helping a new Syrian regime, depending on its orientation and composition, with a serious peace initiative. Progress on the Israeli-Syrian front, of course, might open the way for Lebanon and the Palestinians to join in a comprehensive peace process. This may sound overly optimistic in the grim circumstances of 2012, but one should not rule out the possibility that changes in Syria might make comprehensive Arab-Israeli peace both more compelling and more doable than it now seems.

IRAN AND ITS REGIONAL ROLE

If Prime Minister Benjamin Netanyahu were to have his way, the United States, Europe, and moderate Arab regimes would forget about the Palestinian issue and focus like a laser beam on Iran and its nuclear program. To a degree, Netanyahu has succeeded already in putting the Iran issue front and center in the American political debate. The Obama administration to date has resisted pressure to take military action, arguing that there is time and opportunity for diplomacy to work. There is little appetite in Washington, especially at the Pentagon, for another war in the Middle East.

But there is clearly political pressure on the United States to consider some form of military action beyond the shadow war that is already being waged against the regime in Tehran. In short, it is not impossible that in 2013 the United States could find itself at war with Iran over its nuclear program.

Unlike the previously analyzed regional developments that were judged not likely to have a decisive impact on Israeli-Palestinian peace prospects, this one would surely have far-reaching consequences. It is hard to imagine that the Islamic regime in Iran would easily be swept away or would not respond to an American or possibly American-Israeli attack on its nuclear facilities. How and where Iran might try to retaliate is harder to predict, but one cannot preclude rocket barrages from Lebanon that would lead to something of a repeat of the debilitating Israeli-Hezbollah War in 2006. Whatever their real feelings toward Iran and Hezbollah, Egyptian, Saudi, and Palestinian leaders would be reluctant to be seen as going along with the American-Israeli plan. Tensions within the region would soar, anti-American sentiment would deepen, and prospects for serious peace diplomacy would be lost, perhaps for a very long time.

So, a serious threat to the already slim chances for Israeli-Palestinian peace could take the form of a crisis involving the United States, Israel, and Iran. There is nothing inevitable about this happening. In fact, it is unlikely to take place unless an American president makes the conscious decision that the time has come to deal with Iran's nuclear program by forceful means. In brief, this would be a choice, not an inevitable development or an accident. Iran is unlikely to be the one that deliberately provokes such a crisis, nor is Israel likely to act unilaterally if the United States makes crystal clear its strong opposition. So this scenario, while very dangerous, will depend primarily on decisions made in Washington.

PALESTINIAN REACTIONS TO RECENT EVENTS

While political developments within the Palestinian community are dealt with elsewhere in this volume, a few words are appropriate here on how the Arab Spring and other regional developments are likely to be perceived by Palestinians. There is no single point of view, but several very important changes have affected Palestinians across the region. First, the demise of the Mubarak regime has raised the possibility that the new Egyptian government will act more independently toward Israel and the Palestinians than its predecessor did. Egypt is unlikely to enforce the tight boycott of Gaza that was in place from the time Hamas came to power there. Indeed, Egypt seems to be the likely replacement as the primary patron of both strands of the Palestinian national movement, Fatah and Hamas. The near–civil war in Syria has obliged Hamas to relocate its leadership from Damascus, and that too will have an impact. The Palestinians, with recent memories of sustained political violence, do not seem eager to join the Arab revolution. Instead, there seems to be eagerness on Fatah's part to get on with the project of state building, while Hamas seems to be slowly adjusting its militant stance toward Israel, the most notable expression of which is its willingness to observe a long-term truce with Israel.

ISRAELI POLITICS

As with Palestinian politics, the internal dynamics of Israel are dealt with elsewhere in this volume. But the general reaction to the Arab Spring is worth noting. Israelis across the political spectrum seemed surprised and alarmed by the upheavals that struck the Arab world early in 2011. The ouster of the Mubarak regime was particularly alarming, since Egypt was the pillar of the peace process that, since 1973, kept Israel from having to fight a state-to-state war.

The rise of the Muslim Brotherhood to power caused many Israelis to worry that Egypt might soon join the ranks of its enemies. The overall effect of this sudden change in Israel's strategic setting seemed to be to reinforce the bunker mentality that was all too prominent—Israel is surrounded by enemies, there is no real chance for peace, and therefore the best option is to build barriers and settlements and to ensure that the United States remains a strategic partner.

Developments in Syria largely seem to have added to these concerns, although occasionally Israeli voices could be heard saying that Asad's departure would be welcome, since the tie to Iran and to Hezbollah would presumably be broken. But as the possibility that Asad might be replaced by a Sunni fundamentalist regime has seemed to grow, Israeli officials have been less vocal. In short, developments in Syria also seem ominous.

Even before the Arab Spring, Prime Minister Netanyahu showed no enthusiasm for peace talks with the Palestinians, so it is hard to conclude that the Israeli position in 2013 will be much less obdurate than in the past. At least with elections on the horizon, there may be some debate in Israel about what to do about the occupation and the settlement enterprise. Some Israelis have obviously given up on the idea of peace and think that time is on their side, but the realities of demography and politics may still persuade others that occupation and the maintenance of Israel as a predominantly Jewish democracy do not go together over the long term.

SAUDI ARABIA AND THE GULF COOPERATION COUNCIL

In the frequent moments of intense frustration that occur whenever American officials tackle the Israeli-Palestinian conflict, someone is bound to come up with the bright idea that the Saudis might be persuaded to step in and pressure the Palestinians or reassure the Israelis, or somehow use their wealth and connections to make the job of peacemaking easier. And on rare occasions, the Saudis have indeed taken steps that might have been helpful—Saudi participation in the 1991 Madrid Conference and the multilateral negotiations in the mid-1990s and the Arab League peace initiative in 2002 are two such examples, even if neither was followed with much of a strategic thrust. On balance, however, Americans have been disappointed with the Saudi and GCC (Gulf Cooperation Council) role in the peace process. Is there any reason to expect a change in the near future?

The Saudis in particular have been wary of Iran and its regional influence, especially since the consolidation of Shiite power in Iraq. This concern with Iran has gone hand in hand with a loss of confidence in the United States, both because of the 2003 invasion of Iraq and, more recently, because of the abandonment of the Mubarak regime in early 2011. While one might have thought that the Saudis would be pleased to see the rise of Islamist influence in Egypt, this has not been the case. The Egyptian Muslim Brethren are not natural allies of the Saudis.

Still, as the Saudis and others in the GCC look at regional developments, they must see an opportunity to reduce Iran's regional influence. This accounts for their enthusiastic support for the Syrian opposition. If Asad is forced from power, the Saudis and others in the Gulf will hope to see a friendly regime in Damascus that can serve as a counterweight to Iraq, help to undermine Hezbollah in Lebanon, and cooperate with Egypt and the GCC countries in keeping Hamas from coming under Iranian influence. All of this could mean that the Saudis and GCC would support a serious Arab-Israeli peace effort, but most likely not by taking any leading role. The term "lead from behind" perfectly describes the Saudi leadership style.

Apart from their long-standing caution and conservatism, the Saudis are going through a period of change in the most senior ranks of their leadership. The remaining sons of the founder, Abdul Aziz al-Saud, are all getting on in years, and before too long there will have to be a succession to a new generation. All of this comes at a time of regional disturbances, troubles with the Shiite minority in the Eastern Province, popular sentiment that is stimulated by the exciting scenes from the Arab Spring uprisings, and perhaps volatility in oil prices that would make it hard for the Saudis to rely on petrodollar diplomacy. In brief, any attempt by an American president to relaunch the Arab-Israeli peace process can probably count on cautious Saudi and GCC support, but past experience suggests that such support will be tepid in the best of circumstances.

TURKEY AND ITS POSSIBLE ROLE

At a time when so much of the Middle East seems to be in turmoil, it should be reassuring to Washington that Turkey, a long-standing ally, is doing quite well in terms of economic growth and democratization. Its moderately Islamist AKP (Justice and Development Party) government has won three successive elections, each time with a larger share of the popular vote. Turkey has, of necessity and inclination, turned its attention to regional issues such as Iraq, Iran, Syria, Libya, and the Arab Spring, as well as the Palestinian issue. Until 2009, and even beyond, it was possible to say that Turkey saw a role for itself as a mediator in a wide range of regional disputes. It had relations with Israel, but was also supportive of the Palestinian cause. Without much fanfare, it worked strenuously in 2008 to mediate between Syria and Israel, and both sides noted Turkey's professionalism in doing so.

But Turkey has found it difficult to pursue its "zero problems with neighbors" policies amid the troubled currents sweeping the Middle East. Once a close partner of Asad's Syria, Turkey has now thrown its support to the opposition. Once on fairly good terms with Israel, Turkey reacted strongly to the *Mavi Marmara* affair in May 2010, when Israeli commandos forcibly prevented a Turkish ship from proceeding to Gaza, resulting in the deaths of eight Turkish citizens and one Turkish-American. Israel's unwillingness to apologize, along with the hard feelings on the part of Turkey's prime minister toward Israel for its overall polices in the region, brought this once strong bilateral relationship to its nadir.

One non-trivial advantage of a revived Israeli-Palestinian peace effort might be the easing of tensions between Israel and Turkey. In such circumstances, Turkey could lend its quite considerable prestige as a regional power to the peace process. It could reinforce the efforts of Egypt and possibly the GCC to support the Palestinians as they confront the hard choices that they will face. And Turkey will most likely also be playing an important role in a post-Asad Syria, whenever that moment arrives. The fact that the United States and Turkey currently enjoy very good relations is important in this context; it would be wise for the president to consult with Turkey as he develops a strategy for advancing Israeli-Palestinian peace.

CONCLUSION

This essay started with a claim that Israeli-Palestinian peace would serve American national interests. It also argued that a serious effort at achieving a two-state solution has never really been made. And it acknowledged that the odds of success in any such venture have declined in the past twenty years. The purpose of the remainder of the chapter was to assess whether recent developments in the region, and their likely unfolding in the next few years, provide reasons for concluding that Israeli-Palestinian peace is any more difficult to achieve or less important than it used to be, as many have argued.

On the whole, recent developments do not change the odds very much. The Arab Spring, while meaning that many Arab societies are going through a very introspective moment, has also meant that Arab publics are now very vocal about what they want their governments to do. This makes the Palestinian issue as prominent in public discourse as it has been at any other time. It has not meant a loss of interest among Arabs in this central issue. On the whole, it has created an environment in which a number of important regional actors may see merit in pressing for reconciliation between Palestinian parties on relatively moderate terms. Arab regimes that in the past might have ignored public sentiment on the Palestinian issue are likely to be less willing or able to do so in the future.

In the course of surveying main currents in the region, this essay did identify several possible barriers to a resumed Israeli-Palestinian peace effort. An American-Israeli war with Iran would be one such development. The other worrisome development would be a prolonged civil war in Syria that could lead to widespread regional intervention. At least in the short term, either of these developments would probably be fatal to progress on Israeli-Palestinian peace.

A final word is in order. Israeli-Palestinian peacemaking is not for the faint of heart. An American president who is tempted to take on the challenge must be convinced that it is in the American national interest to do so and must be able to explain those interests to the American public and to Congress. If the decision is to move ahead, the best time to do so will be in 2013 and early 2014. By waiting much longer, a president will run up against the late-term problem of trying to steer a complex foreign policy initiative through domestic political currents that will militate against success. Lame ducks are rarely good peacemakers.

If the decision is to try one more time, the president will need to put someone clearly in charge—preferably the secretary of state—and that person should select a skilled and dedicated team of well-informed professionals. We have not had the "A team" working on these issues for a long time, at least not with effective leadership from the president and the secretary of state.

If the president is prepared to make one more effort at Israeli-Palestinian peace, the last point to consider is a strategic one. He should not fall for the notion that the parties need a prolonged period of confidence building in order to establish trust. Trust will come, if at all, in the course of forging and implementing the final deal. The president's job will be to help the reticent parties face the moment of truth by putting forward well-conceived trade-offs on substantive issues, along with the promise of broad international support for the negotiations, concrete promises of assistance on security and economic issues, and a sophisticated effort to reduce the threat to peace that will be mounted by regional spoilers. This is a daunting task, indeed, but one that is both doable and important.

NOTES

1. General David H. Petraeus, prepared statement for the Senate Armed Services Committee on the posture of US Central Command. http://www.armed-services.senate.gov/statemnt/2010/03%20March/Petraeus%2003-16-10.pdf.
2. General James Mattis, prepared statement for the Senate Armed Services Committee on the posture of US Central Command. http://www.armed-services.senate.gov/statemnt/2011/03%20March/Mattis%2003-01-11.pdf.

2

THE ARAB PEACE INITIATIVE

Marwan Muasher

In early 2002, then-Crown Prince Abdullah of Saudi Arabia initiated an effort to break the impasse in the peace process. He told Thomas Friedman of the *New York Times* that Saudi Arabia had been contemplating a plan by which the Saudis would consider normalizing relations with Israel and persuading the Arab world to do likewise if Israel would reciprocate with a full withdrawal from Arab territories occupied by Israel in 1967. "Full withdrawal for full normalization" is how he framed it. At an Arab summit in Beirut in March 2002, the whole Arab world endorsed the Saudi initiative in a document that became known as the "Arab Peace Initiative."[1]

MAKING PEACE MORE ATTRACTIVE TO BOTH SIDES

Intensive negotiations took place in 2000 to try to reach an agreement that would end the Palestinian-Israeli conflict. The two sides met first at Camp David in July but failed to reach a deal. By December, outgoing President

Bill Clinton called both sides to the White House and presented them with parameters that they had to take on a yes or no basis as a framework for negotiations. Subsequent negotiations based on these parameters took place in January 2001 in Taba, Egypt, and those talks managed to bring the Palestinians and the Israelis closer to a settlement but still did not result in an agreement. By then Clinton had left office, and Israeli Prime Minister Ehud Barak was facing an election in February that he was sure to lose.

A full-blown campaign by the new administration of George W. Bush and by Israel then placed the blame for the failure of negotiations squarely on the Palestinian president Yasser Arafat. The Israelis were said to have presented far-reaching proposals that Arafat rejected. The notion that there was no Palestinian partner for peace was strongly argued by the incoming Israeli prime minister, Ariel Sharon, and others after him to promote the perception that no matter how much the Israelis were willing to concede, the Palestinians were not interested in compromise.

The truth, of course, was more nuanced. A 2001 article by Hussein Agha, a Palestinian-British scholar, and Robert Malley, a Clinton White House official who participated in the negotiations at Camp David, presents the best argument against the black-and-white picture painted by the Israelis.[2] Agha and Malley argue that by going for an all-or-nothing approach and preserving his assets "for a 'moment of truth,' Barak's tactics helped to ensure that the parties never got there . . . Obsessed with Barak's tactics, Arafat spent far less time worrying about the substance of a deal than he did fretting about a possible ploy."

Beyond Malley and Agha's argument, however, one frequently ignored reason for the failure of the negotiations was that Arab states were excluded from the process. As former American official Martin Indyk explains,[3] the Americans kept important Arab states like Egypt and Saudi Arabia out of the loop, probably because Ehud Barak was worried that any leaked information from the summit would severely undermine his position at home if the compromises he was ready to offer were exposed prematurely. External communications, including those through mobile phones, were blocked.[4]

When Arafat was asked to make compromises on Jerusalem and refugees, and was prevented from consulting with Arab leaders, he balked. He felt he needed Arab cover. In short, Barak's fear of leaks made it clear that the

Israelis were making offers they were not sure would pass at home, and the Palestinians were asked to give compromises without some needed Arab support. *Both* sides were not in a position to meet the needs of the other. That, in my view, is the main reason that the negotiations that started in Camp David and ended in Taba failed.

It became apparent that the goalposts needed to be shifted if peace was to become attractive and possible for either side. If the challenge was to find the right set of conditions that would enable Israel and Palestine to make the necessary compromises for peace, then the focus must be on a comprehensive accord between Israel and the entire Arab world. Such an agreement would provide both parties with a regional safety net.[5] For Palestinians and Arabs, it would provide Arab support for the compromises that would eventually be made on Jerusalem, borders, and refugees. For Israelis, it would provide the assurance that they would get peace and security not just with some of the Palestinians, but with the entire Arab world around them.

That is the principal idea behind the Arab Peace Initiative (API): making peace both possible and desirable for both sides. Indeed, a careful examination of the Arab Peace Initiative reveals four important offers to Israel from the entire Arab world:[6]

1. **A collective commitment to end the conflict with Israel**. As a former ambassador to Israel, I witnessed firsthand the importance of this promise to the average Israeli, who remains concerned that Palestinians or Arab states might make further claims to Israeli territory even after Israel withdraws to its pre-1967 borders and a solution to the refugee problem is reached.

2. **Security guarantees for all states in the region, including Israel**. This was a significant offer because, for the first time, Israel was assured that its security would be guaranteed not only by neighboring Arab states but by all Arab states. And a major strength of the initiative that has been widely overlooked is the implicit obligation for Arabs to deliver Hamas and Hezbollah through the security guarantees mentioned. In other words, by including Hamas and Hezbollah in the agreement—with Arab states assuming the responsibility of overseeing the transformation of the two organizations into purely

political parties—the onus falls on the Arab world to ensure that this takes place.

3. **A collective peace treaty and normal relations with Israel**. This signaled full recognition of Israel and normal relations similar to those between an Arab state and any other state in the world.

4. **An agreed solution to the refugee problem**. For the first time, the Arab world committed itself to a workable solution to the refugee problem, thus addressing Israel's concern that four million refugees could be sent to Israel. The initiative acknowledged that the solution needed to be mutually agreed upon, based on a realistic application of UN General Assembly Resolution 194, which deals with the right of return. In other words, there is no possibility of a solution that will lead to changing the Jewish character of Israel.

In return, the Arab Peace Initiative calls on Israel to give up Arab territories occupied in 1967, including the West Bank and East Jerusalem, Gaza, the Syrian Golan Heights, and the Lebanese Shebaa Farms. Subsequent negotiations revealed that the principles of the Clinton Parameters and the Arab Peace Initiative, coupled with full withdrawal from the Golan Heights to the June 4, 1967, borders on the Syrian front, formed an acceptable basis not just for the Palestinians and the Syrians, but for the whole Arab world and almost the entire Muslim world as well.

It is difficult to think of another set of parameters that form a reasonable framework to arrive at a solution that addresses the needs of both sides. The Palestinians would get a viable state, an end to the longest occupation in the contemporary world, and self-determination, while the Israelis would get peace and security with the entire neighborhood, forever.

Yet then-Prime Minister Sharon rejected the offer outright, citing the reference to UN Resolution 194, which calls for the right of Palestinian refugees to return to Israel or be compensated. Sharon ignored the key phrase in the proposal that any solution needed to be agreed to by both sides. More important, Sharon did not present any ideas of his own until the unilateral withdrawal from Gaza three years later.

The Bush administration, for its part, gave the proposal lip service, but lukewarm support at best. It was clear that by the first half of 2002, when the

API was passed, the Bush administration was already focused on preparing for war with Iraq and the peace process was relegated to a very low priority. Sharon had convinced Bush that his war with Arafat was part of Bush's war against terror. As a result, the US administration had little interest in actively supporting an initiative that was met with strong resistance by the Israelis— even while that Arab initiative promised to deliver the whole Arab world.

But after considerable efforts by Jordan, the European Union, and others to gain American support, the API finally made it to the preamble of the Middle East Roadmap that was launched in Aqaba, Jordan, by President Bush in 2003. It was never taken seriously or actively pursued, however, by either the Americans or the Israelis.[7] Serious negotiations would not take place until six years after the API was endorsed, when Israeli Prime Minister Ehud Olmert and Palestinian President Mahmoud Abbas engaged in secret bilateral talks. This would end in failure yet again as the proper conditions were not assured for both sides.

IMPACT OF THE ARAB AWAKENING

Despite the political stagnation of the last decade, and two wars against Lebanon and Gaza by Israel, not one Arab country has withdrawn its signature from the Arab Peace Initiative. But this hardly means that the initiative is a permanent offer, immune from all pressures.

The Arab Awakening is rapidly transforming the political context that produced the Arab Peace Initiative. The Arab public overthrew entrenched Arab leaders and are increasingly disparaging of an Israeli occupation that has become, like the status quo in the Arab world, unsustainable. And while there is little chance that the Egyptian-Israeli or Jordanian-Israeli peace treaties are in jeopardy, as political and economic realities will trump ideological ones, it will be nearly impossible to forge new treaties in the current climate.

The initiative's main allure—an agreement with all Arab states—will become increasingly unlikely as the perception of Israel drops across the region and among its new leaders. New and emerging Arab governments in countries that have undergone transitions, like Egypt, will be more responsive to their publics and far more critical of Israel's occupation. It is hard to imagine that a civilian Egyptian government will not have a far stronger response should Israel wage another war on Lebanon as it did in 2006 or on Gaza as it did in 2008.

The biological factor should not be ignored either. King Abdullah of Saudi Arabia is the last Arab leader who has the stature to protect the Arab Peace Initiative and the principles behind it. As someone who was intimately involved in the development of the initiative and who attended the Beirut Arab Summit where it was signed and launched in March 2002, I can attest that King Abdullah played a crucial role in circumventing possible dissent by some Arab countries and ensuring that it was passed unanimously. He still commands much respect in both the Arab world and his own country. But as he approaches ninety years of age, he could leave the scene at any time, and then the initiative might very well fall apart at the seams.

We might not see an official death notice for the Arab Peace Initiative, but it is unrealistic to expect that it will be on the table indefinitely in light of recent developments. And reaching a peace agreement between the Israelis and the Palestinians will be infinitely more challenging without the support of the Arab countries.[8]

CHANGE NECESSARY FOR ISRAEL AND THE UNITED STATES

Israel needs to revisit its policies. As political reform across the Arab world achieves results, Israel will no longer be able to claim that it is the only democracy in the Middle East. And with conditions changing on the ground, it will be harder to ignore the Palestinians' need for independence. Israel's concern that the region will grow more hostile will become a self-fulfilling prophecy if new democracies see that the Israeli government is impeding steps toward a viable and dignified solution. At the same time, a peace process with elected and more legitimate Arab governments will help solidify long-term peace and stability.

Israel is not the only actor that needs to come to grips with the regional transformations. The United States is the most powerful external actor, and, as such, the sooner it adapts to the new reality, the better. For decades, the United States prioritized stability over reform to satiate its demand for oil and considered the Arab-Israeli conflict to be unrelated to both. It is now clear that this policy failed—reform from above has stalled, stability was lost in the uprisings, and Arab-Israeli peace remains elusive.

Any change of policy by the United States toward the region will be severely tested when it comes to peace in the Middle East. In the words of Muasher and Solana, "for the U.S., broad sympathy for Arabs' yearning for freedom cannot exclude compassion for Palestinians dreaming of lives free of occupation. The Arab world wants dignity and this includes ending the occupation. Washington should not be selective in its support for freedom and democracy. If the U.S. is not seen as an avid supporter of a two-state solution, it will stay well behind the curve and damage its own interests in the Middle East."[9]

The United States needs to step up to the plate. Having been the major, if not practically the only sponsor of the peace process, it has not always lived up to the expectation of being an honest and fair broker. Other US priorities, including its commitment to Israel, the war in Iraq, domestic considerations, and the rapid cycle of elections—the peace process is never more than two years away from any major vote—have preoccupied the United States and have meant that it neither led the peace process nor allowed others to lead it. All of these factors contributed to the long time period that has elapsed without a resolution, despite the two sides negotiating and renegotiating the issues over and over again.

The United States has adopted a set of contradictory positions on the process. President Obama, General David Petraeus, and other administration officials have made it clear on multiple occasions that solving the Arab-Israeli conflict is in America's national interest. But American officials, almost in the same breath, add that the United States cannot want a solution more than the parties themselves, thereby effectively holding the national interests of the United States hostage to the spoilers of the process.

Those who argue that peacemaking cannot be successful in a situation in flux ignore the fact that it is precisely in these circumstances that outsiders can help shape the process. Pushing the peace process now can help the West win over the Arab public and give the United States more credibility.[10]

The urgency of finding a solution to the conflict, however, is not lost on the US administration. President Obama made a convincing argument in May 2011 for the world's need to move forward on peace now. He mentioned that military technology will make it harder for Israel to defend itself, implying that security will only come from peace. He described how the shifting demographic balance will not achieve Israeli dreams, saying "a Jewish and democratic state cannot be fulfilled with permanent occupation." He cited the Arab uprisings and the then-pending UN vote on Palestinian statehood as reasons to act quickly. And he declared that "there are those who argue that with all the change and uncertainty in the region, it is simply not possible to move forward now. I disagree."[11]

After such an eloquent description of the urgency of solving the conflict, there is a dire need to present a clear and expedient plan to find a solution rapidly. The assumption that the status quo is frozen and that one can leave the process and return to it at a later date without thinking about the actual developments on the ground is simply false.

The idea that the United States cannot impose a solution on the parties may seem reasonable at first glance, but it does not stand up to scrutiny. The United States has made its views known in the past—in positive and less positive ways. When President Clinton offered his parameters in 2000, no one talked about Washington "imposing" a solution. More than anything, the Clinton Parameters reflected where the two sides basically stood at the time.

For his part, President George W. Bush, in a negative development, did not have any problem in 2004 writing a letter to Israeli Prime Minister Sharon stating that "it is unrealistic to expect that the outcome of final status negotiations will be a full and complete return to the armistice lines of 1949 . . . it is realistic to expect that any final status agreement will only be achieved on the basis of mutually agreed changes that reflect these realities."[12] President Bush essentially changed the US position that the borders must be based on the 1967 lines with minor adjustments.

Despite a setback during the Bush years, the fact remains that after twenty years of different sets of negotiations, the parties were able to define the parameters for a solution in rather minute details. In fact, today no parameters that the United States presents can be defined as "imposed" or starting from scratch. Rather, they would likely be built on years of negotiations as well as past initiatives such as the Clinton Parameters and the Arab Peace Initiative.[13]

Finally, there are demographics to consider. Israel today is a country of 7.9 million people (5.9 million Jews, 1.6 million Arab-Israelis, and about

300,000 others).[14] Palestinians in the West Bank and Gaza number around 4.3 million, making the total number of Arabs and Jews living today in areas under Israel's control about equal.[15] In the absence of a two-state solution, Israel might perhaps be able to continue to limit Arab influence by perpetuating a two-tier citizenship model for another decade or two, but the end result is clear. No minority group in history has been able to rule democratically over the majority for an indefinite period of time. Given that Palestinians have higher birth rates than Israelis, they would not remain the minority for long.[16]

SPECIFIC WAYS TO MOVE AHEAD

The US president who is inaugurated in January 2013 will find himself confronting these biological and demographic issues, as well as the challenge of building healthier relations between the United States and the emerging Arab world. He will also have to deal with a situation in which time is no longer working on the side of the Israeli state if a two-state solution is not reached quickly.

All this requires a policy of immediate, sustained engagement not only with the Palestinians and the Israelis, but also with the wider Arab world if a viable solution is to be salvaged before it is too late. Returning to an incremental approach is a formula for instability and further loss of credibility for the United States in the region. This method has exhausted its possibilities and lost the trust of almost everyone. More important, it is a policy that will spell the end of the two-state solution and usher in an era of no short-term solution and a move toward a one-state solution in the long term.

If the administration that takes office in January 2013 wants to solve the Arab-Israeli conflict, the president must engage the region almost immediately after being inaugurated. Waiting to do so or engaging in another "peace process" will effectively mean the death of the two-state solution. Negotiators need to undertake two simultaneous efforts. The first is to prepare the proper conditions for a Palestinian-Israeli settlement through quiet engagement with all the major players with the objective of securing "end-game deposits"—positions on key aspects of the conflict that can be deposited with the US administration and implemented only if the other parties are ready to implement theirs—ahead of the launch of a major initiative. The second is to present parameters for a solution in coordination with the other members of the Quartet, which includes the United Nations, the European Union, and Russia.

ENGAGING WITH THE SAUDIS AND THE ARABS

The United States needs to convince the Arabs, and most importantly the Saudis, that it has no plans to engage in another endless process and that the effort must have a limited duration of only a few months. The terms of reference need to be firmly based on the Clinton Parameters, previous negotiations, and the Arab Peace Initiative.

Given the George W. Bush administration's track record, this is understandably not an easy feat. The Saudis in particular are deeply suspicious of processes that never end and promises that are not fulfilled. The US president must establish a personal relationship with King Abdullah and convince him that the United States is serious about bringing the two sides together to agree on a settlement within several months. Justifiably, the issue that Saudi Arabia (like most Arab and Muslim countries) cares most about is East Jerusalem. So any package needs to include East Jerusalem as the capital of the new Palestinian state.

Once the US president convincingly lays out his case, he can ask the Saudis for two particular deliverables. First, the Saudis should take the lead in providing an Arab and a Muslim umbrella for an eventual deal reached between the two sides. This should not be difficult, given that the Arab Peace Initiative has already been endorsed by every Arab state, as well as by the Organization of the Islamic Conference (OIC). A renewed commitment should even come from new governments led by Islamists, such as in Egypt. In a conversation I had with Khairat al-Shater, the Muslim Brotherhood's chief strategist in Egypt and its first candidate for the presidency,[17] he made it clear that Egypt will respect all previous agreements and will not take a position different from that taken by the Palestinians through their free will.[18]

Second, the Saudis should spearhead an effort to secure a commitment to transform Hamas and Hezbollah into purely political parties after an agreement is reached on the Palestinian, Syrian, and Lebanese fronts. The Saudis will need to work with the Palestinians, the Lebanese, and any new Syrian regime. The collapse of the current Syrian regime will provide an opening to distance both Hamas and Hezbollah from Iran and to work with the new Syrian leadership to make that a reality. But this requires securing a full withdrawal from the Golan Heights (including the Lebanese Shebaa Farms) to the 1967 borders.

These are hypothetical "end-game deposits" that the president can get from the Saudis at the onset, provided the Israeli side meets its commitment on withdrawal from territories occupied in 1967.

ENGAGING WITH THE ISRAELIS AND THE PALESTINIANS

The US president can then secure similar "end-game deposits" from the Palestinians and the Israelis. The parties would offer hypothetical commitments that they might not be willing to give at the outset to each other, but that can be deposited with the United States and committed to only if the other side is willing to do the same.[19]

These deposits, as well as the regional safety net provided by the Arab Peace Initiative, would make it much easier for both to provide creative solutions on otherwise thorny issues. A deposit by the Israelis, for example, to establish a viable Palestinian state with East Jerusalem as its capital might allow the Palestinians to back away from a maximalist position on the refugee issue.

But the United States needs to make it clear to the Israelis that the occupation cannot continue, which will not be an easy feat, and that the death of the two-state solution is contrary not only to US national interest, but also to Israeli interests. In return, the US president can agree with Israel on security arrangements beyond the guarantees mentioned in the API that would assure Israel that the United States would be a guarantor of Israel's security as it moves forward with a permanent peace deal.

Once the United States engages in quiet diplomacy for a few months to prepare the ground for a settlement, convince all sides of its unflinching intention to help bring about an end to the conflict, and obtain deposits from all sides, it can move ahead on a second track and present parameters for a solution in coordination with the other members of the Quartet. If it does this correctly, the parameters will not come as a surprise to anyone.

The parameters will be the result of twenty years of on-again, off-again negotiations between the two sides. On borders, the solution will involve the return of the West Bank and Gaza to Palestine with minor and mutually agreed-upon reciprocal swaps to accommodate the Jewish settlements near the Green Line. On Jerusalem, the solution should include East Jerusalem as the capital of the new Palestinian state, and the entire city should stay open to all without Israel's keeping exclusive sovereignty over it. On refugees, the parameters need to include different options for how to implement Resolution 194 in a realistic and agreed-upon manner. Negotiations have shown that these goals are well within reach.

If coupled with a serious timeline and arbitration that provides a clear mechanism for holding the parties accountable for their commitments, such a proposal could provide the catalyst necessary to reach a solution that meets the needs of the two parties and the constraint of time. Still, the United States would need to overcome two hurdles: Israel's current governing coalition, which seems uninterested in moving beyond the status quo and accepting a settlement that would abandon its ideological position to keep the entire land, and a weak and divided Palestinian National Authority.

Ironically, a two-state solution would not only ensure the fulfillment of the Palestinian quest for independence and self-rule, but also the long-term survival of the Jewish state. But the United States needs to take the lead in ensuring implementation of solutions that have already been reached by the parties themselves. The agreement will naturally include security guarantees, financial aid, and other arrangements by the international community to ensure that it is sustainable and permanent.

THE IRANIAN "EXISTENTIAL" FEAR REVISITED

The Israeli government is preoccupied today with an Iranian "nuclear threat" that consumes all its thinking. While not belittling the fear of an Iranian nuclear attack that the average Israeli citizen feels, one can argue that the *hypothetical* "existential threat" to Israel may not come from the outside, but rather from a domestic demographic factor that can no longer be ignored.

The Israeli government portrays the Iranian threat as the principal one facing the country, but this only diverts attention from the *real* threat to peace and stability that is posed by a failure to resolve the Palestinian conflict, quite possibly for decades to come. Furthermore, a poll conducted in February 2012 shows that only 42 percent of Israelis would support a military strike by Israel, with US support, against Iran's nuclear facilities and only 19 percent believe Israel should strike without the backing of the United States.[20] And 34 percent would not support a strike at all. The Iranian threat cannot, and should not, be used as an excuse for not moving forward on the issue of peace as soon as possible.

Iran is not an Arab country and is therefore not a signatory to the Arab Peace Initiative. Iran has been supporting radical groups like Hamas and Hezbollah in the region. But it would be difficult to imagine a scenario in which all Arab states sign a peace treaty with Israel, with the inclusion of Hamas and Hezbollah and with the support of all Muslim states, while Iran continues to oppose peace in a militant fashion.[21]

It is important to recognize that Iran is emerging as one of the biggest losers of the Arab Awakening. The regime's argument that it has always stood on the side of the oppressed rang hollow after its domestic crackdown on its own people during the Green Revolution of 2009. By mid-2011, Iran's popularity in the Arab world had already decreased dramatically, and this was before it adamantly supported the Syrian regime as it killed thousands of its own people.[22]

Iran can no longer present itself as a model for reform in the Arab world. The organizations it supports, particularly Hezbollah, have also suffered severely at the polls for the same reasons. With the emergence of a new Syrian regime that will likely keep a distance from both Iran and Hezbollah due to their support of the Asad regime, and in the context of a comprehensive Arab-Israeli agreement with monitored security guarantees, Iran will be hard pressed to keep providing logistical and military support to Hamas or Hezbollah, even if these groups choose to break the agreement, a very unlikely possibility.

THE TIME IS NOW

Many analysts have dismissed the idea of an effort now to resolve the Palestinian-Israeli conflict as naïve and unrealistic wishful thinking that ignores reality. But the bottom line is that, while it is indeed difficult to solve the conflict today, it may be impossible to solve it in the near future.

The resolution of this issue is not cost-free and will require significant compromises by both sides. And it will also require determined leadership from the United States. The US president who takes office in 2013 needs to engage the entire region, and the Arab Peace Initiative provides an opportunity because it makes peace desirable and possible for all interested parties.

A lasting solution will not come about by waiting for a better time, which facts suggest is not on the near or distant horizon. The result of this sit-and-wait policy fails to provide guarantees for a solution in the future. In fact, it only makes matters worse as it promises no solution at all in the short term and a possible one-state solution in the long term.

NOTES

1. For a full account of how the Arab Peace Initiative was developed, see Marwan Muasher, *The Arab Center: The Promise of Moderation* (New Haven, Conn.: Yale University Press, 2008), 102-133.
2. See Robert Malley and Hussein Agha, "Camp David: The Tragedy of Errors," *New York Review of Books*, July 12, 2001.
3. Martin Indyk, *Innocent Abroad: An Intimate Account of American Peace Diplomacy in the Middle East* (New York: Simon & Schuster, 2009), 288-340.
4. I was Jordanian ambassador to the United States at that time, and I remember how frantically I tried to get in touch with Palestinian officials attending the talks at Camp David, to no avail.
5. Marwan Muasher, "Palestinian-Israeli Direct Talks: The Case for a Regional Approach," *Carnegie Endowment for International Peace*, August 2010, http://carnegieendowment. org/2010/08/24/palestinian-israeli-direct-talks-case-for-regional-approach/bly7.
6. Muasher, *The Arab Center*, 132-133.
7. The Middle East Roadmap stated in its preamble that "a settlement, negotiated between the parties, will result in the emergence of an independent, democratic and viable Palestinian state living side by side in peace and security with Israel and its other neighbors. The settlement will resolve the Israel-Palestinian conflict, and end the occupation that began in 1967, based on the foundations of the Madrid Conference, the principle of land for peace, UNSCRs 242, 338 and 1397, agreements previously reached by the parties, *and the initiative of Saudi Crown Prince Abdullah—endorsed by the Beirut Arab League Summit—calling for acceptance of Israel as a neighbor living in peace and security, in the context of a comprehensive settlement*" (emphasis added).
8. See Marwan Muasher, "The Death of the Arab Peace Initiative?," *The Atlantic*, November 23, 2011, http://www.theatlantic.com/international/archive/2011/11/the-death-of-the-arab-peace-initiative/248910/.
9. Marwan Muasher and Javier Solana, "Push Ahead Now for a Solution on Palestine," *The Financial Times*, March 9, 2011, http://www.ft.com/intl/cms/s/0/5f4c4c68-4a87-11e0-82ab-00144feab49a.html#axzz22KN0Uipg.
10. Ibid.

11. "Remarks by the President on the Middle East and North Africa," The White House, May 19, 2011, http://www.whitehouse.gov/the-press-office/2011/05/19/remarks-president-middle-east-and-north-africa.

12. For the full text, see "Letter from President Bush to Prime Minister Sharon," available at http://www.whitehouse.gov/news/releases/2004/04/20040414-3.html.

13. One need only point to agreements or initiatives such as the Clinton Parameters of 2000, the Taba talks that followed after that, the Geneva initiative in which ex-negotiators from both sides came up with a detailed agreement in 2003, the Arab Peace Initiative of 2002, and the Abu-Mazen-Olmert talks in 2008.

14. Israeli Central Bureau of Statistics, "On the Eve of Israel's 64th Independence Day—Approximately 7.881 Million Residents," April 25, 2012, http://www1.cbs.gov.il/www/hodaot2012n/11_12_106e.pdf.

15. Palestinian Central Bureau of Statistics, "Ahwaal al-Sukkan al-Filasteeniyeen al-Muqimeen fi al-Aradi al-Filasteeniyyah, 2012," July 2012, http://www.pcbs.gov.ps/Portals/_PCBS/Downloads/book1897.pdf.

16. Muasher, "Palestinian-Israeli Direct Talks."

17. He was disqualified from running because he had served time in prison.

18. Interview with Khairat al-Shater, Cairo, Egypt, June 17, 2012.

19. For a detailed discussion of such "end-game deposits," see Muasher, "Palestinian-Israeli Direct Talks."

20. "The February 2012 Israeli Public Opinion Survey," Brookings Institution, February 29, 2012, http://www.brookings.edu/research/reports/2012/02/29-israel-poll-telhami.

21. Muasher, "Palestinian-Israeli Direct Talks."

22. James Zogby, "Arab Attitudes towards Iran, 2011," *Arab American Institute Foundation*, http://aai.3cdn.net/fd7ac73539e31a321a_r9m6iy9y0.pdf.

II

THE ISRAELI AND PALESTINIAN DIMENSIONS

3

ISRAEL'S STRATEGIC DILEMMAS: DON'T WAIT FOR THE DUST TO SETTLE; ACT NOW

Avi Gil

The shockwaves reverberating throughout the Arab world over the last two years pose significant challenges to Israel. The uncertainty that traditionally characterizes the Middle East is exacerbated by the current anxiety and crisis-like atmosphere marking the entire geopolitical arena. When reality is that fitful, the instinctive human response is one of entrenchment: to react tactically and refrain from initiating any new strategic moves until after "the dust settles." Unfortunately, the dust will not settle in the near future, and when it finally does, Israel's *current* policies will have played an important role in what emerges. Indecision is as much a decision as any other, and Israel's leaders are not exempt from the need to make difficult choices. In light of recent developments, however, proactive Israeli policy, especially with regard to the Palestinian issue, can significantly improve Israel's strategic position, while hunkering down will only further complicate its morass of problems, especially in light of geopolitical developments in the following four major arenas.

The global arena, in which the prevailing world order of the Cold War era and the "American moment" that followed the collapse of the Soviet Union have been replaced by a "world disorder" that has yet to consolidate into a stable and functioning system. The United States—whose friendship is so critical to Israel, and which is home to an exceptionally thriving half of the Jewish people—continues to experience a steady diminution of power and international stature.

The Middle East arena, in which the historical pillars that long provided relative strategic regional stability are tottering while the chances of stabilization and a resulting semblance of calm remain slim in the near future. To this, one should add the ouster of Egypt's President Hosni Mubarak, the uncertainty surrounding Bashar al-Asad's reign in Syria, the ongoing crisis in Israel-Turkey relations, and, above all, the dramatic achievements of political Islam (especially in winning the Egyptian parliamentary and presidential elections). All of this is happening as Iran continues to make progress in obtaining nuclear weapons capability, challenging Israel (and the United States) with the dilemma of whether to launch a preemptive military attack should diplomacy and sanctions fail to stop the Iranian program.

The Israeli-Arab arena, in which the stalemate continues to threaten both the security and the Jewish-democratic character of the State of Israel, which in turn helps to fuel the phenomenon of Israel's de-legitimization. The continued failure of the model of direct talks with US mediation has driven the Palestinians to prefer an alternative course: The internationalization of the conflict-resolution process focusing on an enforced solution under international diktat. The stalemate has also helped to encourage settler activity in the West Bank, and the settlers' consequent rise in political power, which may soon reach a point at which it will be impossible to secure Israeli Knesset approval of a two-state agreement.

The Jerusalem-Washington-American Jewry triangle, which constitutes a critical strategic resource for Israeli power. On the one hand, the past year has demonstrated the strength of both Israel and the Jewish people (for example, in preventing steps by the American administration that contradict the Israeli government's stance on Israeli-Palestinian issues); on the other hand, events of the past year have revealed the danger that can emerge in exercising this power, such as positioning Israel as a wedge issue between Republicans and Democrats.

Obviously, these complexes are intertwined and interdependent. Many of the trends within them are not amenable to Israeli intervention; however, any policy chosen will be evaluated as a success or failure to the extent that it can deal effectively with the following threats facing Israel.

Deterioration in Israel's security position, which in the extreme case could lead to all-out war in which Israel is forced to defend itself against a combined offensive spanning multiple fronts, including its home front (for instance, following an Israeli or American operation against Iran, or following a violent deterioration in Gaza, Syria, or Lebanon).

Damage to Israel's international stature as a result of the growing perception that Israel is responsible for the deadlocked Israeli-Palestinian conflict. The erosion in international standing of Israel's American ally, the collapse of the strategic axes of Jerusalem-Cairo and Jerusalem-Ankara, and the rise of political Islam in the Middle East all serve to weaken Israel's international standing.

An economic downturn in Israel as a result of deterioration in the security situation, and/or as part of the de-legitimization campaign waged against Israel, and sanctions enacted against Israeli products, tourism, investments, and the like. The global economic crisis only exacerbates such scenarios.

Damage to Israeli-US relations in light of perceptions in some American circles that the price of friendship with Israel is steadily increasing, that

Israel is an ungrateful ally, that the US image in the Muslim world is damaged by Israel's policies, and that Washington is being cornered in international forums and subjected to sharp criticism for its support of Israel.

On the eve of the upheavals in the Arab world, the Middle Eastern picture was clear and widely understood—ineffective governments, poverty, economic hardship, high unemployment rates, large numbers of young people without any hope for a decent future, rampant corruption, revocation of basic freedoms, and human rights violations. However, the best experts, including intelligence agencies, failed to foresee what was coming and could not imagine Arab crowds flooding town squares risking death in front of live fire. It would be surprising if there were no further surprises in the Middle East. Yet, while the Arab upheavals could go on for years, certain developments and dilemmas are already discernible and should be taken into account in shaping any policy vis-à-vis the fermenting Middle East arena.

The flourishing of political Islam. Political Islam is emerging as the major victor of the Arab revolt. It remains to be seen whether the entry of the Muslim Brotherhood on the political stage in Arab countries will moderate their positions, lead them into coexistence with secular parties in ruling coalitions, or engender dark theocracies. While the Muslim Brotherhood has thus far indicated that it will not support the abrogation of the peace accords with Israel, we are likely to see a hardening of bilateral Egyptian-Israeli relations, more Egyptian support for Palestinian positions, and less willingness to help American mediation efforts. On the other hand, if progress is achieved in the peace process between Israel and the Palestinians, Muslim Brotherhood backing could confer popular and religious legitimacy to the idea of peace with Israel and, perhaps, help tone down Hamas hostility toward Israel. Israel is not able to stem the growth of political Islam, but it can implement policies in coordination with the United States and particularly with respect to the Palestinian issue that can moderate the Islamist regimes' attitude toward Israel, creating—as much as possible—constructive relations.

The increased power of the "Arab Street." Without drawing any conclusions regarding the final outcome of the Arab revolts, it is already clear that future rulers of Arab countries will have to be much more attuned to popular sentiment that is saturated with hatred of Israel and gives priority to the Palestinian issue. This limits the options available to Arab governments and makes it difficult to ignore issues such as Israeli settlements, episodes of Israeli-Palestinian violence, and the absence of any progress toward peace. This also constrains Israeli policy choices: Egyptian attitudes and the possibility of further deterioration in bilateral relations will surely prompt Israel to act more cautiously in the future when dealing with violence emanating from Gaza. Israel does not have the capability to directly mitigate the animosity of the Arab Street, but its policies toward the Palestinians can significantly affect Arab anger and attitudes.

The worsening economic crisis. The dismal economic situation in many Arab countries, which helped ignite the Arab uprisings, has worsened in their wake. In the immediate term, there is a considerable decrease in economic growth. Local tourism and foreign investment have suffered, and local investors are transferring their money out of the region due to uncertainty about the future. The economic crisis may force Arab governments to focus their efforts on economic recovery and domestic affairs, but it could also create a temptation to redirect internal frustrations against "the Zionist archenemy." Israel must consider policies that reduce the potential for this to happen.

The perception of US decline and disengagement. This perception is growing in the region, in part based on the American decision to withdraw from Iraq and Afghanistan, US failure thus far to stop Iran's nuclear weapons efforts, the failure to advance an Israeli-Palestinian agreement, America's "pivot" to Asia, and the American economic crisis. These factors combine to paint a picture of a steadily weakening American superpower, unable to attain its goals, increasingly preoccupied with its own predicaments, and progressively less willing to assume a leading role in the region. Further, the US response to the Arab revolts has been perceived in the Middle East as inconsistent and unwise. Israel's power—both its actual strength and the way it is perceived—is directly correlated to the prevalent perception of American power and the intensity of American friendship with Israel. It is thus in Israel's self-interest to adopt policies that help the United States to restore its standing in the Middle East.

The decline of traditional regional strategic arrangements. The uprisings moving throughout the Arab world are toppling the strategic alignments that characterized the Middle East in the past. The pro-American "moderate axis" has been shaken: Mubarak's ouster and the deterioration in relations with Turkey have intensified Israel's strategic isolation. At the same time, however, the "axis of resistance" hostile to Israel—Iran, Syria, Hezbollah, and Hamas—is also being undermined by the threat to Asad's regime. Will this strategic reality be faced promptly and creatively by Israeli decision makers, especially vis-à-vis Egypt and Turkey?

The dilemmas outlined require Israel to choose between stark alternatives: whether to hunker down and wait passively for things to get better, or whether to act now, seize opportunities, and try to change the status quo in ways that enhance Israeli security and political interests.

The option of hunkering down is attractive in some quarters. It rests on the belief that the threats to Israel have increased substantially as a result of the Arab upheavals, and that this is therefore not the time for taking risks based on wishful thinking and strategic naïveté. In the coming years, according to this view, political Islam, which is understood to be extremely hostile to Israel, is expected to dictate the conduct of Arab states. This uncertainty calls for extreme caution, especially regarding territorial issues, because any territory conceded by Israel today could fall into the hands of hostile forces tomorrow. Prime Minister Benjamin Netanyahu expressed this approach in his speech in the Knesset on October 31, 2011:[1]

> Chances are that an Islamist wave will wash over the Arab countries, an anti-West, anti-liberal, anti-Israel and ultimately an anti-democratic wave . . . They are moving, but they are not moving forward towards progress, they are going backwards . . . I will not ignore reality, I will not ignore the dangers, I will not ignore history . . . or give up on any of our security requirements that have increased because of the recent crises and not diminished . . . This is not the time to rush into things, it is the time to be cautious in our connections with the Palestinians.

A different logic, predicated on a proactive Israeli policy designed to impact the current situation in ways beneficial to Israel, imagines a strategic alternative in which the Arab world is addressed by Israel as follows:

> We respect the rights of the Arab peoples to move forward, determine their own future, and democratically elect their own leaders. We are interested in

peaceful and good neighborly relations, and in this spirit we offer a comprehensive peace initiative based on the 1967 lines and including swaps of equal size. We will be generous in the context of peace negotiations, and we will relentlessly pursue cooperation and normalization. We will stand our ground with determination regarding our real security needs. We believe that both the Jewish and Palestinian peoples enjoy a fundamental right: each should live in their own independent state. We stand ready to enter immediate negotiations with the Palestinians and, indeed, with the rest of the Arab World—based on the Arab Peace Initiative—to reach a comprehensive final status agreement that will end all mutual claims.

Clearly, there is no one magic bullet to resolve all of Israel's many dilemmas, but just as clear is the fact that Israel holds a real strategic key, the careful but determined use of which would improve its position vis-à-vis the challenges noted above. Such a key, in essence, is an initiative to end the Israeli-Palestinian and Israeli-Arab conflicts and to move smartly toward a comprehensive regional peace agreement. For an Israeli initiative to be credible, it must adopt the principle of borders based on the 1967 lines with some adjustments for which equal land swaps would provide adequate compensation. Such a willingness would add significant credibility to Israel's security requirements, tough as they may be, as well as to the demand that the implementation process of such an agreement would be gradual and benchmarked—one that would not only be based on a timetable but also on meticulous, monitored, and verifiable performance tests.

Even if the Palestinians hesitated in accepting such an Israeli initiative, the argument that Israel refuses peace would no longer apply. Such an Israeli initiative would be of strategic importance because of the move toward, and prospects of, setting Israel's permanent borders, ensuring its Jewish majority and democratic nature, and laying the foundations for peaceful and normal coexistence between Israel and its neighbors. From the Israeli perspective, the Arab Spring has enhanced the strategic importance of resolving the Palestinian question:

1. Peace with the Palestinians will help to remove the Israeli issue from the Arab Street's agenda;

2. It will reduce the incentive for Arab countries to alleviate internal tension by initiating violent confrontations with Israel;

3. It will dissolve many of the bonds holding the region's extreme axes together;

4. It will pave the way to normal relations between Israel and the entire Arab and Islamic world;

5. It will help repair damaged strategic axes (Egypt, Turkey) and consolidate a regional strategic alignment against Iran;

6. It will further cement Israeli-US relations by crediting Washington with a "historic achievement" as the sponsor of the agreement, which would, in turn, re-establish US standing in the Middle East;

7. It will improve Israel's political standing and image around the world and substantially curb the de-legitimization trend;

8. It will boost Israel's economic growth and its ability to tackle internal social problems;

9. It will ease the challenges of co-existence with the Arab minority in Israel;

10. It will secure Israel's future as an attractive democratic Jewish state.

With American assistance and active encouragement, Israel should choose a policy that proactively impacts its future. Israel cannot afford to hunker down or entrench itself in the status quo; this has never been the way Zionism has acted. A confident Israel can take charge and advance its own security and well-being through a coherent strategy of engagement and diplomacy, based on its strength. This is not a time for strategic passivity since the price for Israel increases as long as it waits for the dust to settle. This is a time for Israel to act for peace.

NOTE

1. "Prime Minister Netanyahu Addresses Opening Session of the Knesset," October 31, 2011, http://www.mfa.gov.il/MFA/Government/Speeches+by+Israeli+leaders/2011/PM_Netanyahu_opening_Knesset_winter_session_31-Oct-2011.htm.

4

PALESTINE AS A PARTNER IN PEACE

Samih Al-Abid and Samir Hileleh

We have been asked to address two questions: Is the Palestine Liberation Organization (PLO) a partner for peace, and can the PLO actually reach and implement a fair and reasonable peace agreement with Israel? In many respects these questions are presumptuous. If the PLO is not perceived as a partner for peace, why has Israel been negotiating with the PLO since 1993? If Israel really believes the PLO is no longer a partner, why doesn't Israel simply walk away now and do whatever it wants? And if the PLO does negotiate peace, how could anyone think that it would enter a process on any other basis than to try to reach and implement an agreement?

On deeper reflection, it appears to us that these questions—although valuable as a means of gaining greater understanding about the PLO's thinking and the challenges it faces in its policies concerning the peace process—may actually be a device to enhance the public relations value of Israeli policy and to give Israel an excuse to continue its occupation policies and practices. For if Israel can convince the world that the PLO is not a partner for peace and that the PLO is unwilling and/or too weak to reach and implement an agreement, Israel is off the hook.

Where do these questions originate? Many years ago, Abba Eban—one of Israel's foremost and most loquacious diplomats—coined the phrase "Palestinians never miss an opportunity to miss an opportunity." Indeed, Palestinians—as well as Israelis and Americans—missed many opportunities in the past to try to make peace, and we are all worse off for those missed opportunities. But Eban's maxim took on a life of its own, and it became a rallying cry for opponents of peace in Israel to blame the PLO and the Palestinians for every ailment that afflicts the peace process. For example, two former Israeli military and policy officials recently asserted in *Foreign Affairs* that Palestinian "rejectionism" is the key impediment to peace. They devoted considerable verbiage to recounting every perceived misdeed of the PLO in past years and concluded that the PLO was to blame for the failure of the peace process.[1]

We assume our share of the responsibility for the absence of peace today, and we need to continue to do our utmost to find a fair and just resolution of the conflict. But we also wonder whether Israeli critics are ready to turn the mirror around and take a hard look at their own policies and actions. We wonder whether they are ready to be asked whether *they* are partners for peace, and whether *they* really believe they can sign and implement an agreement that will result in a viable, contiguous, sovereign Palestinian state living next door to Israel. We wonder whether they have taken a hard look at their own society—the radical settlers who seize Palestinian land, the so-called price-tag activities of some young settlers, even the role of rabbis who place a higher value on retaining the West Bank than on obeying army orders and Israeli law.

Should Israelis go down this path, the results might be very surprising. How would Israelis explain the actions of a Baruch Goldstein, who murdered innocent Muslim worshippers in the holy place of Hebron in 1994 and who is now venerated as something of a saint by some Israelis? How do Israelis explain the murder of their own prime minister, Yitzhak Rabin, by a religious Israeli Jewish student? How do Israelis justify the billions of dollars of their own budget—and of American aid—that gets poured into Israeli settlements and outposts in the occupied territories, a pernicious process that is eating up the very territory that is supposed to become a part of the state of Palestine? Don't Israelis understand that these and so many other indignities and aggressions are persuading Palestinians that it is Israel that is not a partner for peace?

TRADING PLACES, TRADING ACCUSATIONS

Frankly, we see little value in pursuing this line of argument. We are certain that Israel has a long list of grievances against the PLO—many of which are serious and real—and we are certain that we could match that with an equally long list of grievances against Israel—many of which are also serious and real. This process, however, doesn't get us very far. Indeed, engaging in such a process only makes sense if the purpose of the exercise is to justify one's own inactions before one's own people. We hope that is not Israel's intention; we know it is not the PLO's intention.

If this is the case, should the PLO be asked to "prove" its peace partnership? For the past three years, PLO chairman and Palestinian Authority (PA) president Mahmoud Abbas has insisted that the PLO is ready for serious negotiations and intent upon reaching an agreement. He has asked that Israel stop the one activity—settlements—that is contrary to international law, contrary to American policy, and disruptive of the very process of peacemaking. In 2009, Abbas watched as President Obama sought a freeze on settlements from the Israeli government—a commitment, in fact, that Israel had already undertaken in the Roadmap but had not fulfilled. Obama did not succeed. Despite the administration's hailing a ten-month moratorium on housing starts as an "unprecedented" achievement, in fact there was not one day in the West Bank when ongoing construction within settlements stopped. After ten months, new housing starts resumed, and settlement activity continued on the basis of what some Israeli government spokesmen said was a debt owed to settlers for the moratorium.

Look at the political circus under way in Israel over the evacuation of Migron, an outpost that even the Israeli government conceded was established illegally; the Israeli Supreme Court demanded that it be evacuated.

The government went through contortions to delay, obfuscate, and ignore the court's ruling. All of this took place against the backdrop of an unfulfilled Israeli pledge to the United States in 2004 to evacuate *all* outposts set up since 2001. Israel does not honor its commitments, allows its own laws and courts to be ignored, tolerates illegal settlement activity, and yet presumes to label the Palestinians as non-partners for peace.

Even when the Obama administration tried to launch negotiations—without, it must be said, any particular terms of reference—the PLO laid its positions on the table, but the Israeli government did not. Palestinians put forward positions on territory, Jerusalem, and refugees. On the other hand, Prime Minister Benjamin Netanyahu made demands, primarily in the field of security and recognition of Israel as a Jewish state, but he did not reciprocate the actions of President Abbas by putting forth a full exposition of positions on the core issues.

Again, we are not persuaded that this exercise is fruitful, but if we are asked to engage in it, we respectfully submit that the questions of partnership and readiness to reach an agreement are double-edged swords. The answers to the questions that we were asked are clear and unambiguous: the PLO is a serious, committed partner for peace with Israel; and the PLO is ready and able to sign and implement a just, fair, and conclusive peace agreement with Israel.

PLO PEACE ASPIRATIONS

Some will ask: If the PLO is ready for peace, then why did Yasser Arafat not accept Ehud Barak's offer at Camp David in 2000, and why did Mahmoud Abbas not accept Ehud Olmert's offer in 2008—offers that are routinely portrayed as extraordinary and generous? Others will ask why rocket fire followed Israel's withdrawal from Gaza in 2005. Still others will wonder how the PLO can implement any agreement when Palestinian society is fragmented politically and geographically. The narratives that have developed over the years to explain what has happened in the peace process all seem to weigh against the Palestinians. The problem is that many of the accepted narratives are either wrong or so skewed as to make it difficult even to know where to start to try to correct the record. Let's look first at some of the issues in the negotiations.

Territory

This is hardly the place to try to review the history of Israeli-Palestinian negotiations, but it is important to advise the reader to approach the memoirs and
autobiographies of many Israelis and Americans with great caution. Ehud
Barak's so-called generous offer at Camp David fell far short of the minimum
required by any Palestinian leader on almost every core issue. Palestinians
believe that in 1988 they took a historic decision in favor of the partition of
Palestine, conceding 78 percent of Palestine to Israel, and expressing a willingness to accept a Palestinian state on 22 percent of their homeland. When
Barak came to Camp David with a proposal for Israel to retain additional
percentages of land, the Palestinians balked: not only did this fly in the face
of the historic decision taken by the PLO in 1988, but it also catered to the
demands of the Israeli settlers and expressed an expectation that the PLO
should sanction in an agreement what the settlers had taken illegally.

In 2008, Ehud Olmert changed the numbers, but not the concept. Israel
reduced the amount of territory it sought to retain, increased the amount
to be handed to the Palestinians and offered "swaps," that is, Israel would
retain the area on which large settlement blocks were built and would hand
over to Palestine an area of perhaps equal size. Again, the Israelis missed
the point: To accommodate their own long history of turning a blind eye or
even encouraging illegal settlement activity, they expected the Palestinians
to bend to their—and the settlers'—will. And when the PLO did not respond
affirmatively, Israel blamed the PLO for being the obstructionist party.

It is important to note that over the years, the PLO did make proposals on
territory (and on Jerusalem and refugees, discussed below). The Israelis did
not accept the PLO positions, just as the PLO did not accept the Israeli positions. This is a normal part of negotiations. What is not normal is for one side
to accuse the other of stonewalling, when in fact that has not been the case.

The bottom line on territory is that a peace settlement will have to ensure
that Palestine controls 100 percent of the 22 percent of historic Palestine.
Are there creative ways to deal with practical problems? There certainly
are, but those solutions have to be reached mutually, not by Israeli diktat. In
this respect, the United States did no one any favors by injecting itself into
this issue in 2004 and committing itself to supporting Israel's retention of

unspecified settlement blocks. If the United States wanted—and wants—to be helpful, it may be time to hear its full views on a settlement, not a piecemeal approach that caters only to Israeli domestic politics.

Security

Palestinians have always been sensitive to Israeli requirements on security, but they cannot abide unilateral Israeli demands to deploy their forces inside the Palestinian state, monopolize control of Palestinian airspace, and reserve large areas of Palestine—such as the Jordan Valley—for an undefined period of Israeli security control. If the objective is to reach an agreement by which the two sides live next to each other in peace and security, it is not reasonable for only one side to define what peace and security mean.

Palestine will require the security that any state requires: to protect its people, to ensure law and order, and to maintain the legitimate government in power. We are realistic enough to know that Palestine cannot aspire to become a regional military power. Frankly, we don't need an army that would drain the financial resources of our country. But we also cannot accept a situation in which the state of Palestine is created, but Israel maintains security control over all the territory between the sea and the river. For some period of time, there will be a need for outside help—monitors, observers, peacekeepers—and they will actually help both Palestine and Israel. For us Palestinians these international mechanisms will give us a sense of psychological freedom; for Israel, they will provide a proxy for the direct Israeli control and deployment that are unacceptable in a situation of peace.

Jerusalem

Ehud Barak believes he made a far-reaching offer on Jerusalem in 2000. The truth is, it wasn't so far-reaching, and it was clear even at the time that he had no political support for the offer he made. Indeed, no political groundwork had been laid, either in Israel or among Palestinians, that could have sustained serious movement on the Jerusalem question at that time. Could Arafat or Barak have been expected to renounce a claim of sovereignty over the Haram al-Sharif or Temple Mount? Could either leader have gone home

in peace under such a circumstance? Were the Americans serious in proposing an upstairs-downstairs idea of sovereignty over this holiest of sites? No
one had done the substantive psychological or political homework necessary
to even engage on the issue. Arafat, it should be recalled, believed that it was
premature to meet in a summit in 2000. The Jerusalem issue alone proved
how right he was.

In 2008, Ehud Olmert proposed one of the creative ideas that had been
developed in the so-called Track II community—an international board
that would be responsible for administering the city. Here, too, however, no
groundwork had been laid. Between 2000 and 2008, Palestinians and Israelis
had fought an Intifada that shattered relationships and trust. When Arafat
died in 2004 and Abbas took over, Israel was self-absorbed in its unilateral
policy of disengagement from Gaza. Olmert is to be commended for trying
to move the ball down the field, but even he proved impatient for an answer
on the spot, a reflection of the legal problems he faced that ultimately brought
down his government. In such a context, it would have been impossible for
both Palestinians and Israelis, including Olmert, to seriously tackle the
Jerusalem issue.

Refugees

The PLO is not a state, but rather a movement reflective and representative of disparate constituencies within Palestinian society. No constituency
engenders the emotion and historic respect among Palestinians as much as
the refugees. We are not unaware of Israel's opposite view of the situation,
seeing refugees as symptomatic of Palestinian intransigence and unrealistic
expectations. But is Israel aware of how deeply embedded in Palestinian psychology the notion of dispossession and exile represented by refugees is? We
think not.

Camp David yielded nothing serious on the refugee issue, and the 2008
Annapolis talks appeared to focus on a numbers game—that is, how many
refugees would Israel agree to accept as part of a long-term family reunification plan? Unfortunately, this approach misses the point. If Palestinians
are asked to understand the importance to Israel of its being recognized as
a Jewish state, Israelis need to understand the importance to Palestinians of

maintaining their rights and collective connection to their historic homeland. Any formula that seeks Palestinian relinquishment of the right of return as a precondition to negotiations—however such a demand is phrased—cannot succeed.

That does not mean this issue is unresolvable or that Palestinians will insist that millions of their people be allowed to return to live in what is now the State of Israel. But just as Palestinians realistically cannot expect Israel to accept the Palestinians' right of return as a principle, Israel cannot expect Palestinians to relinquish or forgo that right as a principle.

This also responds to the short-sighted and, frankly, pernicious Israeli demand that Palestinians accept Israel as a Jewish state. In 1993 the PLO and Israel exchanged letters of mutual recognition, the language of which had been negotiated and agreed on by both sides. Such a demand was not made at that time. No other country in the world—including the United States, Israel's closest ally—has been asked to offer such recognition, and Israel won't make such a demand because it knows that the demand itself is foolish. Israel's name is the "State of Israel." How it defines its character and culture is its own business, and it is the subject of intense internal interest among many elements of Israeli society. Asking Palestinians alone to declare such recognition is nothing more than a façade behind which the Israeli government is trying to mask its own unwillingness to negotiate peace.

Unilateral Disengagement and Violence

Some Israelis point to the Hamas takeover of Gaza and the rocket fire directed against Israeli towns as evidence that Palestinians don't want peace: After all, they say, Israel withdrew its army and its settlers from Gaza but Palestinians kept attacking Israel anyway. The argument is specious on several counts.

First, Ariel Sharon's senior advisor Dov Weissglas revealed in 2004 that Sharon's primary strategic goal at the time of the Gaza disengagement was to put the Roadmap and the possibility of dealing with the West Bank in "formaldehyde."[2] If there had been any interest among Palestinians in disengagement before this, Weissglas effectively killed that interest. Second, Sharon had no interest in discussing his strategy or even many of the operational details with the Palestinians. At the time, it was said that Israel was effectively walking out of Gaza, locking the gate, and throwing the keys back over the fence. Palestinians had almost no say about disengagement and thus little sense of responsibility when the withdrawal took place. Third, Palestinians were surprised that the United States supported the unilateral nature of the disengagement after years of American preaching about the dangers of uni-lateral activity. Not only that, but as noted above, the Americans in effect compensated Sharon for taking a unilateral step by making their own uni-lateral commitments on final status issues. This was a major step backward from the American approach begun at Madrid in 1991.

Political and Territorial Fragmentation

In addition to Weissglas's "formaldehyde" article and Sharon's unwillingness to negotiate disengagement with the Palestinian Authority, a third argument directed against Palestinians is that we are a polity divided both politically and geographically and thus incapable of taking the kind of strategic deci-sions that peace will require. Especially after 2007, when Hamas forcibly took control of Gaza, Israelis have raised questions as to whether the Palestinian Authority and the PLO are still paramount in Palestinian politics. These doubts not only reveal a basic misunderstanding of Palestinian affairs, they also fail to note the role that Israel (and the United States) plays in maintain-ing the political and geographical split within Palestine.

Since the 2006 elections in Palestine and especially since Hamas's 2007 takeover in Gaza, Israel and the United States have pursued a policy of pun-ishing the people in Gaza as a means of encouraging them to rise up and throw out Hamas.[3] American and international threats and actions to cut off aid to the PA because Hamas had won the election strongly undermined the PA's authority and called into question the commitment of the West to the democratic elections that they had long demanded.

Yet, even if the allegation of American-Israeli collusion to undermine Hamas is only partly true—and it looks true from the vantage point of those who live in this area—Israeli policies have systematically weakened the Palestinian Authority and strengthened Hamas. The blockade against Gaza, ostensibly in place to prevent arms smuggling, has been totally ineffective, as the tunnel business has grown to replace trade coming in through Ashdod. In fact, whereas the PA used to get the tax and customs payments from the legal trade through Ashdod, the blockade provided Hamas with a financial bonanza, for they began to regulate traffic through the tunnels, collect customs and fees, and tax the businesses that made the tunnel traffic profitable. Palestinians simply do not believe that Israel was unaware of the effect of its policies; and if Israel was aware of the impact, then why was Israel doing something that hurt Abbas and helped Hamas? Most Palestinians believe, in fact, that Israel conducted itself in this manner in order to undermine the ability of its Palestinian partner, the PLO, to function.

On several occasions, the PLO has seen it in its interest to try to bring about reconciliation with Hamas. The firm position of Abbas is that reconciliation would need to leave the PA and his authority strengthened, or he would not agree to it. Yet, when Fatah and Hamas appeared near agreement, Israel and the United States balked, blocked the process, and threatened all kinds of consequences were the process to continue. Palestinians would understand help from the outside to prevent a process demanded by or beneficial to Hamas, but why stop a process that Abbas had, on occasion, seen as being in his and the PA's best interest?

To be sure, it will be very hard to conduct negotiations while Palestine is split—hard, but not impossible. The PLO has promised that any agreement will be put to a referendum, and thus far virtually all Palestinian elements have agreed to abide by the results of the referendum. There is therefore a pathway for negotiations to take place even if reconciliation does not precede those talks. If Abbas thinks reconciliation can help him negotiate, it would be wise for Israel and the United States to support him.

SO, CAN THE PLO NEGOTIATE AND IMPLEMENT PEACE?

By this time, there should be no doubts about the PLO's continued commitment and intention to make peace with Israel on a fair and equitable basis. In fact, despite what many think, now is a good time to invest in efforts to reach that goal. Arab upheavals have caused as much uncertainty in the Palestinian community as elsewhere. If certainty within Palestine can be advanced—through productive negotiations with Israel that yield real benefits to the Palestinian people—this will calm the national mood. Palestinians do not want a return to violence, threats, reprisals, and animosities.

In addition, the fact that the Arab Peace Initiative remains on the table means that Palestinians can still draw on the support—the safety net—that Arab states can provide when we have to take hard decisions for peace. As important as the Jerusalem issue is to Palestinians, for example, it is also important to Arabs and Muslims worldwide. With an Arab policy position in favor of the two-state solution and the emergence of a Jerusalem in which both Palestine and Israel have their respective capitals, this is a tremendous encouragement for the peace process.

In looking ahead, Palestinians ask our Israeli colleagues to avoid pro-paganda and the blame game, and to focus instead on ways in which our peoples can benefit mutually from progress in the peace process. Israel has so many places to invest—in the Negev, the Galilee, in high tech, in the Israeli Arab community—that it can take a break from the wanton expenditure of resources on settlements. Palestinians don't need to hear the words "settle-ment freeze"; they need to see the results on the ground.

Palestinians also ask our American friends for more understanding and support, not at the expense of Israel, but in the cause of peace. We know you are going to provide Israel with its military and security needs; and to the extent that this helps Israel feel confident enough to take risks for peace, we cannot complain. But if your assistance is used by Israel to maintain a sta-tus quo that is dangerous for themselves, for us, and for your own interests, it is time to re-evaluate your policy. There is no justification for American silence in the face of Israel's annual request for assistance from the United States, on the one hand, and its expenditures for settlement activity, on the other.

In addition, we need more help. The PA has launched some very strong initiatives to build our institutions and economy, including in the security area, with your help. Let us work together to build on that success. We do hope for strong, balanced, fair, and sustained American leadership to help both Palestinians and Israelis reach our shared goal of peace.

NOTES

1. Yosef Kuperwasser and Shalom Lipner, "The Problem Is Palestinian Rejectionism," *Foreign Affairs*, November-December 2011, http://www.foreignaffairs.com/articles/136588/yosef-kuperwasser-and-shalom-lipner/the-problem-is-palestinian-rejectionism.
2. Ari Shavit, "Top PM Aide: Gaza Plan Aims to Freeze the Peace Process,"*Haaretz*, October 6, 2004, http://www.haaretz.com/print-edition/news/top-pm-aide-gaza-plan-aims-to-freeze-the-peace-process-1.136686.
3. David Rose, "The Gaza Bombshell," *Vanity Fair,* April 2008, http://www.vanityfair.com/politics/features/2008/04/gaza200804.

5

ISRAEL AND THE US ROLE

Yossi Alpher

Throughout the years 2009–2012, success in advancing the Israeli-Palestinian peace process essentially eluded the Obama administration. This development was detrimental to American, Israeli, and Palestinian strategic security interests. Here we consider, from an Israeli standpoint, what led to this state of affairs and, accordingly, what new departures might be useful for the administration that will take office in January 2013 to consider in order to revive the process and keep the two-state solution alive.

A brief review of relevant aspects of the US role in recent decades under-lines two important features. First, Washington historically has seldom been able to catalyze an Israel-Arab peace process on its own. Second, the prevail-ing assessment by the Israeli mainstream holds that neither Washington nor any alternative interlocutor can, under present and conceivable near-term circumstances, bring the Israeli-Palestinian process to a comprehensive con-clusion. The area where the United States can make a fruitful contribution that serves its own strategic interests, and where it has done so successfully in the past, lies somewhere in between.

THE US ROLE OVER THE YEARS

In the perception of many Israelis, the United States has only rarely sponsored the contacts that led directly to a peace breakthrough between Israel and an Arab neighbor. The Anwar Sadat trip to Jerusalem in November 1977, the Oslo Accords of September 1993, and the Israel-Jordan peace treaty of October 1994 were all the products of preliminary contacts that did not involve Washington. On the other hand, in all these cases the parties involved immediately followed their breakthrough by requesting massive American involvement in the ensuing negotiating process. In another important instance, in late 1991, the United States was the primary convener of the Madrid Conference that produced several significant bilateral and multilateral channels. Over the years, the heavy American commitment has included financial incentives to the parties, substantial security aid to Israel, side letters of assurances, understandings, or commitments, numerous investigative missions, and the 2003 Roadmap.

In the Palestinian context, Washington has been sponsoring and accompanying bilateral Israeli-Palestinian Oslo talks since 1993. These produced sustained negotiations at the highest level on two occasions (Camp David, July 2000; Olmert-Abbas, 2007–2008) and several interim agreements, but no two-state solution. The George W. Bush administration facilitated Israel's unilateral withdrawal from the Gaza Strip and the northern West Bank in 2005. Bush also expanded the American third-party facilitator role into the Quartet (involving Russia, the United Nations, and the European Union), though without any appreciable result.

The most advanced instances of Washington's specific involvement in Israeli-Palestinian peacemaking were the Clinton Parameters of late 2000 and the George W. Bush/Condoleezza Rice sponsorship of the Olmert-Abbas talks that led to Prime Minister Ehud Olmert's far-reaching final-status offer of September 2008. Both endeavors sought to engage all final-status issues based on the "nothing is agreed until everything is agreed" credo that has been a consistent feature of Oslo-based negotiations. Neither attempt was successful.

Sadly, the process itself and the US role have witnessed a sustained set-back ever since Palestinian leader Mahmoud Abbas turned down Olmert's 2008 proposal. In doing so, Abbas asserted that the gaps were too wide: he was referring apparently to the extent of territorial swaps beyond the 1967 lines and particularly to the refugee/right of return and Temple Mount issues, where the two sides remained far apart. Abbas was undoubtedly constrained in his decision making by the Hamas takeover of Gaza and the split within the Palestinian polity, but also by his personal views and those of his refugee constituents. Within months, Olmert had left office and Abbas confronted a new/old prime minister in Israel, Benjamin Netanyahu, who clearly would come nowhere near Olmert's offer.

In 2009, under some American pressure, Netanyahu accepted in prin-ciple the two-state solution, but in much the same way that he later accepted a partial settlement freeze: he had already established an essentially right-wing pro-settler coalition and was signaling that his negotiating demands would leave East Jerusalem, expanded settlement blocs, the Jordan Valley, and critical sites like Hebron under Israeli sovereignty or control—obvious non-starters from the Palestinian standpoint.

For his part, Abbas initially appeared to believe, mistakenly, that Obama would "deliver" Israel with no further need for Palestinian concessions. This reflected the generally poor understanding of the Washington dynamic that has consistently characterized the PLO leadership. In mid-2012 Abbas was again assuring interlocutors, without apparent foundation, that a second Obama administration would "deliver" Israel.

Meanwhile, the Islamist direction of Arab revolutions and a failure to reconcile with Hamas in Gaza left Abbas and the PLO leadership groping for constructive policy initiatives. The most provocative of these was the attempt to achieve UN recognition of a Palestinian state. It was badly mismanaged by the Palestinians and their Arab allies and totally rejected by the Obama administration.

Netanyahu's record over the past four years, in contrast to that of Abbas, reflects a considerable display of manipulative skill. He finessed and even ignored administration demands while relying on congressional and American Jewish and evangelical support. He shifted attention away from the Palestinian issue toward the threat from Iran and the impact of Arab revolutions. All the while, Netanyahu has succeeded in maintaining security and economic cooperation with the Palestinian Authority while nevertheless thickening and expanding settlements at an alarming pace.

By 2012, the Obama administration and the Quartet insisted on rhetorically encouraging and sponsoring essentially non-existent negotiations between two genuinely distant and incompatible governments in Jerusalem and Ramallah in the midst of a chaotic and violent Arab Middle East. This inspired mistrust and at times disdain on the part of both the Israeli and the Palestinian publics.

In looking ahead, the next administration must take into account the inevitability of Israeli elections in 2013, as well as the likelihood that Netanyahu will again emerge from those elections as prime minister. It must also factor in the possibility that the rise to power of the Muslim Brotherhood in Egypt and possibly elsewhere on the borders of Israel/Palestine will strengthen Hamas and Gaza at the expense of the PLO and the West Bank, thereby working against the two-state solution. Yet by the same token, because the consequences of the Arab Spring directly affect US national security interests and because the Israeli-Palestinian conflict will be very much on the agendas of the region's emerging leaders, the administration in 2013 cannot simply turn its back on the conflict.

According to the logic of this very brief historical and strategic review, and given that the likelihood of a new bilateral, unassisted Israeli-Palestinian breakthrough is extremely low, the assessment of Israeli centrists, moderate right-wingers, and even many leftists holds that the best chance Washington has to advance the process in 2013 is to persevere with some variation or derivative of the Oslo process that does not require "reinventing the wheel" but that also clearly avoids attempting to proceed along the same unsuccessful path that has characterized the past four years—even if the outcome is less than an end-of-conflict agreement. A deeper look at Israeli public opinion reinforces this premise.

ISRAELI PUBLIC ATTITUDES REGARDING US INVOLVEMENT

At the public level, a consistent and substantial majority of Israelis continues to support the two-state solution. It supports US involvement in the peace process and recognizes that in return for American security guarantees and backing, Israel will be expected to make territorial and other concessions. Israelis also overwhelmingly recognize their country's vital need for American support and expect their elected national leader to demonstrate a capacity to manage Jerusalem's relationship with Washington—otherwise, as in 1992 (Yitzhak Shamir's electoral loss to Yitzhak Rabin) and 1999 (Netanyahu's defeat by Ehud Barak), they will punish that leader at the polls. Note in this connection that in mid-2012, Netanyahu appeared so confident in his capacity to rebuff possible pressure from the next administration regarding the Palestinian issue that he postponed national elections that he had earlier called for September 2012 until mid- or late 2013, when he will have to factor in the theoretical possibility that emphatically stated administration displeasure with his policies could affect Israeli voter preferences.

But alongside their support for a two-state solution, most Israelis do not believe that an end to the conflict is in sight—an attitude paralleled in 2012, incidentally, by Palestinians. In the Israeli case, public lack of confidence in the peace process derives from a number of developments of recent years. One was the aggressive Arab response to unilateral Israeli redeployments from Lebanon (2000) and Gaza (2005). In the case of Gaza—where settlements were removed, the 1949 "Green Line" was respected, and Palestinians were given an opportunity to engage in state building—Arab aggression appeared to signal to Israelis that no reasonable concessions on their part would satisfy Palestinians and that, indeed, ceding territory signaled weakness and invited violence.

Another contributing factor is the schism between West Bank/Fatah and Gaza/Hamas, which is understood by Israelis to mean that Abbas cannot entirely deliver the goods even if an agreement is reached and that Hamas is liable to sabotage an Israeli-Palestinian agreement through violence. A third development, particularly discouraging for Israeli doves, was Abbas's rejection of Olmert's September 2008 offer—an offer that Israelis found singularly far-reaching. Then there is Abbas's subsequent unwillingness to challenge the hard-line Netanyahu to engage in serious negotiations and call his bluff despite the latter's partial acquiescence in a ten-month moratorium on new housing starts—a complex dynamic that generated resentment toward the Obama administration on both sides. By mid-2012, it was possible to describe all three relevant local actors—Israel, the PLO, and Hamas—as either complacent, indifferent to the peace process, or preoccupied with other regional and domestic issues.

These developments have radically reduced the size and eroded the legitimacy of the Israeli peace camp, and they seemingly refute the persistent argument that an end-of-conflict agreement is achievable in short order with the right leadership. And they go a long way toward explaining the emergence of the current right-wing Israeli government. But there are additional factors that have encouraged negative Israeli public attitudes toward the Obama administration and that must be factored into any new attempt to foster a peace process.

One is Netanyahu's perceived success in fostering alternative, non-administration American support for his policies from Congress. Another is Obama's decision in 2009 to visit Ankara and Cairo but not Jerusalem, and his subsequent avoidance of a visit to Israel. Then too, following the emotional warmth toward Israel displayed by both Bill Clinton and George W. Bush (which Israelis, who crave national validation, thrive on), Obama is perceived as cold and calculating—even when he justifiably reminds Israelis that he has delivered more security backing than have any of his predecessors. And the perception that he supported the removal from power in Egypt of Hosni Mubarak, who was seen by the Netanyahu government as a relatively friendly Arab leader, angered not only Israel but many old-guard Arabs and compounded skepticism fostered by the perception of overall US weakness and state-building setbacks in the Middle East.

REALISTIC OPTIONS FOR THE NEXT US ADMINISTRATION

The current government of Israel can realistically be described as preferring no US initiative at all—and contemplating none of its own—in the Israeli-Palestinian peace sphere. It apparently believes it can rebuff, dilute, or otherwise neutralize any administration demands in 2013 that contradict its maximalist territorial and settlement agenda. Any likely alternative Israeli government—even one headed by Netanyahu but comprising more centrist and left-wing players—would be more sensitive to US pressures in this regard. Netanyahu is notoriously prone to bend to pressure when his core political interests hang in the balance.

Israel's and the United States' best interests would undoubtedly be served by an American initiative that focuses first and foremost on breaking the prevailing Israeli-Palestinian stalemate. Too much is happening in the surrounding Arab revolutions; too much is at stake in the confrontation with Iran. Too many American strategic interests are affected, to say nothing of the demographic threat to Israel as a Jewish and democratic state posed by the current drift of events—a threat that Netanyahu recognizes rhetorically but flouts in practice. Nor will Washington long be able to support Israel's security needs against both Iran and possible violent spillover of Arab revolutions and Arab state instability unless it can point to movement toward a two-state solution and reassure itself and others that Israel is maintaining a sufficiently high moral and democratic profile in its dealings with the Palestinian issue.

But the next administration also should not repeat the mistake of rejoining the Oslo process without introducing changes to the Israeli-Palestinian peace paradigm. Oslo did not work for the past four years and will not work for the next term. The two sides simply are not willing and are not able to sit down once again to negotiate all final-status issues. There is too much Israeli settlement spread and too much Palestinian political schism and paralysis. And, as Abbas suggested, the gaps really are too wide to be bridged in a single agreement. Thus, Oslo-related measures such as sending a new American peace envoy or augmenting monitoring of Roadmap provisions would probably generate little progress in this context.

Are there alternative American or locally generated ideas out there— derivatives of Oslo—that can be molded into a peace paradigm that provides a new direction while building on past accomplishments and exploiting the relative calm and success in state building that, fortunately, still prevails? Is this feasible even if the most we can hope for is partial progress that renders the conflict more manageable and reduces the risks it poses? Would any such ideas conceivably gain the support of the Netanyahu government? Or the support of a majority of the Israeli public?

Here the administration should look for inspiration to the initiatives that have emerged either officially or independently of the two sides in the course of 2011–2012. Those initiatives are imperfect and undoubtedly problematic, not least because they offer essentially interim rather than final steps. But they have the distinct advantage of having appeared, so to speak, "in the field," of enjoying at least a measure of local support on one side, and of moving the conflict substantially closer to resolution. Further, precisely because of their interim nature and their origins in the region itself, they may present less risk to an American administration that adopts them than embarking on another attempt to reach an end-of-conflict agreement.

Leveraging UN Recognition into a Delinked, Win-Win, State-to-State Approach

Abbas's experience in direct negotiations with Olmert in 2008—following the first final-status negotiating failure in 2000 at Camp David between Barak and Arafat—must be seen as a critical juncture in Abbas's understanding of his own capacity to end the conflict. He was confronted with the most far-reaching Israeli peace proposal yet, but rejected it because it was still far from the core demands of his constituents, most of whom are Diaspora-based refugees. These focus primarily on the narrative issues of holy places and—as distinct from the finite question of how many 1948 refugees, if any, Israel undertakes to absorb—the Palestinian demand that Israel acknowledge the principle of the right of return of all the refugees.

That suggests that the Oslo formula of linking all final-status issues in an agreement will continue to founder on these two issues. Both the 2000 and the 2008 negotiations demonstrated that the post-1967 disputes over territory, statehood, and security are relatively more amenable to agreement. In contrast, the differences grounded in both sides' deeper, pre-1967 historical narratives is the main reason for nearly twenty years of failed efforts.

As Israelis understand it, the Palestinian demand that Israel recognize the principle of the right of return of Palestinian refugees requires a tacit acknowledgment that the State of Israel was "born in sin" in 1948. Similarly, the Palestinian assertion that "there never was a temple on the Temple Mount" and that Israel has no inherent rights there is perceived as a denial of Israel's national and historical roots. These Palestinian positions in turn explain Israel's demand of recent years—itself undoubtedly also a deal-breaker because it is blatantly unacceptable to the Arab camp—that the Palestinians recognize Israel as a Jewish state. Note that this demand, introduced by the right-wing Netanyahu government, enjoys widespread support throughout the Israeli mainstream.

Abbas, then, has turned to the UN not only because the Palestinian state-building enterprise in the West Bank has proved successful, but also because it is clear that Oslo-based final-status negotiations, even if they reconvene, cannot succeed in ending all claims. In this sense, it is Abbas's intransigence regarding the contents of a full final-status package, no less than Netanyahu's, that brought Abbas to the UN in 2011.

At the United Nations—in contrast to bilateral negotiations—Abbas appears to be prepared to accept international determination of the 1967 borders and a Palestinian capital in Jerusalem as the defining parameters of a Palestinian state, with the refugees and holy places issues delinked from this package and left to further negotiations. Even if Israel and Palestine subsequently fail to agree on these pre-1967 narrative issues—as well they might—we still will emerge from the United Nations with a two-state reality and a conflict whose manageability is no longer held hostage to insurmountable, perceived existential questions.

True, Abbas has shrouded his UN initiative in a cloud of alternative policy options such as dismantling the Palestinian Authority, resigning, or reconciling with Hamas and holding new elections. And he still feels politically obliged publicly to profess adherence to the full Oslo menu. But here we should look at what he does, not what he says: the real significance of his UN initiative is to turn the conflict into a more manageable and limited state-to-state negotiation.

If Washington is willing (the Europeans and the Russians are already predisposed in this direction), the request for UN recognition of a Palestinian state could conceivably be leveraged into a new two-state paradigm that serves Israel's vital needs as well as those of the Palestinians. This would require a radical change in existing US policy regarding a UN or alternative international role, as well as a willingness to incur differing degrees of opposition on the part of both parties to the conflict.

In this sense, administration investment in an internationally backed state-to-state initiative would have to take into account that the diplomatic payoff might take time. On the other hand, it would build on President

Obama's May 2011 proposal that the issues of territories and security be awarded priority in negotiations.

A win-win UN resolution regarding Palestinian statehood—or a formula nurtured in an alternative forum like the Quartet—could go a long way toward satisfying key demands of both sides and the United States. It could take a variety of forms. Here is one sample formulation, whereby the international community undertakes to:

1. Balance the declarative creation of a Palestinian state by recalling that the United Nations created Israel as a Jewish state. Call on both states to provide equal rights to minorities.

2. Balance recognition of the 1967 lines as the basis for a shared border by recognizing the need for agreed territorial swaps—something the PLO has in any event accepted.

3. Balance recognition of a Palestinian capital in East Jerusalem with long-delayed international recognition of Israel's capital in West Jerusalem.

4. Recognize that extending the authority and status of a sovereign Palestinian state to the Gaza Strip will depend on effective control there by the legitimate and internationally recognized government of the Palestinian state.

5. Relegate all relevant issues involved in implementing this resolution to direct, bilateral negotiations, beginning with the issues of borders, settlements, water, and security, while recognizing that negotiations regarding the right of return and holy places will follow in a later stage of negotiations to be held between the two states once they are functioning state neighbors.

6. Offer UN (and, separately, US) guarantees for Israel's legitimate security needs as it concedes West Bank territory and control.

7. Call upon the Arab states to begin seriously implementing their obligations under the Arab Peace Initiative as an additional incentive to Israel.

Such an approach to leveraging the Palestinian UN initiative would not end the conflict or end all claims. A lot of negotiating in accordance with that initiative—about border delineation, the shape of the Palestinian capital, timetables, security, and the like—would still be called for.

PLO objections to such an initiative would presumably be mild. Abbas could hardly reject outright an internationally backed proposal that takes his own idea as its point of departure. The United States could suggest to Palestinian skeptics that a sovereign state is an attainable and important goal that overrides their fixation on the unattainable right of return. Netanyahu, on the other hand, would flat-out oppose such an initiative insofar as it paves the way toward a Palestinian state that requires Israeli territorial concessions unacceptable to his pro-settler political allies. Washington would have to remind the right-wing public in Israel that ending the occupation and ensuring Israel's future as a secure Jewish and democratic state constitute far greater rewards than holding out for unattainable concessions on intractable narrative issues. But important elements in the center and left wing of Israeli politics and public opinion would be able to hoist a significant new policy flag that boosts their standing and generates new pressure on Netanyahu.

Thus a strong American stand would be required to overcome both Israeli and Palestinian opposition. This win-win approach, whose terms correspond fully with existing US commitments to Israel like the 2004 George W. Bush letter to Ariel Sharon, could render the conflict far more manageable as a state-to-state affair rather than as a negotiation between Israel and a national liberation movement whose main constituency lies outside the territory it is discussing. Separately, it might still take a generation to resolve the now delinked pre-1967 narrative issues.

A (Hopefully Coordinated) Major West Bank Withdrawal

But if conditions do not allow for this approach, or if it is tried and fails, or perhaps even in parallel with it, careful American consideration should be given to recent proposals from the Israeli centrist mainstream for an additional Israeli withdrawal on the West Bank. Ideas along this line were presented in 2012 by former defense minister Shaul Mofaz; the Blue-White Future movement, whose leadership features former senior security officials like Ami Ayalon; and the Institute for National Security Studies under the leadership of recently retired IDF (Israeli Defense Forces) intelligence chief

Amos Yadlin. The primary rationale of these plans is their contribution to maintaining Israel as a Jewish and democratic state by reducing the profile of the occupation. In seizing the initiative, they also better position Israel for countering the challenges posed by Arab revolutions and the Iranian threat, all at a time when comprehensive final-status negotiations do not appear possible.

The great advantage of this approach is that, if necessary, it can be implemented without the agreement or cooperation of the Palestinian side. But by the same token, its success would be more likely with Palestinian cooperation—something only Washington may be able to deliver. The PLO leadership has always been wary of unilateral withdrawal schemes for fear that they would leave it with considerably less than the entire territory of the West Bank but fewer means of pressuring Israel to withdraw further. This consideration led Mofaz to introduce the idea of firm international (primarily American) guarantees that a final-status agreement based on the 1967 lines would be negotiated within a short period of time; meanwhile, Palestinian statehood would be recognized in conjunction with the first, partial withdrawal.

Another problematic aspect of the unilateral idea is possible lack of Israeli public support. This could reflect the heavy security price the Israeli public has paid for unilateral withdrawals from Lebanon in 2000 and Gaza in 2005. This led Yadlin to propose that the IDF remain in the Jordan Valley pending a final-status agreement, thereby giving Israel a greater measure of ongoing security control over the West Bank and applying lessons drawn from the mistake, in his view, of withdrawing from the Gaza-Sinai "philadelphi strip" along with the body of the Gaza Strip in 2005. Yet any ongoing Israeli military presence in the territories would undoubtedly render the Israeli withdrawal less attractive to the Palestinians.

How much territory would Israel relinquish unilaterally in the West Bank, and would it remove settlements? The proposals vary: some seek withdrawal to the security fence, leaving Israel in full control of some 9 percent of the territory, including East Jerusalem and all of the settlement blocs, with financial incentives offered to settlers beyond the fence to leave; others suggest a more modest move embodying 10 or 20 percent of the West Bank and little if any settlement removal. Blue-White Future would leave Israeli forces in place in Areas B and C (nearly 60 percent) of the West Bank pending a peace agreement, while declaring a future border along the security fence line and providing incentives for settlers beyond the fence to leave.

Obviously, the more territory turned over to Palestinian rule and the more settlements removed or at least incentives offered settlers, the more likely the withdrawal is to attain the presumed objective of such an interim move: nourishing and sustaining the two-state process and its Palestinian and Israeli supporters and encouraging the sides to follow up with serious final-status negotiations. On the other hand, the more territory and settlements involved, the less likely this measure is to meet a welcome from Netanyahu. Over the past three years, the Israeli prime minister has on occasion agreed to consider ideas for a partial withdrawal. And he is not oblivious to the potential public appeal of the unilateral withdrawal proposals raised by so many prominent security veterans.

Here, then, is an area where a determined US administration could, in 2013, push even Netanyahu for progress. One way or another, US support, along with commitments to the Palestinians regarding the final-status sovereign and territorial outcome and to Israel regarding the security risks it undertakes, would be vital to both sides—even if the PLO officially rejects the initiative.

CONCLUSION

Two important insights emerge from this analysis. First, even with active American support, a return to the "Oslo table" and full-fledged final-status negotiations on all outstanding issues will not succeed—indeed, it could deepen the Israeli-Palestinian divide by adding to current frustrations. The facile slogans of recent years—"nothing is agreed until everything is agreed" (proclaimed by both Israelis and Palestinians), "just get to the damn table" (Leon Panetta), and "the rough solution to the core final status issues [is clear to] well-educated Israelis and Palestinians" (Tony Blair)—may be popular in certain peacemaking circles. In fact, they are wrong and have been made irrelevant by the demise of the Oslo process. The new post-Oslo paradigm that we require may be messy and less than comprehensive, but it might also have a better chance to register desperately needed progress.

Second, in searching for this paradigm, unilateral initiatives presented in recent years by the Palestinian leadership and key Israeli security figures point to the possibility of US-sponsored interim progress that will maintain stability, move us closer to a two-state solution, and enhance Washington's credibility as a serious peace sponsor.

In any event, the next administration will probably have to deal with less-than-cooperative and possibly even obstructionist Israeli and Palestinian leaders. It may have to appeal over their heads to their respective publics and present them with new models for progress that aspire to change their political agendas. Certainly it will have to do so aggressively, based on the conviction that an ongoing Israeli-Palestinian stalemate, against the backdrop of ongoing Arab revolution and developments involving Iran, seriously endangers US national security interests.

6

CONSTRAINED AND NOW CORROSIVE: HOW PALESTINIANS VIEW THE US ROLE

Ghassan Khatib

Many analysts and observers said little when President Barack Obama admitted in a television interview in Washington in July 2012, "I have not been able to move the peace process forward in the Middle East the way I wanted."[1] It was a stunning understatement, given the catastrophic and far-reaching nature of his involvement. Indeed, the manner in which this administration has handled the Palestinian-Israeli conflict goes beyond simply failing to solve the problem during Obama's four-year term or neglecting to relieve suffering by ending the conflict. The failure of the current American administration "to move the process forward in the Middle East" allowed others to move it backward.

The United States is recognized, worldwide and in the region, as the leader in international efforts to help solve the Arab-Israeli conflict. There have always been criticisms of and challenges to its positions in this role. Arabs, especially Palestinians, have typically accused the American government of bias toward Israel. Palestinians have gone further to say that this bias is such as to create an insurmountable defect in US involvement—a defect that has resulted in its weakness and/or failure.

Others, such as some of the European states, Russia, some Latin American countries, and many others, have criticized US involvement for its inadequacy. In addition, they complain of Washington's tendency to monopolize the process at the expense of collective mediation.

Despite the last twenty years of US-led peace efforts, neither side of the conflict has found itself nearer to achieving its legitimate objectives. Palestinians are no closer to ending the Israeli occupation of their land, namely the West Bank, including East Jerusalem, and the Gaza Strip, and establishing an independent and free country of their own. Israelis also do not feel they have moved closer during the two decades of the peace process to lasting and comprehensive peace, recognition, and integration into the region. In fact, with the dramatic developments currently under way in the neighborhood (Arab Spring), many Israelis believe that they might have lost a historic opportunity.

Twenty years ago, Israelis, Palestinians, and the region were all more "ripe" than they are today for a historic compromise of the kind that could end this conflict, one based on the two-state solution and the creation of an independent state of Palestine on the land occupied in 1967. Public opinion in the two respective societies and the regional political environment were more conducive then to the compromise that this requires than it is today.

Given this situation, the two main questions to be asked are: First, to what extent can the leadership of the United States be held responsible for losing this opportunity? Second, is it too late to rescue the two-state solution promoted by successive American administrations—and what can be done by the administration that will take office in January 2013 to save it?

A BRIEF HISTORY OF US INVOLVEMENT IN PEACEMAKING EFFORTS

The first experience in which the United States joined forces with others to solve the Middle East issue (albeit with limited scope and for a short time) was the international Middle East peace conference convened in Madrid in October 1991 upon joint invitation of the Soviet Union and the United States. This conference was followed by the creation of bilateral tracks of negotiations; one of them was between Israelis and Palestinians. This track was hosted for two years by the State Department in Washington, D.C. The "Madrid process," as it was called at the time, was interrupted when the Declaration of Principles (DOP) between the PLO and Israel was signed at the White House in September 1993. (The DOP was developed in a secret side track but was certainly influenced by the discussions under way in Washington.) This initial agreement was followed in September 1995 by the signing of an interim agreement that stipulated the creation of the Palestinian Authority, which was to be a limited self-governing arrangement.

The parties to this process, in addition to their sponsor and main mediator, the United States, were unable to maintain the momentum needed to complete the agreements. The second half of the 1990s witnessed a stagnation of the process accompanied by a dangerous resumption of the pre-peace process symptoms of the conflict, accelerated Israeli settlement expansion (illegal in international law), and a gradual resumption of mutual violence. While each of the parties blamed the other for the deterioration, others, including independent academics, offered an objective analysis. Professor Herbert C. Kelman from Harvard University came to the following conclusion:

> The major structural limitation of the Oslo agreement, which put the new relationship to a severe test, was its lack of an explicit commitment to a two-state solution as endpoint of negotiations . . . both [Israeli Prime Minister Yitzhak] Rabin and [PLO leader Yasser] Arafat did maintain reserve options as a fallback position, in the event that the arrangements and negotiations stipulated on for the interim period did not work out as they had hoped. On the Israeli side, the reserve option was to resume control over the Palestinian territories; on the Palestinian side, it was to resume armed struggle.[2]

At the turn of the twenty-first century, in 2000, the US government tried to push the process forward by convening the first final-status negotiations at Camp David. The clock was ticking; the interim agreement said a final-status document ending the conflict was to be signed in five years.

When the summit ended in failure, the blame game began. With devastating long-term consequences, the US host and sponsor took sides against the Palestinians, probably to enhance the deteriorating public position of Israeli Prime Minister Ehud Barak, who was headed for elections. Wrote Robert Malley and Hussein Agha:

> [President Bill Clinton's] decision to hold the Camp David summit despite Arafat's protestations illuminates much about U.S. policy during this period. In June, Barak—who for some time had been urging that a summit be rapidly convened—told the President and Secretary [Madeleine] Albright that Palestinian negotiators had not moved an inch and that his negotiators had reached the end of their compromises; anything more would have to await a summit. He also warned that without a summit, his government (at least in its current form) would be gone within a few weeks.[3]

By not listening to Palestinian assertions that the parties' positions remained too far apart for an agreement and then blaming them when the summit failed, Washington set the stage for the Second Palestinian Intifada, which grew out of frustration with the process and resulted in deep setbacks in structures and attitudes that the process had set into motion.

The administration of George W. Bush took up the Palestinian-Israeli conflict in an active way only late in its second term. Only in the sixth of his eight years in office did the president initiate the Annapolis process.

President Obama took the opposite tack, showing a great deal of enthusiasm for the needs of the Middle East and signaling a desire to invest in the Israeli-Palestinian peace process. "America will not turn our backs on the legitimate Palestinian aspiration for dignity, opportunity, and a state of their own," he said in an early speech.[4]

In that same statement, he clearly committed the American government to ending Israel's illegal expansion of Jewish settlements in the occupied Palestinian territories: "The United States does not accept the legitimacy of continued Israeli settlements. This construction violates previous agreements and undermines efforts to achieve peace. It is time for these settlements to stop." Nor did Obama stop his engagement with these constructive statements. He quickly appointed respected former Senator George Mitchell, who had been involved in mediating the Northern Ireland conflict, as his envoy to represent him in efforts to revive the peace process.

Obama's close attention to the conflict made him realize the clear contradiction between peacemaking and Israel's settlement expansion. Any peace process based on the vision of two states naturally requires an end to the occupation, whose outposts are the ever-growing settlements. Israel's continued nurturing of the settlement enterprise made a lie of its commitment to the peace process.

This conclusion led to visible tension between the Obama administration and Israel. Obama was explicit in expecting Israel to stop the expansion of settlements in order to allow for the resumption of negotiations that would lead to peace based on the creation of the state of Palestine. Secretary of State Hillary Clinton was quoted in the Israeli newspaper *Haaretz* saying that Obama "made it very clear" to Prime Minister Benjamin Netanyahu that he expects a total freeze in the settlements. "He wants to see a stop to settlements. Not some settlements, not outposts, not natural growth exceptions," she went on.[5] This position created remarkable push-back from Israel (given the two countries' stated "friendship" and Israel's dependence on US largesse) and motivated Israeli Strategic Affairs Minister Moshe Ya'alon to announce that "Israel won't yield to U.S. demands, won't halt settlement construction."[6]

After two years of arguing unproductively over settlements, in May 2011 Netanyahu, seeking to relieve pressure from Washington, resorted to his comparative advantage: internal American politics. This was an effective tactic a year and a half before a US presidential election. As is already conventional wisdom, American candidates for the presidency must go out of their way to express extraordinary support for Israel in election years. As explained by John Mearsheimer and Stephen Walt:

[S]erious candidates for the highest office in the land will go to considerable lengths to express their deep personal commitment to one foreign country—Israel—as well as their determination to maintain unyielding U.S. support for the Jewish state.[7]

This relationship between internal US politics and foreign policy toward Israel is not a new phenomenon.

Instead, the thrust of U.S. policy in the region derives almost entirely from domestic politics, and especially the activities of the "Israel Lobby." Other special-interest groups have managed to skew foreign policy, but no lobby has managed to divert it as far from what the national interest would suggest, while simultaneously convincing Americans those U.S. interests and those of the other country—in this case, Israel—are essentially identical.[8]

Obama was forced, through the wielding of domestic power by Israel, to abandon his vision of ending settlement construction as a path to renewing serious negotiations. Moreover, in order to spend his political capital to work on other pressing issues in the Middle East, he has largely abandoned the Palestinian-Israeli conflict to the winds of change.

THE "UNDOING" OF US MEDIATION

The last few years have seen the beginnings of serious debate among many Palestinians, some Israelis, and engaged international observers and analysts on the viability of the two-state solution. Ahmed Qurie, a member of the Executive Committee of the PLO, former Palestinian prime minister, and a chief negotiator in the Oslo talks, said in a statement last year that, owing to the irreversible facts on the ground being created by Israel, the two-state solution has been eclipsed. As such, he said that Palestinians are exploring a new paradigm: "The Palestinian leadership has been working on establishing a Palestinian state within the '67 borders . . . If Israel continues to oppose making this a reality, then the Palestinian demand for the Palestinian people and its leadership [would be] one state, a binational state."[9]

Khalil Shikaki, one of the most prominent Palestinian pollsters and a measured analyst, essentially concurred with Qurie's assessment: "With no agreement on a two-state solution to the Palestinian-Israeli conflict in sight, one-state dynamics are gaining momentum—a development that will be difficult to reverse or even contain."[10]

The same conclusions are being drawn in Israel. Said Israeli analyst Akiva Eldar: "Facing a default reality in which a one-state solution seemed the only option, Israel chose a third way—the continuation of the status quo. This unspoken strategic decision has dictated its policies and tactics for the past decade."[11]

"The Emperor Has No Clothes," declared a recent analysis by the International Crisis Group. One of the report's main conclusions was to ask: does anybody still believe in the Middle East peace process? "Nineteen years after Oslo and thirteen years after a final settlement was supposed to be reached, prospects for a two-state solution are as dim as ever."[12]

Indeed, the peace process has never been so stagnant, peace prospects never so gloomy, and the two-state solution never so elusive. However, this grim state of affairs was not predetermined, but rather, it was man-made. Radicalization in Israel and lack of attention by the US administration reinforced each other, allowing former Netanyahu aide Michael Freund to conclude the following after observing that in 2011 the settler population in the occupied Palestinian territory grew at pace of 4.3 percent, more than double the national average: "[T]he Green Line is dead and buried, and the Left can kiss it goodbye. It is no longer of any relevance, politically or otherwise."[13]

The long-term nature of the current stalemate is having a detrimental effect on the internal political balance in our societies, especially in Israel, which is the determining power in the conflict. American policy ends up undermining moderates in Israel and the Arab world (including among Palestinians). As Stephen M. Walt put it: "We unwittingly aid the various extremists who gain power from the prolonged stalemate and the sowing of hatred. This bipartisan [i.e., Republican and Democratic] practice may not be the most dysfunctional policy in the history of U.S. foreign policy, but it's got to be damned close."[14]

Despite great hyperbole about the current leadership division between Hamas in the Gaza Strip and Fatah in the West Bank, the fact remains that the Palestinian political scene is conducive to a peaceful settlement on the basis of two states. Public opinion polls continue to show majority support for the two-state solution.[15]

But the status quo is confronting the Palestinian Authority with danger-ous existential threats. The combination of financial shortfalls that increase unemployment and poverty and the lack of political prospects for peace have created a time bomb waiting to explode; when and if it does, the explosion will tear down the last remaining structures of the peace process begun in Madrid.

Furthermore, the Palestinian leadership is unable to deliver on any of the areas the public expects it to. These include not only some services, but also the peace process, reconciliation between Hamas and Fatah, and the holding of overdue elections.[16] The current period is unique in that opinion research shows a remarkable decline in public support for armed struggle against the Israeli occupation. A recent study analyzed the attitudes of Palestinians in the occupied Palestinian territories toward armed resistance against Israel over the last fourteen years. It showed that "The highest point of public support for military operations was in September 2001, measured at 84.6%, and its lowest point was in November 2011, at 29.3%."[17]

AFTER THE ELECTIONS

Given the above conditions, if the United States does not invest in Middle East peacemaking, there is almost no hope of progress. The United States has more ability to influence Israel than does any other country. American sup-port for Israel guarantees its military superiority, its welfare, and probably its survival. The United States has too much leverage over Israel for the latter to ignore its wishes. As Akiva Eldar concluded, "History teaches us that Israelis are only willing to take brave and honest steps toward peace when they know the cost of failing to do so will be even greater. Unfortunately, given the reali-ties of the current situation, there is little reason to think that the Israelis will take these steps anytime soon."[18]

Any discussion of the potential US role after the presidential election in November must try to answer the question of whether there might be a change in approach and level of involvement. The optimistic scenario is that if President Obama is elected to a second term, the administration will be less constrained. Therefore, it will be more engaged, probably more balanced, and consequently more efficient. On the other hand, there are some who believe that the prospects for substantial change in the second term are not supported by the actions of previous administrations.

Another question is whether the US administration in place after these elections will decide to continue a similar strategy of promoting the two-state solution or will develop a new one. The behavior of the current administration thus far has undermined the two-state option. Is this the road to a new strategy or simply a non-strategy brought on by lack of political will?

Objectively, given domestic and regional constraints, the only two possible approaches for the next administration have already been tried.

The first is based on a strategy that stems from pursuing the national interests of the United States in the Middle East region and elsewhere. That strategy was implemented in 1991. The United States was just finishing a war in Iraq in which militant Arab states sided with the United States, thus losing a great deal of their credibility. The Palestinians were successfully challenging the international and ethical position of Israel through non-violent Palestinian resistance to the occupation (the First Intifada). That period witnessed the gradual collapse of the Eastern Bloc, which made the international environment more conducive to Middle East peace efforts.[19]

When right-wing Israeli prime minister Yitzhak Shamir tried to obstruct American efforts to push negotiations led by Secretary of State James Baker, the United States enforced its interests through sanctions. The combination of consistent diplomatic effort and strict expectations of the parties that included possible sanctions was responsible for making the launch of the Madrid peace process possible.

The second strategy is one based on limiting American political initiatives to the outer extent to which Israel is willing to go. The best example of this approach can be found in the annals of the current administration. In the beginning of 2011, and after two years of extensive diplomacy, the administration declared that Israel should stop expansion of settlements in order to resume meaningful negotiations. The Israeli response was firm opposition. The administration then modified its stance and turned to apply pressure on the weaker party, the Palestinians. The Palestinian Authority was too debilitated to endure this shift and subsequently lowered its position to one even less stringent than the initial US policy, thereby diminishing its domestic support even further.

The Palestinians have high expectations from the new administration. At this point, they have everything to lose. Therefore, the administration's failure to deliver will have a detrimental impact on the stability and public support for the Palestinian leadership that has gambled entirely on a US-led peace process (even abandoning its own moves at the United Nations to try to move outside that circle). In addition, a new failure will further encourage Israeli practices that are responsible for the current impasse, thus prejudicing basic peace requirements for the long term, particularly the demands of two independent states.

CONCLUSIONS AND RECOMMENDATIONS

A more effective and productive role from the United States is possible after the elections, however, if the lessons of the past are learned.

The first and most important requirement is the establishment of criteria and benchmarks that the United States will use to judge the two parties. It is no longer enough that the United States merely supports a negotiated two-state solution because such vagueness has increased Israel's appetite for creating more illegal facts on the ground in an attempt to determine the future borders between the two states. The established criteria should be consistent with international law. This is the only way to make the criteria credible and allow Israel to enjoy the support of the rest of the world.

A second recommendation—which complements the first—is introducing elements of accountability to the American relationship by the parties engaged in the conflict. The United States should adjust its relationship and cooperation with each of the two sides based on the parties' adherence to the established criteria; hopefully, other members of the international community will follow—indeed, some are already moving in this direction. Double standards will undermine any new policy and should be avoided at all costs.

In his most recent interview with *The Independent*, Palestinian Prime Minister Salam Fayyad urged the international community to "raise the bar of accountability" by confronting Israel on its occupation without in any way "delegitimizing" the State of Israel.[20]

The third important recommendation is to take into consideration the possible positive influence of ongoing dramatic changes in the Arab world when designing post-election US Middle East policy. This would entail an inclusive approach toward the Islamic movement of Palestine instead of the current exclusion policy. It should also mean replacing the stick with a carrot along with conditions that must be taken into consideration: commitment to regular elections and the normal circulation of power, and adherence to international legality.

Ending the political division in Palestine is a necessary requirement for the two-state solution. The reconciliation measures required for the end of the split between Hamas and Fatah have been blocked by strong opposition from the United States and Israel. The new attitudes of the Islamic movements in leading Arab countries, such as Egypt and Tunisia, particularly their engagement in the democratic process and respect for international commitments, is inspiring for their extension movement in Palestine, that is, Hamas.

Therefore, dropping the standing veto against a Fatah-Hamas reconciliation and forming a joint government committed to democracy and legality will remove another important obstacle to the two-state solution.

Although it might not be explicit, there is a clear linkage between the Arab Spring and the Palestinian-Israeli conflict of which the United States must be observant. The biased American position, its monopolization of the peace process, and its failure to deliver have had a negative effect on US credibility among the Arabs. Consequently, this has limited the extent to which the United States can influence the ongoing decisive developments in the region. More serious efforts in helping to move the conflict to an end will definitely improve the chances of success for American policies in Arab and Muslim countries.

Finally, as a result of a political reality that has marginalized the conflict on the one hand and enhanced American internal political constraints on the other, the next administration must and can "maintain" the peace process. That means keeping the desired options open. It also means preventing the collapse of the current status quo, which is defined greatly by the security situation. Increasing incitement leading to growing levels of violence, especially of armed Jewish settlers against Palestinian civilians as well as the violent reaction of the Israeli military to nonviolent Palestinian protest, could bring the current state of general calm to an end. Leaving Palestinians and their land to the mercy of the Israeli government, army, and settlers is a known recipe for disaster.

Palestinians remain committed to reaching a peaceful solution with Israel based on the two-state paradigm and the precepts of international law and United Nations resolutions. Public opinion consistently reflects this choice, and the Palestinian leadership continues to pursue this as its strategic option. Indeed, most Palestinians see no other way forward. Today, most of the Palestinian public expects to share in creating a peace that will ensure the legitimate rights of both Palestinians and Israelis as laid out in international law. The Palestinian people seek international and American support to fulfill their hopes for independence, freedom, justice, and a peaceful future.

NOTES

1. Jacob Edelist, "Obama Says He Failed to Push Mid East Peace, Vows to Do Better in 2nd Term," *Jewish Press*, July 17, 2012, http://www.jewishpress.com/news/breaking-news/obama-says-he-failed-to-push-mid-east-peace-vows-to-do-better-in-2nd-term/2012/07/17/.

2. Herbert Kelman, "The Israeli-Palestinian Peace Process and Its Vicissitudes," *American Psychologist* 62, no. 4 (2007): 287-303.

3. Robert Malley and Hussein Agha, "Camp David: The Tragedy of Errors," *New York Review of Books*, August 9, 2001, http://www.nybooks.com/articles/archives/2001/aug/09/camp-david-the-tragedy-of-errors/?pagination=false.

4. "Text: Obama's Speech in Cairo," *New York Times*, June 4, 2009, http://www.nytimes.com/2009/06/04/us/politics/04obama.text.html?_r=1&pagewanted=all.

5. Yitzhak Benhorin, "US Calls for Total Settlement Freeze ahead of Abbas Meeting," *Ynetnews*, May 27, 2009, http://www.ynetnews.com/articles/0,7340,L-3722832,00.html.

6. "Israel Won't Yield to U.S. Demands, Won't Halt Settlement Construction," *Haaretz*, May 29, 2009, http://www.haaretz.com/news/israel-won-t-yield-to-u-s-demands-won-t-halt-settlement-construction-1.276570.

7. John Mearsheimer and Stephen Walt, *The Israel Lobby and U.S. Foreign Policy* (New York: Farrar, Straus and Giroux, 2007).

8. John Mearsheimer and Stephen Walt, "The Israel Lobby," *London Review of Books* 28, no. 6 (March 6, 2006): 3-12, http://www.lrb.co.uk/v28/n06/john-mearsheimer/the-israel-lobby.

9. "PA Negotiator: Israel May Make Two-State Solution Impossible," *Haaretz*, August 11, 2008, http://www.haaretz.com/news/pa-negotiator-israel-may-make-two-state-solution-impossible-1.251475.

10. Khalil Shikaki, "The Future of Israel-Palestine: A One-State Reality in the Making," NOREF, May 14, 2012, http://www.peacebuilding.no/Regions/Middle-East-and-North-Africa/Israel-Palestine/Publications/The-future-of-Israel-Palestine-a-one-state-reality-in-the-making.

11. Akiva Eldar, "Israel's New Politics and the Fate of Palestine," *The National Interest*, June 28, 2012, http://nationalinterest.org/article/israels-new-politics-the-fate-palestine-7069.

12. "The Emperor Has No Clothes: Palestinians and the End of the Peace Process," International Crisis Group, May 7, 2012, http://www.crisisgroup.org/en/regions/middle-east-north-africa/israel-palestine/122-the-emperor-has-no-clothes-palestinians-and-the-end-of-the-peace-process.aspx.

13. Michael Freund, "Fundamentally Freund: Kiss the Green Line Goodbye," *Jerusalem Post*, June 20, 2012, http://www.jpost.com/Opinion/Columnists/Article.aspx?id=274599.

14. Stephen M. Walt, "What's Going on in Israel?," *Foreign Policy*, July 12, 2012, http://walt.foreignpolicy.com/posts/2012/07/12/the_veil_falls.

15. In a Palestinian survey conducted in May 2012, a majority of 51.9 percent still supported the two-state solution and only 19.8 percent supported one binational state in historical Palestine. For a detailed account of Palestinian public opinion on this subject, see JMCC public opinion polls: http://www.jmcc.org/documentsandmaps.aspx?id=855.

16. For further analysis on the difficulties facing the Palestinian Authority because of the status quo, see "If the Palestinian Authority collapses?" http://www.bitterlemons.org/previous_ins.php?opt=1&id=50#221.

17. Charmaine Seitz, "Tracking Palestinian Public Support for Armed Resistance during the Peace Process and Its Demise," Jerusalem Media & Communications Centre, February 27, 2012, http://www.jmcc.org/documentsandmaps.aspx?id=850.

18. Akiva Eldar, "Israel's New Politics and the Fate of Palestine," *The National Interest*, June 28, 2012, http://nationalinterest.org/article/israels-new-politics-the-fate-palestine-7069?page=6.

19. For further elaboration on American efforts to initiate peace negotiations between Israel and Palestinians, see Ghassan Khatib, *Palestinian Politics and the Middle East Peace Process: Consensus and Competition in the Palestinian Negotiation Team* (London: Routledge, 2010).

20. Donald Macintyre, "Salam Fayyad: 'We Have Never Been More Marginalised,'" *The Independent*, July 26, 2012, http://www.independent.co.uk/news/people/profiles/salam-fayyad-we-have-never-been-more-marginalised-7976731.html.

7

THE OTHER NEGOTIATOR: THE ISRAELI PUBLIC AT THE PEACE TABLE

Gershom Gorenberg

Histories of peacemaking normally focus on leaders and negotiators, and on what they say inside closed rooms: Henry Kissinger shuttles between Anwar Sadat and Golda Meir to conclude an interim agreement after the Yom Kippur War; Israel's Yair Hirschfeld and the PLO's Abu Alaa meet secretly in Norway and sketch out the Oslo Accord; Bill Clinton, Ehud Barak, Yasser Arafat, and their teams gather at Camp David in 2000, argue, and fall short of a desperately needed agreement. These dramas seem to be filmed close up; the cast is small; a brilliantly chosen formula can close a gap or preserve a vital ambiguity.

Yet the most accurate of such accounts leave out another set of parties to the diplomatic process: the publics in whose name negotiators act. Even in a

representative democracy, the government's positions are not a precise repro-
duction of the views of the electorate or even of the ruling party's voters. This
is particularly true in Israel, with its roiling debate, fragmented society, and
startling electoral swings. An Israeli leader who, by choice or under duress,
joins a diplomatic process must also negotiate with his own public—formally
through the political system and informally through the media. If he fails to
do so, he may pay by losing power and turning the country's critical decisions
over to his opponents.

An American peace initiative must therefore pay close attention to the
views, concerns, and contradictory emotions of the Israeli electorate. To go
further: deliberately or not, the US administration will be engaged in a negotiation with the Israeli public, not just with the government. The chances for
success are greater if that negotiation is pursued consciously. Israeli domestic
opinion is fragmented. The major goals of public diplomacy will be to convince the broad center that peace is possible, safe, needed, and beneficial, and
to soften opposition from the hard right, especially ideological settlers and
their supporters. The strategy should include public actions of the US president and other high-level officials and careful attention to the Israeli media.
The message should include understanding of Israeli concerns and should
stress peace as a victory rather than a setback for Zionism. Most challenging, negotiating with the public may include adjusting proposals for peace to
increase domestic support in Israel.

To understand, let us look briefly at the history of negotiating with the
Israeli public, then at the main currents in opinion today, at possible elements
of the public side of a diplomatic initiative, and finally at the risks posed by
the most hard-line opponents of an agreement.

Outsiders risk assuming that if there is a gap between the Israeli public and its leaders, the public is more reluctant to negotiate or make compromises. Certainly, this has been true regarding particular issues. In 1993,
Prime Minister Yitzhak Rabin secretly offered a full withdrawal from the
Golan Heights for Israeli-Syrian peace.[1] The next year, a Peace Index poll of
Israeli Jews found that only 18 percent would accept a full pullback from
the Golan. A plurality rejected any territorial concession to Syria. Rabin had
staked out a position more dovish than that of the overwhelming majority of
the electorate.

Yet the same survey found that 43 percent of Jewish Israelis supported the Oslo process, considerably more than the 28 percent opposing it.[2] Indeed, asserts veteran Israeli pollster Mina Zemach, director of the Dahaf Institute, the Oslo process was itself a response to public opinion. "What happens in Israel in many cases . . . is that the public is ahead of the leaders. The public's positions showed openness to compromise before the leaders were ready to act. Certainly in the case of Oslo, the public pushed the leaders."[3]

The gap between the electorate and the government has helped drive the repeated changes in power in Israel over the past two decades. The public may be unhappy with its elected leaders for being too dovish, as in Ehud Barak's 2001 landslide loss. But it can also reject incumbents for being too hawkish, as in the defeat of the Likud prime minister, Yitzhak Shamir, by Labor's Rabin in 1992.

In contrast to previous elections, in 1992 the future of the occupied territories was a major consideration for over half of all voters. Government spending on settlements became a wedge issue for the first time.[4] The Palestinian uprising had turned the status quo in the occupied territories into a question for many Israelis. So had the Madrid peace conference of 1991, President George H. W. Bush's push for continued negotiations, and Shamir's refusal to consider trading land for peace. Bush's conditioning of US loan guarantees to Israel on a settlement freeze helped recast settlement as an economic issue, and much of the electorate thought the cost was too high. The quarrel with Washington became a campaign issue, with Rabin stressing the need to repair relations with Israel's essential ally.[5]

On election day, voters narrowly rejected Shamir's intransigence. Rabin's victory broke the decade-long stalemate between Israel's two major political camps. In one view, it also represented a temporary victory in the struggle between two Israeli understandings of reality—one that sees Israel as alone in an "inherently hostile" world, another that sees cooperation and peace as possible.[6] It is worth stressing that many, perhaps most, Israelis read reality in both of these ways, but circumstances can make them trust one intuition over the other.

As 1992 shows, the actions of other actors in the diplomatic arena affect the positions of the Israeli public, but they do so by interacting with long-held attitudes. The potential impact of foreign statements and actions on Israeli views must be carefully weighed. Even a gesture of support may backfire. In 2000, at the end of the Camp David summit, President Bill Clinton praised Prime Minister Barak for moving "forward from his initial positions" more than the PLO's Arafat had done. Administration officials likewise put the full blame for failure on the Palestinians.[7] Leaving aside the historical debate on what happened in the summit, Clinton's quick public verdict did not help Barak at home or encourage peace efforts.[8] Instead, it portrayed Barak to his constituents as willing to make reckless concessions, and it called forth Israelis' fears that Palestinians had no intention of ending the conflict. The narrative of Camp David fit, ready-made, into the existing Israeli narrative about a world that cannot be trusted and continues to haunt efforts to renew peacemaking.

The most powerful example of a diplomatic partner reaching past the Israeli government to the Israeli public is Egyptian President Anwar Sadat's visit to Israel in November 1977. Six months before, running on a Whole Land of Israel platform, the right-wing Likud had won its first election. A year before Sadat's visit, when a poll asked Israeli Jews if they believed the Egyptian leader was sincere when he said he sought peace, only 17.5 percent answered yes.[9] By coming to Israel and speaking in the Knesset, Sadat physically showed recognition of Israel in a public drama that released Israelis' suppressed hopes. Immediately afterward, the same polling institute found that 86.4 percent of Israeli Jews believed Sadat sincerely wanted peace. The numbers dropped after the initial ecstasy but stayed much higher than before Sadat's visit. Willingness to withdraw from part or all of the Sinai tracked closely with trust in Sadat's intentions.[10] In the diplomacy that led from Sadat's visit to the peace treaty with Egypt, the Israeli public became an unrecognized but real party at the table.

The Sadat gambit cannot be repeated blindly this deep into the Israeli-Palestinian process. But its lessons can be learned: Israeli public opinion is not equivalent to the last election result; it can be changed, especially by dramatic events and deliberate acts of symbolism; and it can affect the outcome of an initiative. The power of Sadat's gesture was that it spoke directly to Israelis' most basic question about peace negotiations: is the other side willing to accept Israel and put the conflict in the past? Those lessons are especially relevant today.

THE ISRAELI PUBLIC: BETWEEN DESPAIR AND HOPE

Here are the most salient features of current Israeli public opinion: The traditional positions of both the Left and the Right have lost credibility among many Israelis who once held them. There is widespread despair about negotiating peace with the Palestinians, yet support for permanent Israeli rule of the West Bank has shrunk. The concept of unilateral withdrawal, which briefly dominated Israeli politics, is discredited. Israelis are almost universally unaware of the role of the Palestinian Authority (PA) in ending the terror attacks of the Second Intifada. The internal politics of the Likud push Prime Minister Benjamin Netanyahu's party to positions more intransigent than those of its electorate. For the purposes of peacemaking, the two most significant groups are a wide, deeply confused center and the hard-line Right tied to ideological West Bank settlements.

Recent polling hints at how wide that center is. In the monthly Peace Index surveys carried out between February and June 2012, between 65 and 70 percent of Jewish respondents favored renewing peace talks with the Palestinian Authority. Yet the number who believed that such talks would "lead to peace . . . in the coming years" fluctuated between 25 and 32 percent.[11] That is, a consistent plurality of up to 40 percent backed negotiations but despaired of such talks leading anywhere.

A more specific question yielded slightly greater optimism. In one survey, just over 40 percent of Jewish respondents strongly or moderately believed that the conflict could be resolved by a two-state agreement within ten years. That was still considerably below the 57 percent who said it was urgent or at least moderately pressing to resume peace talks. One-sixth of respondents, in other words, thought it important to renew talks that they do not believe will lead in the next decade to the most commonly discussed arrangement for Israeli-Palestinian peace.[12]

(This analysis focuses on the Jewish majority of Israel. Among Palestinian citizens of Israel, surveys also show a gap between support for and confidence in peace talks. However, the reasons for their doubts are likely to focus at least as much on the Israeli government as on the Palestinian leadership.)

The polling figures point to the nature of the Israeli center. It consists of people who hold views, often passionately, that pull them in opposite directions. They are willing to make territorial concessions but not yet on the order needed to reach an agreement. The word "settlement" may arouse in them associations of both Zionist pioneering and religious extremism.

Over the last two decades, the center has grown. "The two historic camps [in Israeli politics] have collapsed," says Dan Meridor, deputy prime minister and minister of intelligence and atomic energy and the sole prominent moderate in Netanyahu's government. "The hawkish camp . . . which thought, as I did for many years, that it was possible to preserve the Whole Land of Israel including Judea and Samaria and to preserve a Jewish majority and democracy has for the most part concluded that this is impossible." But, argues Meridor, "the left has also shattered," because its approach of achieving a final-status peace agreement with the Palestinians by "conceding all or nearly all of the territories" has been tried and failed.[13]

As diplomatic history, Meridor's account can be challenged on key details; it depends, for instance, on the Barak-Clinton telling of Camp David. As a history of the Israeli public mood, his description is accurate. The signing of the Oslo Accords brought recognition of Palestinian peoplehood and of the PLO—radical positions only a few years before—into the Israeli mainstream. The accords promised nothing more than Palestinian autonomy, and neither of their Israeli patrons, Yitzhak Rabin and Shimon Peres, "wanted the autonomy to usher in a Palestinian state," according to historian and former Labor politician Shlomo Ben-Ami.[14] Yet the perception that Oslo's logical outcome was a Palestinian state quickly percolated into public consciousness. Concern that Palestinians would very soon outnumber Jews in the land under Israeli rule further eroded support for the Right's classic position. Over time, a number of prominent Likud "princes"—sons and daughters of the movement's hard-line founders—publicly broke with the party's ideology. The process culminated when Vice Prime Minister Ehud Olmert came out in 2003 for withdrawal from most of the West Bank.[15]

And yet, throughout the Oslo years, "the majority of the Israeli Jewish public, including a significant minority on the left, mistrusted Palestinian intentions to the extent that they did not believe the historical conflict with the Palestinians would be brought to an end even if the two sides were to sign a formal peace agreement," writes sociologist and pollster Ephraim Yaar.[16] Mistrust grew with the Camp David debacle and the Second Intifada. When

Benny Morris, the once-dovish historian, wrote in 2008 that "each suicide bomber seemed to be a microcosm of what Palestine's Arabs had in mind for Israel as a whole," he articulated a very widely felt response in Israeli society.[17]

With both ideologies in shambles, Olmert and Prime Minister Ariel Sharon offered an alternative: Israel would withdraw unilaterally, first from the Gaza Strip, then to lines of its choosing in the West Bank. It would reduce the number of Palestinians under its rule without giving up the amount of land or evacuating the number of settlements necessary to reach agreement with the Palestinians. Sharon's name for the 2005 pullout from Gaza, "disengagement," had the military connotation of reducing contact with the enemy, not of making peace. His adviser Dov Weissglas described it as way of putting President George W. Bush's Roadmap for a two-state solution into "a bottle of formaldehyde."[18] After Sharon suffered a stroke, Olmert ran for prime minister as head of the new Kadima Party and won on a platform of a further, undefined pullout in the West Bank.

However, the Hamas electoral victory in 2006, the Islamist movement's takeover of Gaza in 2007, and continuing rocket fire from Gaza into Israel have discredited unilateralism. "If you ask the center what happened in the disengagement," says political communications scholar Gadi Wolfsfeld, it would say that "Israel made a gesture to the Palestinians . . . pulled out of Gaza, and what we got in return was missiles."[19] This is an account of perception, not reality. Sharon hardly intended to engage the Palestinians diplomatically. But the public's perception has driven subsequent politics.

Olmert afterward jettisoned unilateralism and engaged in serious negotiations with Palestinian Authority President Mahmoud Abbas—talks that broke off because of Israel's Cast Lead Offensive in Gaza and because corruption allegations made Olmert a lame duck. Olmert has consistently asserted that Abbas was "a fair partner, opposed to terror," and that agreement remained possible.[20] In contrast to Barak's account of Camp David, Olmert's description of the talks with Abbas has not filtered into the Israeli center's perceptions.

Neither has the cooperation between Abbas's security forces and Israel. Meridor describes this as a strategic choice by Abbas, a "revolution in thinking" compared to Arafat, and a change that is well known among Israeli security professionals—but one that has not registered among the Israeli public. "They don't know about it, and their intuition is that Palestinians are terrorists," he says. The possibility that such cooperation may fade unless there is diplomatic progress to legitimize Abbas's strategy among his own people is even more distant from most Israelis' thoughts.

Rather, the most available explanation in Israeli discourse for the end of the Abbas-Olmert talks, the failure to renew bilateral negotiations since Netanyahu's election, and the Palestinian gambit of seeking UN recognition is that the Palestinian side is unwilling to accept generous Israeli offers and instead seeks international help to impose Palestinian statehood without a commitment to peace.

The result is ennui. The ideological Right committed to permanent Israeli rule of the Whole Land has shrunk. Yet hopelessness about peace efforts reaches across the center and into the dovish Left. Meanwhile, fear of terror has faded from daily life; only those Israelis who live within rocket range of Gaza are still in personal danger as a result of the Israeli-Palestinian conflict—and a diplomatic solution for Gaza appears entirely out of reach. Analysts' warnings that the current calm is fragile make as little impact as geologists' warnings that Israel is located on a fault line and should be preparing for an earthquake: A danger without a date attached is easily ignored. By the summer of 2012, the issues of peace and territory were nearly absent from Israel's political agenda.

It is not surprising that most Israelis are more attuned to Barak's account of diplomacy than to Olmert's, or that terror attacks make an impression and the PA's security cooperation does not. Like other groups involved in lasting ethnic disputes, Jewish Israelis share a narrative of the past that fits new events into existing understandings and explains the motives of each side. The Israeli narrative of survival under constant siege screens out positive events and explanations, and accepts negative ones.[21]

This pattern fits what Nobel economics laureate Daniel Kahneman and Jonathan Renshon have described as a "bias . . . built into the fabric of the human mind" to exaggerate the malevolent motives of adversaries while assuming that one's own benevolent intentions are obvious. In one psychological experiment, they write, "Israeli Jews evaluated an actual Israeli-authored peace plan less favorably when it was attributed to the Palestinians than when it was attributed to their own government."[22] The public also depends on an unreliable messenger for information. As Wolfsfeld writes, the news media have a structural bias toward covering violence, which is dramatic and immediate, and toward ethnocentrism.[23] Every news organization has an "us" for whom it produces the news.

Rather, it is the broad center's continued support for peace talks—its hope despite hopelessness—that stands out. The fact that such support exists despite the natural biases shows how conflicted the center is and suggests that there is a foundation on which public diplomacy has a chance of building.

It also emphasizes the need not to equate the positions of Netanyahu and his Likud Party with those of the electorate, or of Likud voters. Historically, the Likud had a small, ideological core and attracted much wider backing from hawkish-leaning voters who shared resentment of Israel's Labor founders. Support for Likud became a family and communal tradition. As mentioned, prominent Likud figures broke with the founding ideology after the Oslo Accords. Yet developments over the past several years have made Likud a more homogeneously hawkish party. After the Gaza pullout, the party split. Most leading figures who had accepted the need for territorial concessions left to join Kadima.

Meanwhile, a radical religious-right faction known as Jewish Leadership has gained influence within the Likud. Jewish Leadership is the creation of Moshe Feiglin, a West Bank settler who in the past has proposed such measures as creating a powerful Jewish-only upper house of the Knesset. After Jewish Leadership ran unsuccessfully for the Knesset in 1999, it joined the Likud and encouraged religious settlers and their supporters to do the same. Since the electorate in Likud primaries is small and Jewish Leadership votes as a bloc, the faction wielded disproportionate power over the makeup of the current Likud Knesset delegation.[24]

Where Netanyahu himself stands is open to interpretation. He, too, is the scion of the party's ideological aristocracy. In the book he wrote before his first run for prime minister, he argued for permanent Israeli sovereignty over the West Bank, with limited Palestinian autonomy in four non-contiguous enclaves.[25] In his Bar-Ilan University speech of June 2009, he declared for the first time that he would accept a "demilitarized Palestinian state" alongside Israel, if Palestinians met a number of preconditions.[26] Whether this was a real shift or a rhetorical one is a matter of debate. The description that he and his surrogates give of a Palestinian state falls short of usual concepts of statehood. Vice Prime Minister Moshe Ya'alon, for instance, has asserted that Israel would retain control of the border between Jordan and the Palestinian state.[27] In practice, Netanyahu has continued construction in West Bank settlements, including those deep in the West Bank, and has sought to push Israeli-Palestinian relations to the bottom of the diplomatic-security agenda.

Were Netanyahu to agree to steps leading toward Palestinian statehood, he would likely face a rebellion within his Knesset delegation and possibly the collapse of his coalition. A diplomatic initiative that garners centrist support in Israel would create a conflict for Netanyahu between satisfying swing voters and preventing a revolt in parliament. Until he faces such a conundrum, the path of least resistance is to satisfy hard-line backbenchers.

THE SETTLER OPPOSITION: A CLOSER VIEW

Not only Netanyahu but any Israeli leader who agrees to withdrawal, evacuating settlements, and Palestinian statehood is likely to face intense opposition from the most vocal and ideologically hawkish sector of the Israeli public—the religious settler movement and its supporters. In preparing for that response, three trends deserve note: The number of settlers continues to increase; their profile in the military is growing; and the withdrawal from Gaza has pushed some settlers, especially in the younger generation, to greater extremism. The practical implication is that postponing a diplomatic solution will make it more difficult to achieve.

Speaking before Congress in May 2011, Netanyahu referred to the "dramatic demographic changes that have occurred" in the West Bank since 1967, and to the "650,000 Israelis who live beyond the 1967 lines."[28] The figure was striking for two reasons: First, the actual number was just over 500,000, according to official data.[29] Second, Israel's government normally insists on distinguishing between Jewish neighborhoods of annexed East Jerusalem, which it regards as part of Israel proper, and settlements in the remainder of the West Bank. By presenting the combined figure and inflating it by 30 percent, Netanyahu apparently sought to bolster his assertion that the settlements where the majority of settlers live are too large to evacuate and must remain under Israeli sovereignty. Referring to changes that "have occurred," he portrayed settlement as a natural process, rather than a state project.

Exaggerations aside, the settlement situation is serious enough. But it must be viewed with nuance. Settlements continue to grow—both those near the Green Line, or pre-1967 border, and those deep in the West Bank. Their growth does increase the difficulty of reaching a two-state agreement and the cost of implementing it—in shekels and in the risk of internal Israeli strife. The danger of internal violence is one more factor discouraging politicians from pursuing negotiations. For precisely those reasons, settlement growth makes a new diplomatic initiative urgent: delay constantly raises the price. On the other hand, the settlements are not cause to give up in advance on reaching and carrying out an agreement.

In assessing settler opposition, let us stress: the settlers are not homogeneous. In broad terms, they are usually divided into three main groups: "quality of life" settlers, meaning Israelis who have been drawn to towns and exurbs in the West Bank by low home prices and other incentives; ultra-Orthodox settlers; and ideological settlers, whose explicit motivation is commitment to the Whole Land of Israel.

The ultra-Orthodox belong to a religious subculture that segregates itself from mainstream Israeli society and that is largely impoverished. Though their political views are overwhelmingly hawkish, their reasons for moving to the West Bank are economic: since the 1990s, government-subsidized housing has drawn tens of thousands to exclusively ultra-Orthodox settlements. Over a quarter of all settlers in the West Bank, excluding East Jerusalem, now live in two ultra-Orthodox towns, Beitar Illit near Jerusalem and Modi'in Illit near Greater Tel Aviv.[30]

The dominant group among the ideological settlers is religious Zionists—members of another strand of Orthodox Judaism that historically supported the project of creating a Jewish state and sought a large degree of integration into Israeli society. After 1967, a theology swept religious Zionism that saw Israel's establishment and its victory in the Six-Day War as steps in God's plan for final redemption. Settling beyond the Green Line was a way of living that theology. In religious settlers' own eyes, they became the vanguard of Zionism. In Israeli stereotypes and foreign news coverage, these are *the* settlers.

In reality, the majority of Israeli settlers in the West Bank live in the Jewish neighborhoods of East Jerusalem, in "quality of life" and ultra-Orthodox settlements, and near the Green Line. The small communities deep in the West Bank, in areas that Israel would have to give up to allow for establishment of a viable, contiguous Palestinian state, are overwhelmingly religious and ideological.

Thus, a contradiction is built into every proposal for Israel to keep large settlements close to the Green Line while evacuating those farther in: Israel would retain a small fraction of the West Bank and the great majority of the settlers. Financially, this would reduce the cost of resettlement. Politically, though, the most serious opposition to an agreement to cede land, and certainly to evacuation, is likely to come from the ideological settlers living deeper into the West Bank and from their supporters within Israel.

The mass protests in 1993–1995 against the Oslo Accords were organized by ideological settlers, and demonstrators came almost exclusively from the religious Zionist community.[31] The same was true of protests against the Gaza pullout, where it was the religious settlers who collectively refused to believe the withdrawal would take place until the soldiers and police appeared at their doors. In the closing act of the pullout, hundreds of young religious activists barricaded themselves in the synagogue at the Kfar Darom settlement and fought police with stakes and steel rods before being dragged away. For the secular Right and for quality-of-life settlers, opposition to territorial concessions has been a voting issue. For the religious Right, it has been a marching issue and sometimes more than that.

Even this is a schematic picture. Some residents of suburban settlements moved there for ideological reasons. Most small religious settlements, especially the older ones, are comfortable exurbs, and this is part of their attraction.

Indeed, their bourgeois character has helped sparked rebellion among a radical minority of young religious Zionists, especially second-generation settlers, who have moved to the tiny settlements known as outposts. Established without government approval, illegal under the laws by which Israel governs the West Bank, the outposts still received assistance from government bodies. By some accounts, their locations were mapped out by former prime minister Ariel Sharon to break up the contiguity of a potential Palestinian state.[32] That sponsorship has not kept them from becoming the loci of anger against the government and the founding generation of settlement leaders, especially since the Gaza withdrawal. In the young radicals' eyes, the secular state has lost legitimacy, and settlement leaders sold out by letting the Gaza evacuation take place without much more forceful resistance. Allegations of violence against neighboring Palestinians by outpost settlers are rife.[33] There are two sides of this picture: The outpost radicals, and residents of a few older settlements known for extremism, are a small fraction even of the ideological settlers. But they pose a particular risk of violent opposition to evacuation.

Meanwhile, the military has become a potential arena of ideological conflict. Since the end of the 1980s, the religious Zionist Right has steadily taken a greater role in the Israeli military. The seeds of change were planted years earlier with the establishment of *yeshivot hesder*—seminaries where students alternate between religious studies and active military duty. The late 1980s saw the birth of a new program, the pre-army academy, in which young men study for a year before conscription. The academies aim at strengthening recruits' faith and boosting motivation to serve in combat units and rise to command positions. Despite their many ideological shades, nearly all the *yeshivot hesder* and Orthodox pre-army academies are identified with the theology of the religious Right.

The academies' impact can be seen in statistics: In 1990, just 2.5 percent of the men finishing the infantry officers' course were graduates of Orthodox high schools. By 2008, over a quarter of new infantry officers were Orthodox.[34] Not all Orthodox soldiers are on the right, and not all on the right base their political views on religion. But a rising portion of combat soldiers and their commanders have studied in institutions stressing the inviolability of the Land of Israel.

The IDF (Israeli Defense Forces) has thus acquired a new cadre of soldiers and commanders whose relationship with highly politicized religious leaders remains ambiguous. The one serious test came before the Gaza withdrawal. Leading rabbis of the religious Right, including heads of several *yeshivot hesder*, proclaimed that soldiers should refuse orders rather than evacuate settlements. Other rabbis called on Orthodox soldiers to "recognize the authority of government" and obey orders. Still others, among them heads of pre-army academies, suggested the middle way of "gray refusal"—quietly avoiding evacuation duty. After the pullout, the army announced that sixty-three soldiers had been tried for refusing orders. The extent of gray refusal is unknown. Moreover, to avoid the risk of mass refusal, the IDF did not assign units with a high proportion of Orthodox soldiers to evict Israeli civilians.[35]

The response of Orthodox soldiers, especially graduates of pre-army academies and *hesder* soldiers, to a larger evacuation from the West Bank is an open question. Delaying a two-state agreement is only likely to exacerbate the potential problem. Yet the response of soldiers could also be a function of how ideological settlers react to an agreement and of the breadth of support among the Israeli public at large.

NEGOTIATING WITH THE ISRAELI PUBLIC: TOWARD A STRATEGY

If the United States pursues a new effort to achieve Israeli-Palestinian peace, the focus of its negotiation with the Israeli public will be the political center. What remains of the Left is likely to resume activism on peace if negotiations with a tangible chance of success are under way. What remains of the Right will oppose any plan to partition what it sees as the indivisible Jewish homeland.[36] If the center continues to regard peace as unattainable, the government can remain intransigent. If the center's existing support for talks is transformed into an active sense that an agreement is achievable, the current government will face a quandary. The Palestinian issue is likely to return to the top of the political agenda. This government or a future one would have much greater reason to show diplomatic achievements than to stonewall.

Certainly, the Palestinian side in a diplomatic process should be concerned with Israeli public opinion, even if Abbas appears to be in a weak position to affect it. His diplomatic strategy and security cooperation have not penetrated Israeli consciousness. A return to direct negotiations may have some impact, especially if the declared goal is an end to the conflict. Any public Palestinian gestures underlining commitment to that goal are valuable.

However, the focus here is on the role of the American administration, on the assumption that Israelis are attuned to what the country's key ally is saying. What follows is meant not as a plan but as a starting point for discussion. The goal is not to intervene in Israeli electoral politics, but to take public opinion seriously as a factor in the process, to place peacemaking back at the top of the Israeli political agenda, and to build as much support as possible for it.

While advocating renewed Israeli-Palestinian negotiations and facilitating them, the administration should find ways to show Israelis publicly that it is listening to their concerns. The administration should seek to create greater awareness of the security risks and economic costs of the status quo, and suggest realistic responses to Israelis' fears—not just in proposals raised in closed rooms, but in public. The diplomatic goal most likely to win support is an end to the conflict, supported and enforced by the international community and especially the United States.

To start, the administration has to *hear* Israelis. The Israeli government presents one position, or at most a narrow range of opinions, within the country's political debate. American pro-Israel organizations present an even more constricted view. Within these organizations, awareness of changes in Israeli politics can lag years behind what is happening in Israel. As part of a negotiating strategy, the administration needs much more direct information and should track the internal Israeli discussion closely. It may even suggest to a third party—a think tank or NGO—to conduct polling on questions relevant to negotiations.

But listening should also be a public act, a statement. Visiting Israel, the secretary of state or the president might have dinner with a family or college students in the town of Sderot near the Gaza Strip. A mediator might make a public point of meeting with ex-generals or other security experts from both Right and Left, and speaking afterward of their concerns—from the possibility that missiles would be fired at Israel from a Palestinian state to the military costs of defending settlements. If the president praises Israeli democracy in a speech, he can also describe the range of opinion heard in those conversations, conveying to Israelis that their views are taken seriously—and to the American audience that Israeli opinion spans a much wider range than lobbyists in Washington portray.

At the same time, administration officials should challenge the popular Israeli perception of the current impasse with the Palestinians as a comfortable, open-ended calm. This is a delicate task: quiet is not news, and lack of an obvious deadline for progress reduces drama and media interest. Strident warnings that violent Palestinian opposition to Israeli rule may erupt again could reinforce the belief that the Palestinians will never accept an end to the conflict. Nonetheless, the administration should look for opportunities to convey in the Israeli media that the calm of the last several years is the result of a Palestinian choice, and that the best way to maintain that calm is diplomatic engagement.

When diplomatic crises arise—such as a possible Palestinian bid to become party to the Rome Statute, or tensions with the European Union (EU) over labeling products from the settlements—they should not be wasted. At a minimum, the administration message to Israeli media, on or off the record, should be that the United States faces growing difficulties defending Israel's international status without progress toward a two-state agreement. If a crisis can be used to create a deadline for progress, media and public attention will be greater.

Against the backdrop of Israeli government austerity measures, heated public discussion of inequality, and an upcoming election campaign likely to focus on economic issues, the administration should aim at putting the costs of settlement back on the Israeli political agenda. Settlement spending is a major government outlay, but it is spread through the national budget and no total is published. Occasionally NGOs or newspapers attempt to add up the pieces. For instance, a former finance ministry official's study of the 2001 budget found $430 million in extra outlays for settlers. This was a fraction of an unknown whole; the analysis did not cover the defense and education budgets, both likely to include major expenditures on settlements.[37] Last July, the business newspaper *Calcalist* reported that Israel annually submits a total for settlement expenditures to the US administration, which deducts the amount from American loan guarantees. For 2011, the newspaper said, Israel reported an outlay of $236 million, but other government documents indicate a total of $300 million—again, not including outlays in the defense budget and possibly missing other expenditures.[38] The government does not report these numbers to the public, and they are not part of the annual budget debate.

At the least, administration officials can regularly insert the settlement outlay as reported by Israel into comments to the media. Going further, the administration can conduct or commission an independent audit—ideally including an analysis of the defense costs of settlement. The United States need not threaten any reduction of aid beyond the existing deduction from loan guarantees. The point is to draw attention to the burden on Israel.

Even if Israelis become more aware of the cost and fragility of the status quo, they will justifiably weigh the current situation against the potential price of an incomplete or failed peace. They ask whether an agreement with the Palestinian Authority will apply to Hamas-ruled Gaza; they want to know what would happen if the Palestinian regime fell and what would prevent rocket fire from the West Bank. Palestinian insistence on the right of return is widely understood as a demand that all refugees be allowed to enter Israel, erasing its Jewish majority. The Israeli Right's argument that a Palestinian state in the West Bank and Gaza would be a base for an ongoing effort to regain all of Palestine resonates widely.

These issues are obviously on the negotiating agenda: the right of return; security arrangements; building an agreement solid enough to outlive a particular government; dealing with Hamas; and bringing Gaza back under PA rule. But if the administration facilitates new talks, it must publicly reiterate that solutions to these questions will be part of an agreement, and that America will help provide the military and financial means to create a stable peace. Where possible, the outline of security measures should be made public. Ensuring that the Israeli-Egyptian peace remains intact under the new Egyptian regime is critical to allaying Israeli fears about peace with the Palestinians.

Because these issues and others appear so challenging, some experienced negotiators advocate interim agreements rather than a final-status accord. In gaining the necessary Israeli political support, however, the interim approach is mistaken. For most Israelis, the essential quid pro quo for relinquishing land is a secure end of the conflict. Concessions without full peace will be a hard package to sell, all the more so after Oslo and the Gaza pullout.

In speaking of an agreement to the Israeli public, the administration should stress what Israel will gain. Israelis, Palestinians, and international actors working for an agreement should "shape the discourse . . . in a way that makes an agreement sound more like a declaration of victory [for both sides] than a concession speech," as former Israeli negotiator Tal Becker writes. A final status agreement, he notes, can finally bring world recognition of Jerusalem as Israel's capital.[39] It will give Israel recognized borders that may include some of the large settlements near the Green Line. It will replace the threat of economic boycotts with new economic opportunities.

Beyond practical gains, there is a psychological dimension. As mentioned, two narratives compete in Israeli Jewish consciousness. In one, Israel faces the eternal hostility of the world toward the Jews. In the other, Zionism has brought a revolutionary change in the Jewish condition, and Israel is the locus of remarkable accomplishments. American spokespeople should describe a peace agreement with the Palestinians as the next achievement in the narrative of success.

INTERNAL STRIFE: THE POLICY CHALLENGE

In the best case, with majority support for negotiations and an eventual agreement, large parts of the Israel public will remain opposed. The strongest opposition will come from ideological religious settlers and their religious Zionist supporters. Those settlers will see a two-state accord as a decree against their homes, their communities, and their religious-political vision. For some, it will be an attack on the project that has given meaning to their lives.

The risks include legitimate protest crossing the line into violence, especially during evacuation of settlements, and a crisis within the military. In an atmosphere of radical rhetoric and desperation, extremists could turn to terrorism against Palestinians or the government—as in the 1994 massacre in Hebron and the assassination of Yitzhak Rabin.[40]

The public message of the administration should be that Israel cannot allow itself to be held hostage by a radical minority, any more than it would like to see the Palestinian state-in-the-making allow extreme groups to set its agenda. At the same time, public diplomacy and the symbolic aspects of an eventual agreement may affect the degree of domestic Israeli opposition. For the Israeli government, the extent of internal strife during a peace process is not a matter of fate, but a challenge to be addressed.

Rather than see this challenge as unique, official Israeli bodies and independent research groups should examine the experience of countries such as France and Portugal that have had to reabsorb significant numbers of citizens. They should also study past cases of negotiating, or failing to negotiate, with radical religious movements, such as the US government's confrontation with the Branch Davidian sect in 1993 at Waco, Texas.[41]

But it is already possible to suggest means—some connected to the diplomatic process—to reduce the fever. The ideological settlers and their backers have their own spectrum of beliefs and conflicting commitments. If an agreement is backed by a large majority of Israelis and thus by a large parliamentary majority, the breadth and intensity of religious opposition may be lessened.

Most religious Zionists within Israel proper are "socially bourgeois, middle-class, concerned with a stable economy and the security of their children," as a prominent religious Zionist intellectual asserts. The same is true even among residents of the more comfortable Orthodox settlements, he argues. "It's true that they have a right-wing perspective but . . . they won't go to war against the state for it." In his assessment, the response of most religious Zionists to a peace accord will depend on whether it is ratified by a large enough parliamentary majority to be seen as an unambiguous democratic choice. Even in that case, he says, rabbis will make declarations against the agreement, and "thousands upon thousands of young people will go into the streets" to protest, but pragmatic acquiescence will win out over more extreme resistance.[42]

Indeed, even among settlers and other religious Zionists with sharper ideological commitments, most identify strongly with wider Israeli society and want to be accepted and appreciated as part of it. A common religious Zionist formula describes the Jewish people, the Land of Israel, and Judaism as equal, complementary values.[43] If an accord gains a broad majority, trying to prevent its implementation would come at the price of divorce from Israeli society. For religious soldiers and officers, wide public support will give additional weight to the military's institutional ethos of fulfilling government decisions; insubordination will become a less attractive choice. This prognosis only underlines the importance of the public side of the negotiating process.

The accord's content will have an impact as well. Two points are worth particular attention. First, an agreement must deal not only with the holy places in Jerusalem but also with major Jewish sites in what will become independent Palestine: the Tomb of the Patriarchs in Hebron, Rachel's Tomb in

Bethlehem, Nabi Samuel (Samuel's Tomb) north of Jerusalem, and Joseph's Tomb in Nablus. These are not only religious but also national symbols, evoking ancient Jewish history for part of secular Israeli society. Determined opponents of a two-state arrangement could use potential loss of Jewish access to these sites to rally opposition beyond the ideological religious Right. Joint religious administration and detailed arrangements for Jewish access—possibly along the lines proposed in the 2003 Geneva Accord—could defuse the issue.[44]

Second, it is worth reexamining the assumption of previous negotiations that Israeli settlers cannot remain in independent Palestine. Raising this question does not mean ignoring Palestinian objections or practical obstacles. However, giving some or most settlers the option of staying in Palestine would defuse emotionally effective arguments that settlers and other opponents of a two-state arrangement often raise: that the two-state model is racist or asymmetrical because Israel will have a Palestinian minority while Palestine does not allow a Jewish minority, or that Jews are being banned from part of their homeland. In internal Israeli negotiations between the government and settlers on compensation, giving settlers the option to stay put would remove the settlers' ability to blackmail the government by threatening to resist evacuation.

In practice, it is likely that few, if any, settlers would want to stay once the practical conditions are clear: They would become residents of Palestine with the option of taking Palestinian citizenship; they would live under Palestinian law, without extraterritorial rights; they could no longer exclude non-Jews from their residential communities; disputes over land ownership would be adjudicated by Palestinian courts.

However, the option of staying cannot be extended to all settlers. Criteria would need to be set, aimed at excluding settlements with a history of violence against neighboring Palestinian communities and settlers whose goal in remaining would be disrupting creation of a Palestinian state. Thus Israel would still face the task of evacuating a hard core of radical settlers. But reducing the number, and therefore the potential for violent resistance, would ease the implementation of the agreement.

Still, an Israeli government making peace will be tested by radical opposition. Learning the painful lessons of the early Oslo years, it must not naively underestimate the danger of terrorism by Israeli Jews who seek to foil territorial concessions. Despite then-IDF chief of staff Ehud Barak's description of the Hebron massacre as "thunder on a clear day," it did not come out of the blue.[45] Nor did the Rabin assassination. Greater vigilance might have prevented both attacks.

The government should also avoid pushing opponents of an agreement toward extremism. Learning again from the early Oslo period, leaders should take care not to dismiss settlers or the crisis they will undergo.[46] Treating the settlers as irrelevant will make more of them feel that mainstream Israel has abandoned them and that its decisions do not need to be honored. Instead, Israeli leaders should acknowledge that settlers have sought to serve the country and should describe the sacrifice imposed on them as another contribution to Israel's future. If the need arises to negotiate with ideological settlers resisting evacuation, the government should seek intermediaries who are respected by the settlers and who speak in a shared religious language.

Whether or not a diplomatic process is under way, the Israeli government should already be addressing politicization and the influence of hardline clerics in the army, which creates potential discipline problems on issues other than settlement evacuation. The military needs to reduce the role of the increasingly nationalist army rabbinate and reevaluate its ties with *yeshivot hesder* that challenge military discipline.

The bottom line: There is no reason to think that waiting will soften the eventual confrontation. Rather, the longer diplomacy is put off, and the more the settlement enterprise grows in numbers and confidence, the greater the internal crisis will be.

For this reason as for many others, a new diplomatic initiative is a pressing necessity. Despite the reluctance of their current government, a new effort could potentially win support among a majority of Israelis. For that to happen, an American diplomatic strategy must treat the Israeli public as another partner in the negotiations.

NOTES

1. Clayton E. Swisher, *The Truth about Camp David: The Untold Story about the Collapse of the Middle East Peace Process* (New York: Nation Books, 2004), 64.

2. Peace Index, monthly survey under the direction of Ephraim Yaar and Tamar Hermann, August 1994, http://www.spirit.tau.ac.il/xeddexcms008/download.asp?did=peaceindex1994_8_9. Monthly Peace Index surveys did not yet include the Arab minority for technical reasons. Ephraim Yaar, telephone interview, August 5, 2012.

3. Mina Zemach, telephone interview, July 26, 2012.

4. Asher Arian and Michal Shamir, "Two Reversals: Why 1992 Was Not 1977," in *The Elections in Israel 1992*, ed. Asher Arian and Michal Shamir (Albany: State University of New York Press, 1995), 24, 42–44.

5. In a pre-election poll of Israeli Jews, 62.3 percent said the state of relations with America would affect their vote; respondents preferred Labor over Likud to handle relations with America by 47.1 percent vs. - 23.6 percent. Guttman Institute, Election Study, June 8–18, 1992. Data provided by the Guttman Center under the auspices of the Israel Democracy Institute (R.A.).

6. Gerald M. Steinberg, "A Nation That Dwells Alone: Foreign Policy in the 1992 Elections," in *Israel at the Polls, 1992*, ed. Daniel J. Elazar and Shmuel Sandler (Lanham, MD: Rowman & Littlefield, 1995), 175–76, 181–84, 193.

7. Jane Perlez, "Impasse at Camp David: The Overview; Clinton Ends Deadlocked Peace Talks," *New York Times*, July 26, 2000, http://www.nytimes.com/2000/07/26/world/impasse-at-camp-david-the-overview-clinton-ends-deadlocked-peace-talks.html.

8. Participants, journalists, and scholars offer conflicting versions of the summit. See, inter alia, Robert Malley and Hussein Agha, " Camp David: The Tragedy of Errors," *The New York Review of Books*, August 9, 2001, http://www.nybooks.com/articles/14380; Benny Morris, Hussein Agha, and Robert Malley, "Camp David and After: An Exchange," *The New York Review of Books*, June 13, 2002, http://www.nybooks.com/articles/15501, http://www.nybooks.com/articles/15502; Swisher, *Camp David*; Shlomo Ben-Ami, *Scars of War, Wounds of Peace: The Israeli-Arab Tragedy* (London: Orion, 2006), 229–264.

9. Guttman Institute, Continuing Survey on Public Issues, November 24–26, 1976.

10. Guttman Institute, Continuing Survey, November 21–23, 1977; January 25–26, 1978; August 14–16, 1978; October 30, 1978.

11. Peace Index, February, April, May, June 2012. http://www.peaceindex.org/indexYears.aspx?num=19, August 2, 2012.

12. Peace Index, April 2012.

13. Dan Meridor, interview, July 31, 2012, Jerusalem.

14. Ben-Ami, *Scars of War*, 220.

15. Nahum Barnea, "Olmert Leaves the Territories" [in Hebrew], *Yediot Aharonot*, December 5, 2003, B2.

16. Ephraim Yuchtman-Yaar, "The Oslo Process and the Israeli-Jewish Public: A Paradox?" in *Educating Toward a Culture of Peace*, ed. Yaacov Iram et al. (Greenwich, CT: Information Age, 2006), 138.

17. Benny Morris, "From Dove to Hawk," *Newsweek*, May 8, 2008, http://www.thedailybeast.com/newsweek/2008/05/07/from-dove-to-hawk.html.

18. Ari Shavit, "Beshem Marsho" ("Speaking for His Client"), *Haaretz*, October 8, 2005, http://www.haaretz.co.il/hasite/pages/ShArtPE.jhtml?itemNo=486151.

19. Gadi Wolfsfeld, telephone interview, August 2, 2012.

20. Bernard Avishai, "A Plan for Peace That Still Could Be," *New York Times Magazine*, February 7, 2011, http://www.nytimes.com/2011/02/13/magazine/13Israel-t.html; "Olmert: Abbas Never Responded To My Peace Offer," *Haaretz*, February 14, 2010, http://www.haaretz.com/news/olmert-abbas-never-responded-to-my-peace-offer-1.263328.

21. Marc Howard Ross, *Cultural Contestation in Ethnic Conflict* (Cambridge: Cambridge University Press, 2007), 24–25.

22. Daniel Kahneman and Jonathan Renshon, "Why Hawks Win," *Foreign Policy*, December 27, 2006, http://www.foreignpolicy.com/story/cms.php?story_id=3660.

23. Gadi Wolfsfeld, *Media and the Path to Peace* (Cambridge: Cambridge University Press, 2004), 15.

24. Moshe Feiglin, "Tokhnit Me'at Hayamim" ("The 100-Day Plan"), http://he.manhigut.org/content/view/2457/153/. This document, Feiglin's program for his first 100 days as prime

minister, disappeared from Jewish Leadership's website shortly before the Likud's December 2008 primary as the faction drew more attention. See also "Netanyahu 'Stars' Dim on Likud list, as Hawks Dominate Primary," *Haaretz*, December 9, 2008, http://www.haaretz.com/news/netanyahu-stars-dim-on-likud-list-as-hawks-dominate-primary-1.259155.

25. Benjamin Netanyahu, *A Place among the Nations: Israel and the World* (New York: Bantam, 1993), 353–354.

26. "PM's Speech at the Begin-Sadat Center at Bar-Ilan University," June 14, 2009, http://www.pmo.gov.il/English/MediaCenter/Speeches/Pages/speechbarilan140609.aspx.

27. Moshe Ya'alon, interview, May 3, 2011, Tel Aviv.

28. "Transcript: Israeli Prime Minister Binyamin Netanyahu's address to Congress," *Washington Post*, May 24, 2011, www.washingtonpost.com/world/israeli-prime-minister-binyamin-netanyahus-address-to-congress/2011/05/24/AFWY5bAH_story.html.

29. At the end of 2010, the number of Israelis living in the West Bank, not including East Jerusalem, was 311,000, according to the Central Bureau of Statistics, a unit of the Prime Minister's Office. *Statistical Abstract of Israel 2011-No. 62*, Table 2.4, http://www.cbs.gov.il/reader/shnaton/templ_shnaton.html?num_tab=st02_04&CYear=2011. At the end of 2010, the number of Jews and "people not classified by religion" in East Jerusalem was 190,976, according to the *Statistical Yearbook of Jerusalem, 26th edition* (Jerusalem: Jerusalem Institute for Israel Studies, 2012), Table III/10, http://www.jiis.org.il/.upload/yearbook2012/shnaton_C1012.pdf.

30. At the end of 2010, the population of Beitar Illit was 37,600 and of Modi'in Illit 48,600. *Statistical Abstract of Israel 2011-No. 62*, Table 2.15, http://www.cbs.gov.il/shnaton62/st02_15.pdf. There are smaller ultra-Orthodox communities elsewhere in the West Bank. See Dror Etkes and Lara Friedman, "The Ultra-Orthodox Jews in the West Bank," October 2005, http://peacenow.org.il/eng/content/ultra-orthodox-jews-west-bank.

31. Yisrael Harel, telephone interview, November 1995; *Jerusalem Report* Staff, *Shalom, Friend: The Life and Legacy of Yitzhak Rabin*, ed. David Horovitz (New York: NewMarket, 1996), 205ff.

32. Talia Sasson, *Havat Da'at (Beina'im) Benose Ma'ahazim Bilti Murshim* (Opinion Concerning Unauthorized Outposts) (Jerusalem, 2005); Amos Harel, "Mofaz Makshiah Et Yahaso Lema'ahazim, Sharon Megabeh Otam" ("Mofaz Takes Tougher Stance toward Outposts, Sharon Backs Them") *Haaretz*, May 16, 2003, news.walla.co.il/?w=//388380; Gershom Gorenberg, *The Unmaking of Israel* (New York: HarperCollins, 2011), 125–128.

33. Lior Yavne, *A Semblance of Law: Law Enforcement upon Israeli Civilians in the West Bank* (Tel Aviv: Yesh Din, 2006), 42, 45, 47, 83, 103–106, 108–110, 112–120.

34. B., "Mekomam Shel Hovshei Hakipot Bapikud Hatakti Shel Tzahal" ("The Role of the Orthodox in the IDF's Tactical Command,") *Ma'arakhot* 432 (2010), 50–57.

35. Gorenberg, *Unmaking*, 148–152.

36. Parties backed mainly or completely by Israel's Palestinian minority hold 11 of 120 seats in the Knesset. Though some Palestinian citizens support a one-state future, the Palestinian-supported parties are likely to back a two-state agreement. However, the unwritten rule of Israeli politics is that the Arab parties are never offered a place in the governing coalition. In the view of part of Israel's Jewish majority, Rabin's dependence on Palestinian parties to ratify the Oslo Accords reduced the legitimacy of the agreements. This is a blatantly undemocratic attitude, but must be taken into account in evaluating the size of a majority needed to support an agreement.

37. Dror Zaban, *Omdan Helki Shel Taktzivei Memshalah Hamufnim Lehitnahaluyot Bagadah Hama'aravit Ubiretzu'at Azzah Veshel Tiktzuv Ha'odef Bishnat 2001* (*Partial Estimate of Government Funding to Settlements in the West Bank and the Gaza Strip and of Surplus Budgeting in 2001*) (2003). Commissioned by Peace Now.

38. Shaul Amsterdamsky, "Hamismakh Hasodi She'af Ehad Lo Rotzeh Shetiru" ("The Secret Document That No One Wants You to See"), *Calcalist*, July 30, 2012, http://www.calcalist.co.il/local/articles/0,7340,L-3578591,00.html.

39. Tal Becker, "The End of the 'Peace Process'?" *Policy Notes*, Washington Institute for Near East Policy, March 2012, http://www.washingtoninstitute.org/uploads/Documents/pubs/PolicyNote10.pdf.

40. An earlier example was the failed conspiracy to destroy the Dome of the Rock in order to pre-
     vent Israel's 1982 withdrawal from the Sinai.

41. See James Tabor and Eugene V. Gallagher, *Why Waco? Cults and the Battle for Religious Freedom
     in America* (Berkeley: University of California Press, 1995).

42. Interview, July 26, 2012, Jerusalem. Name withheld by author.

43. In Hebrew: *Am Yisrael, Eretz Yisrael, Torat Yisrael.*

44. "The Geneva Accord: A Model Israeli-Palestinian Peace Agreement," http://www.geneva-
     accord.org/mainmenu/english.

45. Shmuel Mittelman, "Hatevah Bama'arah Nafal Aleinu Kera'am Beyom Bahir" ("The Massacre
     in the Tomb of the Patriarchs Hit Us Like Thunder on a Clear Day"), *Ma'ariv*, March 24, 1994,
     via *Ma'ariv* archive; Gershom Gorenberg, *The End of Days: Fundamentalism and the Struggle
     for the Temple Mount* (New York: Free Press, 2000), 203–208.

46. *Jerusalem Report* staff, *Shalom, Friend*, 213–214.

8

THE PEACE PROCESS AND THE PALESTINIAN NATIONAL MOVEMENT

Robert Malley

For US policymakers, Palestinians have long been both an object of confusion and a source of frustration. The list of misjudgments runs long. By meddling in domestic Palestinian affairs, Washington has more often than not produced the reverse of what it set out to accomplish, strengthening those it hoped to weaken and undermining those it wished to bolster. Its pressure has generally backfired, and its incentives have tended to miss their mark. The substance of Palestinian positions has repeatedly been misinterpreted, as has the weight of various internal constituencies, the role of Islamism, the influence of outside powers, and the importance of Arab states.[1]

A HISTORY OF MISJUDGMENTS

Puzzlement began with the person of Yasser Arafat, the father of the national movement, whom Washington alternatively considered a terrorist, a possible peace partner, or a hybrid of the two. His ability to remain the leader of his people over several decades and despite serial defeats was a cause of constant bafflement. American policymakers thought he would be assessed on the basis of how well he governed and what he achieved. On both counts, they found him wanting and expected Palestinians to follow suit. Palestinians did not—not out of blindness to his failings, but rather out of a sense that Arafat embodied the nation in all its torment and all its aspirations. That central assumption—that Palestinians would be more sensitive to material than to political or psychological well-being—is a misconception that bedevils US policymaking to this day.

Puzzlement continued during the 2000 Israeli-Palestinian summit at Camp David, at which both personalities and substantive positions were mis-apprehended. The United States sought to play the younger, supposedly more flexible generation against its older, more established counterpart—and it ended up undercutting the former while alienating the latter. Substantively, although Israel was prepared to concede far more than in the past, and far more than the United States had anticipated, the proposals put forward were not close to the minimum any Palestinian leader could accept, whether on the status of Jerusalem, the scope of Israel's territorial withdrawal, or the fate of the refugees. Tellingly, the man who was not yet president, Mahmoud Abbas, and whose pragmatism has often been contrasted to Arafat's purported intransigence, was first in line to denounce the proposals. Camp David mis-fired, too, because by excluding participation by any Arab nation, Americans ignored the Palestinian need for regional buy-in, for Arab legitimization of their eventual compromises.

Years later, faced with Hamas's participation in the 2006 Palestinian legislative elections, US policy went awry—again. The threat to withhold diplomatic and material support in the event of an Islamist victory pro-vided Hamas with the final nudge it needed to cross the finish line ahead as Palestinians, who had grown tired of being told what to do by a country that, in their eyes, had done virtually nothing to promote their cause, opted for a vote of defiance. After Hamas's victory, the attempt to oust them from power by starving them of resources and, in the wake of their Gaza takeover, juxtaposing prosperity in the West Bank against misery in Gaza, stumbled badly as well. In reality, the situation unwittingly helped Hamas tighten its hold by drying up the private sector and enabling the Islamic movement to monopolize scarce resources, which it allocated as it wished to a needy population. As is so often the case, economic punishment designed to hurt the rulers hurt the ruled instead. Those intending to undermine Hamas ended up giving it an assist.

But what most perplexed the United States has arguably been the Palestinian reaction to President Obama's tenure in office. Obama came in with the highest of expectations, moving quickly to put the Israeli-Palestinian issue at the top of his agenda, naming a special envoy, delivering an inspiring speech in Cairo in June 2009 that was aimed at reconciling the Arab world and America, and talking tough about the need to stop Israel's settlement expansion. Four years later, the record appears bleak: President Abbas rebuffed Obama's successive pleas to resume direct negotiations unconditionally, that is, without a settlement freeze and without Israeli agreement to the 1967 line as the basis for talks; to refrain from pushing for a UN Security Council resolution condemning settlements; and to desist from seeking UN membership.

In virtually each case, American officials expected the Palestinian leader, eager to maintain good relations with Washington and fearful of possible retribution, to ultimately give in. They assumed that Abbas would not risk undermining the central pillars of his political life: negotiations with Israel and strong US ties, as well as the preservation of stability and the well-being of his people. Abbas, under this view, was prone to put up a fight only until he chose not to do so any longer. His mettle was deemed the kind to buckle under duress.

The assessment turned out to be wrong. It mistook a strong preference for talks for an absolute dependency on them; optimism about US presidents for blind faith in them; rejection of violence for passivity; and concern about the Palestinian Authority's survival for a determination to preserve it at all costs. Most of all, it mistook inordinate patience for infinite patience, and while Abbas arguably exhibited the former—in what has often struck many

Palestinians as a manifestation of excessive naïveté—he was never possessed of the latter. Even Abbas had a breaking point. It was reached.

American misreading of Palestinian politics and psychology by no means constitutes the only or even the principal reason for the impasse at which the peace process finds itself. Nor is the misreading one-way. But it is an important ingredient, and one that the next administration would do well to address. Seeking a better understanding of Palestinian dynamics is all the more critical at a time when virtually everything in the makeup of the national movement—its leadership, attitudes, relative importance of domestic constituencies, and regional alliances—is in the midst of or on the verge of a radical overhaul.

THE CRISIS OF THE MAINSTREAM NATIONAL MOVEMENT

The mainstream Palestinian national movement—embodied in the Palestine Liberation Organization (PLO) and Fatah—is experiencing its most acute crisis in decades. As the prospect of a two-state solution has receded and as the goal of liberation is replaced with the reality of managing the status quo, it is searching for a cause and fighting its own decline. It can boast name recognition and a rich historical legacy, but little more.

The most visible manifestation of this dynamic has been the Palestinian attitude toward President Obama. In many ways, it has been a source of paradox. Palestinians, suffering most from the status quo, and therefore most in need of a resolution, balked at resuming talks. In Obama, they had a president more willing to focus on the issue and to confront Israel, yet they denied him the chance to advance talks. Almost two decades after the Oslo Accords, the best he could do was engineer the briefest of direct negotiations and slightly less brief indirect talks—even then, not without overcoming huge Palestinian reluctance.

To many US officials, the Palestinian approach has appeared both tactically suspect and politically self-defeating. Settlement expansion continued despite Palestinian insistence that they would not talk until building ceased, and the administration's patience with the Palestinians eroded even as the contrast with the hard-line Israeli government should have served them well. Nor, as seen, was Abbas's resistance to returning to the negotiating table consistent with his own personal history and political convictions.

He had obvious short-term motives for adopting such a stance, and these have sometimes been cited as explanations. Since late 2008, indignities have been piled upon him: his apparent impotence during the Gaza War; the election of a right-wing Israeli government; the American change of heart on a settlement freeze; and his own decision to postpone a UN vote on the Goldstone Report—condemning both Israel and Hamas for war crimes—which unleashed a wave of Palestinian and Arab criticism. These hardly formed a propitious background for risk taking. For Abbas to await somebody else's next move seemed the surer bet.

But it would be wrong—and, to Palestinians, profoundly misguided—to see in the leadership's current attitude a matter of mere personal frustration or political apprehension. Quite to the contrary: Abbas was simply, if belatedly, following a broad and deep national consensus. He and his colleagues retained, if not faith, then at least a form of habitual reliance on bilateral talks as the only viable way forward for much longer than their constituents did. As seen from presidential headquarters, these talks were premised on a necessary and essential quid pro quo: that if Palestinians did their part—negotiate in good faith, ensure Israeli security, and pursue a good governance agenda—then Israel would reciprocate by allowing for the establishment of a sovereign, independent state; if it did not, the United States would bring Israel around. For most Palestinians and for quite some time, this theory has been exposed as illusory. They became convinced that, far from prompting Israeli concessions, good behavior would only produce Israeli complacency and satisfaction with the status quo, and the United States would never exercise its muscle.

As of now, Abbas and his colleagues have yet to come to that conclusion. The PLO has invested too much in negotiations for too long, and its power depends too heavily on the process to accommodate a swift and radical shift. Instead, they oppose a resumption of talks under their traditional format on the grounds that they cannot yield an agreement and that each unsuccessful round of negotiations carries increasing political costs. As the leadership sees it, the strategic implications of a tactical failure at this point could be enormous; they believe another setback would assuredly be their last and would seriously undermine Fatah's domestic standing while simultaneously boosting Hamas's standing by demonstrating once and for all that negotiations are futile.

In this sense, the obstinacy Abbas has displayed over the past two years is less a curt about-face or surrender of his prior convictions than a last-ditch attempt to resuscitate what most other Palestinians see as dead. Since the implicit quid pro quo that formed the basis of his strategy never material-ized, he is looking, if not for guarantees that talks will succeed, then at least for a way to increase their chances. This, in his eyes, requires redressing what he considers the inherent structural inequality between the parties, a power imbalance outside the negotiating room that is inevitably reflected within.

Toward this end, Abbas has variously demanded a definite timeline, clearer terms of reference, and, in particular, acceptance of the 1967 bor-ders as the point of departure, as well as a comprehensive settlements freeze. Palestinian officials wish to turn the page on nearly two decades of focusing on details and hoping that incremental progress would culminate in agree-ment on a complete package. Instead, they want to turn the paradigm on its head: to enshrine principles first, and from there, work backward to fill in the details. There is some ambiguity in this, however. Pressed as to what principles they would want the United States to put forward, they focus on borders and East Jerusalem; about refugees, by contrast, they say very little, asking merely for a reiteration of the Arab Peace Initiative's vague language (an "agreed, just solution to the problem of Palestinian refugees in confor-mity with [UN General Assembly] Resolution 194").

Hovering over Palestinian decision making throughout this recent period has been a central question: whether their leadership could still rely on the United States to do what needs to be done to make negotiations with Israel work. For Abbas, believing good relations with Washington were a key to persuading or pressuring Israel had been a quasi article of faith. Indeed, it was both premise and paradox of the peace process that Palestinians would depend on their foe's staunchest ally to achieve their goals.

In yet another delayed manifestation of more widely held popular views, Abbas has begun to harbor serious doubts regarding both America's reliability and its ability to make a difference. This is a reaction not so much to the Obama administration—though disappointment in this regard has been proportional to the expectations that greeted the new president's election—but to a broader historical experience with Washington. That Obama has had to bear the brunt of Palestinian disenchantment is but one of the conflict's many ironies.

This impasse notwithstanding, the leadership has yet to develop realistic substitute strategies. Instead, it has begun to tinker with different approaches. "Tinker" is the appropriate term: in its quest to reshuffle the deck, it has flitted from one idea to another and pursued tracks simultaneously without fully thinking through the alternatives or committing to a single one. President Abbas and his colleagues have left the door open to negotiations with Israel should the opportunity to renew them on conditions that are considered acceptable present itself. They have contemplated the possibility of internationalization—namely, going to the UN to pressure Israel directly and the United States indirectly. They have spoken of intensifying acts of popular, nonviolent resistance. Every so often, they move toward domestic reconciliation. And, though more as threat than as reality, they have evoked the option of dissolving the Palestinian Authority and reverting to direct Israeli rule.[2] Tensions over these options are bound to grow as Prime Minister Salam Fayyad becomes more politically assertive and many—even within the leadership's ranks—become more convinced of the need for bolder action.

The ad hoc, irresolute character of the Palestinian leadership's approach has been striking, yet it is not without reason. Whatever it chooses to do would carry a potentially heavy price and at best an uncertain gain. Negotiations are viewed by a majority of Palestinians as a fool's errand, so a decision to resume them without fulfillment of Abbas's demands could be costly. A Palestinian move at the UN would likely prompt a cutoff in US aid and a suspension of tax clearance revenue transfers by Israel. A joint government with Hamas could trigger similar consequences without assurance that elections could be held or territorial unity between the West Bank and Gaza restored. Getting rid of the PA could backfire badly, leading to a further deterioration of living standards, leaving public employees and their families penniless, and depriving the mainstream national movement of a base in the occupied territories even as Hamas remains ensconced in Gaza.

Equally debilitating, the movement lacks the institutional mechanisms to develop a genuine strategy. For a variety of reasons, Abbas finds himself essentially alone, with more decision-making power concentrated in his hands than even Arafat accumulated. Little wonder then that even personal considerations—including his legacy and retirement—instantaneously become national ones or that decisions reflecting personal proclivity take on strategic importance.

All in all, the Palestinian leadership in Ramallah finds itself in an unenviable position at a historical crossroads. It suffers from a legitimacy deficit. Negotiations, after decades of failure, have been discredited. Reconciliation with Hamas is frozen. Israeli settlement building continues. Elections are long overdue, and there is no prospect they will be held anytime soon. The PA is under financial strain. The regional mood is inhospitable to slow and deliberative progress. The leadership is thus unable and unwilling to maintain its course of the past two decades—but so too it is unwilling to jettison it.

HAMAS, GAZA, AND THE ARAB UPRISINGS

In assessing how to handle the Palestinians, US policymakers will need to heed the lessons of years of mishandling of its Islamist wing. Constraints over direct engagement with Hamas are likely to endure no matter who occupies the Oval Office. But that does not mean that US policy toward Hamas need remain static, particularly at a time when US policy toward the Muslim Brotherhood region-wide is in exceptional flux.

Since the collapse of the Oslo process, the decline in Fatah's fortunes has coincided with an upsurge in those of Hamas. Its rise reflected dissatisfaction with PA rule, anger at the inability of the mainstream Palestinian movement to achieve its self-proclaimed objectives of liberation and establishment of a sovereign state. But it reflected something else, a psychological dimension that often eludes political analysis. As Hussein Agha and I wrote in the wake of Hamas's 2006 electoral victory:

> The vote was more than a rejection of corruption, an expression of frustration with the peace process, or even an act of defiance. It was an expression of deeply felt, if unarticulated, anger at years of lost dignity and self-respect, coupled with a yearning to recover a semblance of both . . . Because of all it did, said, and stood for, a vote for Hamas became one way to exorcise the disgrace. The Palestinian Authority had been unable to protect its people, and Hamas evidently could do no better on that score. But though its brutal attacks on Israelis did not provide safety, they provided revenge, and, for many Palestinians, in the biblical land of primal urges, that was second best . . . . Unlike Fatah, Hamas did not succumb to international pressure

to alter its views, which explains both why the West warned against voting for it and why, as hope for a peaceful settlement disappeared, Palestinians did so nonetheless. Hamas's performance was made possible, evidently, by acute dissatisfaction with the Palestinians' material situation, but its roots lay deeper, in their psychological condition. Voting for Hamas was not merely an act of rejection. It was, in the only way many Palestinians knew how, an act of self-determination.[3]

Since then, the policy of isolating Hamas and sanctioning Gaza has proved bankrupt and, by all conceivable measures, has backfired. It has not put an end to periodic flare-ups of violence between Gaza and Israel. The credibility of President Abbas and other pragmatic leaders has not been bolstered. The peace process has remained at a standstill, further burdened by the Palestinians' territorial and political divisions, which have prevented them from speaking authoritatively, in one voice. Meanwhile, Hamas's hold on Gaza, purportedly the policy's principal target, has been consolidated.

To the extent that the movement has lost some popularity, the attempt to enfeeble it by squeezing Gaza is arguably working, but the success is politically meaningless. Hamas's losses are not Fatah's gains; Gazans blame Hamas for being unable to end the siege, but they also blame Israel for imposing it, the West for supporting it, and Fatah for acquiescing to it. What is more, poverty and hopelessness boost the appeal of jihadi groups, particularly among under-sixteen Gazans—half the population.

Recent events in the Arab world—most significantly, the rise to power of the Egyptian Muslim Brotherhood, Hamas's mother organization—offer an opportunity to revisit past policy and turn the page. Over time, such regional developments will inevitably have far-reaching implications for Hamas and for the Palestinian national question itself. They are likely to undermine Fatah and the PLO as they currently exist, and both, in an environment moving toward the Islamists, will increasingly appear odd men out.

But the impact on Hamas will not be straightforward. At first glance, the Arab uprisings could hardly have caused a more stark—and more positive— reversal of Hamas's fortunes. In the stagnant years preceding the uprisings, Hamas had been at an impasse: isolated diplomatically; caged in economically by Egypt and Israel; crushed by Israeli and Palestinian Authority security forces in the West Bank; warily managing an unstable ceasefire with a far more powerful adversary; incapable of fulfilling popular demands for reconciliation with Fatah; and more or less treading water in Gaza, where some supporters saw it as having sullied itself with the contradictions of being an Islamist movement constricted by secular governance and a resistance movement actively opposing Gaza-based attacks against Israel.

Facing reduced popularity since the 2006 Palestinian legislative elections that brought it to power, Hamas had to contend with criticism from without and within, the latter accompanied by defections from a small but important number of militants who left to join groups more committed to upholding Islamic law and to engaging in attacks against Israel. All in all, the movement could take comfort in little other than the fact that Fatah was doing no better.

The Arab revolts seemed to change all that. Positive developments came from across the region: the toppling of Fatah's strong Arab ally, Egyptian President Hosni Mubarak; the rise in Egypt of Hamas's closest supporter and mother movement, the Muslim Brotherhood; the opening of the Gaza-Sinai crossing at Rafah, control of which the former Egyptian regime had used to pressure, constrict, and impoverish what it perceived to be Gaza's illegitimate rulers; the empowerment of Islamist parties in other countries; growing instability in states with large Islamist oppositions; and the promise of a new, more democratic regional order reflecting widespread aversion to Israel and its allies and popular affinity with Hamas. As Hamas undoubtedly saw it, these and other events promised to profoundly affect the advancement of each of its primary goals: governing Gaza; weakening Fatah's grip over the West Bank; spreading Islamic values through society; ending its diplomatic isolation; and strengthening regional alliances in opposition to Israel.

Upon a closer look, however, it appears that regional changes have not been universally helpful to Hamas. It abandoned its headquarters in Damascus, harming its ties with its largest state supporter, Iran. Even the most prized change of all, that affecting Egypt, is not without its challenges. The Egyptian Brotherhood's short-term priority will not be Palestine, and its interest in maintaining good relations with the West could dictate restraint in its approach to the Palestinian question. Hamas could thus find itself pressured to further shed the mantle of resistance and, like Islamist organizations across the region, move further toward becoming a strictly political movement.

All in all, the implications for Hamas seem contradictory. On the one hand, its association with the new rising regional power will bolster its hand; the sense of discouragement within Fatah, of history passing it by, is a good indication. On the other hand, Hamas risks finding itself, even more than it does today, without a clear purpose—notably without the purpose of immediately confronting Israel. In the absence of a different Hamas strategy, and with criticism of its rule in Gaza persisting, this could both lead Palestinians to further question the movement's raison d'être and erode its domestic popularity.

The Arab uprisings have also brought to the surface and exacerbated internal contradictions and rifts among the movement's varied constituencies. In a sense, the impasse in which Hamas had been stuck before the events that have shaken the Arab world allowed the movement to keep its many differences largely beneath the surface; with few significant opportunities before it, no contest among visions needed take place. But once Hamas found itself in a dramatically altered environment with novel challenges and possibilities, long-standing tensions came to the fore and new forms of friction emerged. Broadly speaking, these reflect several interrelated factors: the group's geographic dispersion and its leadership's varied interests and calculations; ideological distinctions, particularly those not exclusively related to varying assessments of the impact of the Arab upheaval; and pre-existing personal rivalries.

Hamas's differences over national strategy, particularly over how far to go in reconciliation negotiations with Fatah, stem in large part from contrasting perceptions of what near-term effects the Arab uprisings will have on the movement. These have in turn been shaped by the distinct firsthand experiences of the leaderships in Gaza and, until recently, Damascus. Broadly speaking, the strategic divide corresponds to two views, themselves related to two different sets of interests: that, on one hand, because regional changes are playing largely to Hamas's favor, the movement should do little other than hold fast to its positions as it waits for the PA to weaken, for economic conditions in Gaza to improve, and for its allies to grow in strength; and that, on the other, it should take this rare occasion to make tough decisions that might bring about significant long-term gains—notably in terms of regional and international acceptance.

For the moment, unity within the movement has prevailed—but chiefly by putting both tactical and strategic choices on hold and falling back on the default position of inaction. But that cannot last indefinitely. Over time, an impact is likely to be felt on Hamas's outlook and strategic choices regarding such critical issues as reconciliation, relations between Gaza and Egypt, regional alliances, approach toward Israel, and armed struggle.

THE RISE OF OTHER PALESTINIAN CONSTITUENCIES

The crisis affecting the mainstream national movement, the exhaustion of the founding generation of its leaders, disenchantment with Hamas, the enduring geographic and political division, and, more than that, the collapse of the peace process, are potentially scrambling the deck, shifting the balance of power within the Palestinian community as a whole. Without a strong, representative national body, constituencies that have been politically marginalized for the past several decades are feeling emboldened. Over time, they could seek to play a far more influential role in policy debates, in particular with regard to Israel.

For as long as the PLO was viewed as the uncontested, legitimate representative of the Palestinian people, these voices were largely silent or could be ignored. But that is decreasingly the case and, in the event of a succession at the top of the national movement, this dynamic is likely to accelerate. Hussein Agha and I put it as follows:

> There may be potential successors [to Mahmoud Abbas], though none with the legitimacy required to straddle geographic and political divides. Some will focus on state-building, others might seek to revert to resistance; most will be adrift. Hamas waits in the wings; the diaspora is beginning to stir; East Jerusalemites and Palestinian citizens of Israel are more active. So far, however, none of these groups has the means to match its ambitions. The national movement might reassemble but it will take time. In the interim, it is likely to express itself in numerous disparate parts.[4]

Two of these constituencies in particular appear to have been energized of late, often displaying greater activism than either their West Bank or Gaza counterparts. The first is the diaspora. Until recently, there had been no clear evidence that it has had a significant impact on Palestinian decision making, the community being neither structured nor organized in a manner adapted to Palestinian political structures. A hybrid creature that was composed in the main of a loose and leaderless international alliance of activists without an organized popular base and that more often than not was disconnected from Palestinian factional politics, its primary aim appears to have been to raise international public awareness of Palestinian refugee rights and, to a lesser extent, to connect directly with refugee communities. Conventional political activity of the type normally undertaken by a lobby seeking to influence senior decision makers on a single issue has been sporadic at best.

That could be changing. The weakening of the PA and the PLO, coupled with the significant geographic and organizational fragmentation of the national movement, will inevitably affect the ability of Palestinian political institutions to represent national constituencies. In turn, the diaspora could assert a greater role, mirroring the decline in power of the national leadership. The absence of consultation and internal dialogue, particularly as far as formulating a coherent strategy toward the refugee question is concerned, and the perception that some among the leadership were prepared to use the refugee issue as a mere negotiating card, could potentially accelerate this process.

The second constituency is Palestinian citizens of Israel. In their case as well, political shifts are contributing to renewed assertiveness. Since 2000, a series of dramatic events have both poisoned Jewish-Arab relations in Israel and reinvigorated its Palestinian minority. The collapse of the peace process and the ensuing Intifada harmed Israel's relations not only with Palestinians in the occupied territories but also with its own Arab minority. As Palestinians in Israel organized rallies in solidarity with Gazans and West Bankers, Israeli Jews grew ever more suspicious of their loyalty. Palestinian citizens' trust in the state plummeted after Israeli security forces killed thirteen demonstrators during protests in October 2000.

A rapid succession of confrontations—the 2006 war in Lebanon, the 2008–2009 Gaza War, and the bloody 2010 Israeli raid on the aid flotilla to

Gaza—further deepened mistrust, galvanizing the perception among Israeli Jews that Palestinian citizens of Israel had embraced their sworn adversaries. Among Arabs, in turn, it reinforced the sense that they had no place in Israel. Several have been arrested on charges of abetting terrorist activity. Meanwhile, the crisis of the Palestinian national movement—divided, adrift, and in search of a new strategy—has opened up political space for Israel's Arab minority.

All of this is taking place against the backdrop of a peace process in which very little is happening—and what is happening only makes matters worse. Prime Minister Benjamin Netanyahu's insistence that the PLO accept Israel as a Jewish nation-state in the context of a final status agreement resonates widely with Israel's Jews, but raises all sorts of red flags for its Palestinian citizens, who have vigorously pressed the PLO to reject it. They might not have a veto, yet President Abbas cannot easily dismiss their views on such matters and has shown no inclination to do so. All of which has only elevated the centrality of the demand, in turn making it all the more important for Israel's government and all the more unacceptable to its Palestinian minority.

The potential implications for the peace process are profound. Originally, the notion had been that progress in the peace process would help improve Arab-Jewish relations in Israel. Instead, simultaneous deterioration on both fronts has turned a presumably virtuous circle into a dreadfully vicious one. Neither the State of Israel nor its Arab minority will be willing to reach a historic understanding before the Israeli-Palestinian conflict has been settled; and settling that conflict will be near impossible without addressing the question of Israel's nature—which itself cannot be done without the acquiescence of Israel's Arab citizens. Indeed, the PLO cannot afford to ignore an important Palestinian constituency, and Israel understandably insists that an agreement put an end to all Palestinian claims, including those of its Arab citizens.

The two constituencies, to date, when it comes to the shape of a future Israel-Palestinian agreement, have been held at a distance by the national leadership, which assesses, perhaps, that their demands would complicate its achievement. Yet both have become more assertive in voicing their expectations that their interests (protection of refugee rights and rejection of any recognition of Israel as a Jewish state) will be taken into account in future talks with Israel. And both have begun to see overlap in their efforts: the interests and rhetoric of Palestinian citizens of Israel on the one hand and of refugees in the West Bank, Gaza, and the diaspora on the other increasingly coincide with respect to the symbolic dimensions of recognizing Israel as a Jewish state. It is hardly surprising, then, that Palestinian citizens of Israel have stepped in to champion their brethren in the diaspora.

Ignoring either of these constituencies could prove costly as they possess the means to challenge any putative deal and render an agreement somewhat less than conflict-ending. From Israel's perspective in particular, an accord that leaves alive the refugee issue or the question of its Arab minority would be deeply flawed. All of which explains why an increasing number of voices can be heard arguing that the Israeli-Palestinian conflict cannot be fully or sustainably settled unless matters pertaining to the conflict's origins—the creation of the State of Israel, its character and identity, and the fate of Palestinians in both the diaspora and Israel—are also addressed.

IMPLICATIONS FOR AMERICAN POLICY

The Palestinian arena, with which the United States has traditionally had a hard time dealing, is undergoing a historical transformation. The national movement is facing one of the most serious crises in contemporary times. It is sharply divided, ideologically, politically and geographically. Neither of its two principal organizations, Fatah and Hamas, has been able to chart or pursue a clear agenda. Its leader, President Abbas, drifts between alternative courses of action. Its administrative expression, the Palestinian Authority, is economically stressed and, as the prospect of independence recedes, finding it harder to justify measures that many Palestinians see as ensuring Israeli security rather than promoting their own national interests. At the same time, all must adjust to new fluctuating regional realities.

These are not the only changes the United States will need to take into account. The height of the Oslo process coincided with the post–Cold War moment when the United States could largely dictate the diplomatic agenda. Today its influence has waned, and its credibility has taken a severe beating in the region as a whole and among Israelis and Palestinians in particular. As covered elsewhere in this volume, Israel's political system, having shifted to the right, is less amenable to the traditional peacemaking paradigm; this shift has been magnified by regional uncertainty, which makes it ever more difficult to take historic decisions. The Arab state system on which Washington once relied to alternatively pressure the Palestinians, provide them cover, and reassure Israel has disintegrated. Its regimes, both new and old, are more assertive in pursuit of their own agendas.

But correctly assessing the state of play among Palestinians is an indispensable ingredient to any forthcoming US policy, and for that reason several important lessons regarding the Palestinians ought to be kept in mind.

Understanding Abbas

Mahmoud Abbas was among the first Palestinian leaders to believe in engagement with Israel, and he will be among the last to give up on that idea. He remains convinced at heart that a peace agreement can only be reached through negotiations. Yet, though his disenchantment has come far later and slower than for most, he is fast approaching the point where he too will believe that the peace process has been an illusion. He is the restrained and belated expression of a visceral and deep popular disillusionment with the peace process as Palestinians have grown to know it. Should he decide that renewed efforts at a negotiated settlement are futile, it is hard to imagine how any of his successors could conclude otherwise. In this sense he is, as Hussein Agha and I once put it, the "last Palestinian for some time to come, with the history, authority, and legitimacy to sign a deal on behalf of all Palestinians that could end the conflict."[5]

The implications are twofold: First, that the opportunity presented by Abbas's leadership likely will not soon recur, that his eventual successors will find it far more difficult to engage in the kind of process he has supported and far harder to contain risks of a violent explosion, and that every effort should thus be made to reach an agreement while he is in office. But second (and somewhat contradictorily), a premature endeavor—based on pressuring Abbas to resume talks without sufficient preparation or assurance of success, particularly in pursuit of an agenda that does not enjoy broad support among Palestinians—could have devastating consequences: a public backlash and serious erosion of credibility were Abbas to renege on his own oft-repeated conditions for a resumption of negotiations, and a potentially fatal blow to the very idea of bilateral negotiations were they to fail. In short, attempts to persuade or pressure Abbas to resume talks without some tangible achievement or greater guarantee of success would be to make short shrift of—or worse, misread—the realities of Palestinian politics.

Risks and Benefits of Negotiations

A corollary to the above is thus that the United States needs to carefully think through the desirability of a quick return to talks. In fact, the mystery at this stage is not why the administration has failed at this writing to get talks restarted so much as why it would have tried as hard to do so. The explanation most often produced is that it is important to maintain some hope and that a process—even one almost certain to fail—is better than none. Yet this argument—to preserve the existing mechanism for lack of an alternative and fear of a vacuum—is becoming more and more tenuous. It overestimates the process's remaining credibility, assumes that Palestinians continue to believe it might end the Israeli occupation, and sees it as a substitute for a vacuum when in fact it is increasingly considered vacuous itself. In this sense, Palestinians are already living in the void that the United States fears recognition of the bankruptcy of the current process would produce. More broadly, it is hard to understand how negotiations can help get the parties out of their fix when (failed) negotiations are what led them there in the first place.

In addition, maintaining the illusion that merely restarting talks may yet yield success is not without costs. It further erodes the already damaged credibility of all principal actors, making the prospect of serious talks even more elusive. For this same reason, trying to bolster Mahmoud Abbas through piecemeal concessions or confidence-building measures is almost certainly an exercise in futility: there is no longer confidence to build. Equally questionable is the presumption of imminent violence in the absence of negotiations—which assumes both that Palestinians are held back by belief in the efficacy of talks and that they are incapable of making strategic calculations about which forms of resistance to employ and when. The argument that they will explode in reaction to the loss of something in which they do not believe is as tendentious as the claim that its continuation somehow will pacify them.

This is not to dismiss the utility of negotiations or of diplomacy; indeed, there can be no solution that ends the occupation and realizes the two peoples' aspirations in their absence. But with mounting evidence that the current approach will not bring about the desired accord, simply repeating it as is makes little sense.

Changing the Paradigm: New Constituencies and New Substance

Transformations in the Palestinian political landscape over the past two decades suggest that other changes in the negotiation structure will be needed. The failure of past talks has many causes, but almost certainly among them is the inability of proposed solutions to satisfy the parties' deep-seated aspirations. At the core of the Oslo process was the notion that a peace agreement would need to deal with issues emanating from the 1967 War—the occupation of the West Bank and Gaza—as opposed to those that arose in 1948 from the establishment of Israel, the trauma of the accompanying war, and the displacement of the vast majority of Palestinians.

But if that logic was ever persuasive, it is no longer. The diplomatic process has increasingly run up against two core issues—Israel's insistence on recognition of the Jewish character of the state and Palestinian refusal to extend that recognition or to concede on the right of return—that resonate deeply with both peoples. Associated issues—recognition of Jewish history; the place of the Arab minority in Israel; and, more broadly, the role of religion in political discussions and its influence on peacemaking—loom larger than before. As difficult as it is to imagine a solution that addresses these issues, it is harder still to imagine one that does not.

The matter of addressing different issues is closely tied to the question of who has been involved in the negotiating process. For the most part, it has been least welcoming to those who could do most to torpedo it. The process traditionally has been led by a relatively narrow array of actors whose authority and legitimacy have been eroded even as the influence of those who have been excluded has risen. This chapter deals with the Palestinians, and in their case, neglected constituencies include Islamists, Palestinian citizens of Israel, and the diaspora. Insofar as those groups collectively represent the majority of the Palestinian people, it is hard to imagine how a process that ignores their interests might succeed. But the same applies to Israel, where the Right, religious and national, as well as settlers, has grown in size and political weight without commensurate participation in diplomatic endeavors. In both cases, forces opposed to the kinds of compromises that will be necessary are the more dynamic, most actively mobilized, and least involved in discussions about a settlement.[6]

A reformed process would need to address—at its core, not as peripheral add-ons—the question of the character of the State of Israel, the rights of refugees,[7] the status of the Palestinian minority in Israel, and recognition of religious imperatives in peacemaking. And it will need to reach out to those groups for whom such considerations are central and consider whether and to what extent their interests can be accommodated in order to widen the spectrum of those with a stake in a positive outcome.

Rethinking the Question of Palestinian Reconciliation

To date, much of US thinking has assumed that Palestinian reconciliation would be an impediment to the peace process. Putting aside the fact that for some time there has been no peace process to derail, the theory turns reality on its head. As discussed in this chapter, perpetuation of the political division between Fatah and Hamas and territorial division between the West Bank and Gaza stands as one of the (many) obstacles before a final status agreement. It reduces Abbas's overall legitimacy, makes it harder for Palestinians to speak in one voice, stymies internal Palestinian political activity and elections, raises the risks of violent conflagration in Gaza, and diminishes Israel's incentives to compromise since it can question the Palestinian leadership's ability to deliver, notably with regard to Gaza.

So far, the US and Quartet conditions regarding a possible unity government have focused on its ideological position: whether it recognizes Israel, renounces violence, and accepts past agreements. Words certainly matter, but actions matter more. An alternative approach would be for the United States and the Quartet as a whole to announce that they will judge any future Palestinian government based on considerations that truly ought to count if the goal is to move toward a peaceful settlement: willingness (or not) to enforce a mutual ceasefire with Israel, acceptance of Abbas's authority to negotiate an agreement with Israel, and respect for a referendum on an eventual accord.

Dealing with Hamas

A related question, of course, involves how the United States should deal with Hamas. Substantively difficult and politically fraught, it does not lend itself to simple answers. But the fact remains that the movement will continue to play a vital role in Palestinian politics, affecting the prospect of renewing Israeli-Palestinian negotiations as well as their odds of success. For these and other reasons, the world—and the United States in particular—should do more than merely stand on the sidelines as Hamas wrestles over its future.

As discussed above, changes in the region and the uncertainty these have introduced within the Palestinian Islamist movement offer opportunities to rethink past approaches. Two related developments in particular stand out: first, the rise to power (notably in Egypt) of Islamist movements that are keen on improving relations with the West, crave stability, and are signaling that they do not wish to make the Israeli-Palestinian issue a priority. The Egyptian Brotherhood also happens to be Hamas's mother organization. No party will be more important to Hamas than the Brotherhood, whose future relations with Israel and Gaza could take any number of forms. More broadly, in this nascent environment, other important US regional allies—Turkey and Qatar—enjoy ever closer relations with the Palestinian movement. They are in a position to seek to influence Hamas.

The second development involves intense internal debates taking place within Hamas. It is a movement more divided than in the past and more uncertain about its future course. That makes it potentially more open to outside proposals, which could help push the movement in one direction or another. All this suggests that the United States could reach out to Egypt, but also to Turkey and Qatar, with concrete ideas about what Hamas might do and what Hamas might expect in response.

Even if Hamas is susceptible to influence by third parties, however, the United States should be careful not to overreach. The movement might be unsure about how to adapt to the current era, but that does not make it desperate. Indeed, it feels the wind in its sails and is increasingly focused on its regional environment at the expense of a Western community it sees as both unreliable and less and less relevant. Many in the leadership would still prefer some form of engagement with the West, but Hamas is unlikely to suddenly abandon its principles; nor will it endorse the Quartet conditions to the letter.

Instead, acting in concert with Egypt and others, the United States should set out to achieve changes that relate to its priorities—a sustained cessation of violence and the possibility of productive negotiations between Israel and the PLO. Among desirable changes: Hamas entering into a more formal ceasefire agreement with Israel over Gaza; exerting efforts to help stabilize the situation in Sinai; reaffirming, as part of a unity deal, President Abbas's mandate to negotiate a final status agreement with Israel; and pledging to respect the outcome of a popular referendum by Palestinians on such an accord. In return, Hamas could benefit from reciprocal Israeli guarantees over a Gaza ceasefire, an improvement in the Strip's economic status, and an assurance by the United States that—as discussed above—the Americans would engage with a Palestinian unity government that carried out those commitments.

In this respect, intriguing areas of convergence potentially exist between Muslim Brotherhood-ruled Egypt and Israel. Both Jerusalem and Cairo favor a period of sustained quiet in Gaza, the former for obvious reasons, the latter because instability at its borders would interfere with its domestic priorities, force it to sharpen its stance toward Israel, and complicate its relations with the West. Hamas, too, at this point appears to prefer to consolidate its rule rather than incur Israeli attacks. Long overdue, a more solid arrangement involving mutual commitments to a ceasefire and improvements to Gaza's economic status could be mediated by Egypt.

Most counterintuitively, the Muslim Brotherhood arguably might see it as in its interest for negotiations to resume between Israelis and Palestinians and for them to succeed. It is, at a minimum, a proposition worth testing. The Islamists know this is an important American objective; moreover, progress on the Israeli-Palestinian front would contribute to improving the overall regional climate, remove a possible irritant in US-Egyptian relations, and facilitate contacts between Cairo and Jerusalem. Having Abbas lead the talks means that Islamists would not be tainted by what, inevitably, would be difficult concessions. In the past, Hamas has signaled its preparedness to agree to Abbas-led negotiations in the context of a Fatah-Hamas unity deal, as long as any agreement that resulted would be subject to a popular referendum by Palestinians in Gaza, the West Bank, and the diaspora. Hamas would not have to formally endorse the deal, merely defer to the expression of the Palestinian people's will, thus remaining true to its principles without directly obstructing the agreement.

Egypt (and, possibly Turkey, as well as Qatar) could encourage Hamas to clearly reiterate this position while simultaneously intensifying efforts at producing some form of reconciliation agreement. Were it to resume its work in the context of such an agreement, the Hamas-dominated legislature could even pass a law committing all Palestinian factions to abide by a peace deal approved in a referendum.

The objective, in other words, should be to break from a mindset that sees any improvement in Gaza as a gain for Hamas and any gain for Hamas as a loss for Israel and the Palestinian Authority. Such a shift cannot happen if the United States does not alter its approach toward the Islamist movement. This does not mean full-fledged, unconditional acceptance but a greater degree of flexibility in US policy and tolerance in the actions of others vis-à-vis the Islamist movement.

Presentation of US Ideas?

Over the years, the popularity of the notion that the United States might put forward its ideas for how to resolve the Israeli-Palestinian conflict has waxed and waned. President Obama moved in that direction, but stopped in midsentence, presenting terms of reference for territorial and security solutions but not for the rest. As this chapter has suggested, there are good reasons for the next administration, at some point, to consider such a move. Indeed, one of the more obvious lessons from the past is that any future talks will need to be characterized by greater confidence in—and advance knowledge of—the endgame. This requires greater clarity as to the terms of reference going in to negotiations and a better sense of the negotiations' likely outcome, both of which an American initiative could provide.

But there also are good reasons to proceed cautiously. As seen, conditions have changed dramatically in the last decade and not in ways that

self-evidently boost the chances of success of a US plan. A proposal introduced at a time when Palestinians are deeply polarized, when the region is
deeply divided, incapable of producing a credible Arab consensus, and when
important Israeli constituencies doubt Washington's commitment and reliability would likely become the target of intensive and effective attacks. The
rifts created could be such as to render acceptance, let alone implementation,
of a plan extraordinarily complicated. Failure would not be inevitable, and
there certainly would be benefits from the expression of a broad international
consensus on the endgame. But a positive response and genuine follow-up
from the region's key actors would be more uncertain. The upshot is that the
United States ought to take the time necessary to implement steps that will
maximize odds of success.

Some of these are outside this chapter's purview—repairing strained
relations between Washington and Jerusalem without backing down from
core US principles, for example. But others flow directly from the above
assessment: a more nuanced approach toward Palestinian politics, including at a minimum a hands-off approach toward reconciliation; rethinking
policy toward Hamas; reaching out to typically ignored constituencies such
as refugees and Palestinian citizens of Israel, settlers, and religious groups;
addressing head-on issues previously given short shrift; and making sure not
to force a Palestinian leader to choose between angering the United States
and angering his own people.

If the next administration is serious about avoiding the fate of prior peace
proposals—from the 1969 Rogers Plan through the 1982 Reagan Plan to the
2000 Clinton Parameters—its effort should be the culmination of a period
of intensive diplomacy designed to create a more propitious climate. To say
conditions are not ripe for a US initiative does not mean waiting for them
to ripen; it means taking deliberate, sustained, and active steps designed to
bring them to fruition.

NOTES

1. This chapter draws heavily on my work with the Israel-Palestine team of the International
   Crisis Group over the past several years.
2. As Hussein Agha and I wrote, "Palestinians have looked for other nonviolent options. It's a
   curious list: unilaterally declaring statehood, obtaining UN recognition, dissolving the PA, or

walking away from the idea of negotiated partition altogether and calling for a single, bina-tional state. Not one of these ideas has been well thought out, debated, or genuinely consid-ered as a strategic choice, which, of course, is not their point. They are essentially attempts to show that Palestinians have alternatives to negotiation with Israel even as the proposals' lack of seriousness demonstrably establishes that they currently have none." "Who's Afraid of the Palestinians?" *New York Review of Books*, February 10, 2011.

3. Hussein Agha and Robert Malley, "Hamas: The Perils of Power," *New York Review of Books*, March 9, 2006.

4. Agha and Malley, "Who's Afraid of the Palestinians?"

5. Ibid.

6. "The process of the past sixteen years also has been least effective in dealing with those who can do the most to derail it. The elements of a two-state deal as traditionally mooted carry little appeal to the more mobilized constituents—Israeli settlers and right-wing activists; Palestinian refugees and Islamist militants. If the objective is a legitimate and sustainable deal, their inter-ests and aspirations too need to be borne in mind." Hussein Agha and Robert Malley, "Israel and Palestine: Can They Start Over?" *New York Review of Books*, December 3, 2009.

7. The need to more seriously address refugee rights is not tantamount to accepting an unre-stricted right of return, something Israel will never accept. But it also is not tantamount to treating Palestinian insistence on the refugee question as a mere tactical ploy to extract conces-sions on other issues. The fact is that the question of the right of return is, for Palestinians, an existential issue; compromise likely is possible, but it will entail treating the issue as a genuine one and finding a package deal that addresses all permanent status issues.

III

THE UNITED STATES AND THE PEACE PROCESS

9

MEMORANDUM TO THE PRESIDENT: THINKING THROUGH AN ISRAEL-PALESTINIAN INITIATIVE

Aaron David Miller

Having worked in the administrations of several of your predecessors, I appreciate the opportunity to offer you some observations on whether and under what circumstances you might consider an American initiative to broker an Israeli-Palestinian peace agreement and what it will take to succeed.

What to do about the Israeli-Palestinian issue will be one of the most difficult foreign-policy challenges of your administration.

You're going to receive a great deal of advice from many quarters. Some will argue that this is the last chance for a two-state solution, that it might well expire on your watch, and that you must launch a major initiative to save it no matter what the risks. Others will advocate caution and suggest a lower-key management approach.

Whatever you decide, the key is to think matters through before acting. I know this seems rather self-evident and galactically obvious.

But don't take it for granted. The ill-advised decision in 2009 and 2010 to go after a comprehensive freeze on settlements demonstrates the perils of not thinking matters through.

Faulkner wrote in *Requiem for a Nun* that the past was never over; it's never even past. And while you cannot allow yourself to be imprisoned by the failures of the past, you also can't ignore the history on which those failures, as well as some previous successes, were based. I will say that when it came to American initiatives, many factors contributed to failure; but the most important was our own misreading of what was required to reach an agreement and whether the two sides were willing and able to do so. That means being brutally honest with yourself and with the Israelis and the Palestinians. Getting this assessment right will be critical the next time around, as will our ability to deal fairly with the needs and requirements of both sides.

Middle East peacemaking isn't for the faint of heart or for dreamers, even those with the best intentions. It's a tough business because it reflects the toughness of the neighborhood and the search for political and religious identity and physical security that drives the Israelis and Palestinians.

That it is in the vital national interest of the United States to see Israelis and Palestinians at peace and that you may be personally committed to it are necessary but not sufficient bases on which to hope for, let alone expect, success. American will is critically important, but it's no substitute for that of the Arabs and Israelis.

Indeed, given American failures in peacemaking over the past twenty years, it's simply not good enough to argue that we must try to achieve an agreement because this is the last chance or that trying—even if we fail—is better than not trying at all. Inaction certainly carries a price, but so will another failure—threatening the very notion that negotiations can be a credible instrument for ending conflict. Sadly, many Israelis and Palestinians have already reached that conclusion.

No, an assessment of whether you should commit to a serious initiative can't be driven by good intentions, a last-chance mindset, desperation, your own desire for a foreign-policy legacy, or even just by our own national inter-est. There must be enough elements in place to have a reasonable chance of succeeding. And you must be cruel and unforgiving in your own assessment of whether you believe they are in place.

There are certainly no risk-free initiatives. When Jimmy Carter brought Anwar Sadat and Menachem Begin to the first Camp David Summit in September 1978, there was no assurance of success. It was only very late in the nearly two-week summit that a basis for an agreement was reached. And the first Camp David Summit was about as perfect a peace process as you might imagine: strong leaders who wanted a deal, a committed US president, and an agreement that both the Egyptians and the Israelis could handle.

Still, to maximize success and to reduce the odds of failure, a number of elements are required. You can't defy the laws of political gravity by compen-sating with personal/political commitment. There isn't going to be a perfect moment when the sun, the moon, and the stars align. There will always be risk.

The question for you, Mr. President, is whether the risks are calculated and manageable when measured against the nature of possible opportunity and against those risks incurred by not acting. And if you choose to pursue a major initiative that doesn't produce an accord, can you leave the situation better than you found it with a legacy on which others can build? This is an essential requirement. The negotiating process cannot withstand another set of circumstances similar to those following the second Camp David Summit in the fall of 2000 in which expectations were raised, follow-up was too slow, and the process was buried by violence, confrontation, and terror.

I have identified ten elements that are vital to success in pursuit of a conflict-ending agreement between Israel and the Palestinians. They are all strategic considerations; I have spared you the details of the tactics and the substance of an actual initiative. If you have these ten in place, the odds are that you'll get the details right. Without enough of these ten ingredients in place (you won't get them all aligned), you can't possibly succeed.

The most intriguing and complex strategic issue you'll confront is whether or not the two-state solution remains viable. My own view is that at the moment the two-state solution is too big to succeed or to fail, that is to say, the decisions required now to make two states a reality may be beyond the Israeli and Palestinian capacity to take; and yet neither side—let alone the international community—wants or can afford to abandon its pursuit. This, of course, raises a question that the solutionists still need to consider: if a conflict-ending accord isn't possible, is there an alternative that the two sides would endorse, if only as a way station to a final settlement that America can support? Until now, the answer to that question has been no. One of the issues that you will face is whether or not such a middle ground exists.

FIRST, BE HONEST ABOUT THE LAY OF THE LAND

Only a willfully delusional observer would conclude that the current situation offers favorable circumstances for a major American initiative to end the Israeli-Palestinian conflict.

Israel has a tough conservative prime minister and a right-wing government whose conception of a settlement is far from that of the Palestinians. Nor does the Israeli public—even while open to the idea of a two-state solution—see much urgency in pressing their leaders for one.

The so-called Arab Spring has introduced enormous uncertainty into Israel's relationship with Egypt, its most important Arab partner. Egypt now has a president tied closely to the Muslim Brotherhood, and its Shura Council is ideologically hostile to the very notion of acceptance, let alone peace with, a Jewish state. And if the Israeli-Egyptian relationship frays badly, the odds of a deal with the Palestinians that involves sensitive security issues will only grow longer. Israel's relationship with Jordan may also come under greater strain.

The Iranian nuclear issue continues to be Israel's main preoccupation, and it is arguable whether the current Israeli government would move on a major initiative with the Palestinians until there is more certainty in the Iranian situation—a prescription for continued delay, or, if the Israelis strike Iran's nuclear sites, regional turmoil. Either way, the Iranian issue spells trouble for a negotiated settlement.

The Palestinian national movement is deeply divided, politically and geographically—a veritable Noah's Ark with two of everything from prime ministers to security services to constitutions to different visions of what Palestine is and where it's supposed to be. The chances of creating real unity— one gun, one authority, one negotiating position—offer up very long odds indeed.

And yet, despite all of this bad news, the peace process and its preferred conclusion—the two-state solution—persists, limping along to be sure, but still very much a part of the regional and international landscape. It isn't diplomacy that is keeping the prospects of two states alive, but reality.

Israel's future as a healthy, normal state—Jewish and democratic in character—depends on resolving the Palestinian issue. The proximity of Israelis and Palestinians and the perverse dance they do in their roles of occupier and occupied promises only false stability and more violence and confrontation. Indeed, while Benjamin Netanyahu may not be seized with the Palestinian issue, he is surrounded by Israeli politicians who are far more interested and who recognize the importance of a solution. Minister of Defense Ehud Barak, former Prime Minister Ehud Olmert, and Opposition Leader Shaul Mofaz have all taken positions on the issue that are far more flexible than that of Netanyahu.

As divided and dysfunctional as the Palestinian Authority (PA) is, it continues to create its own facts on the ground through institution building in the West Bank and its campaign abroad to gain recognition for statehood and membership in UN agencies. Even Hamas—now with fewer options in the wake of its departure from Bashar al-Asad's Syria—has put more stock in controlling its own statelet in Gaza. The Arab states are, to be sure, preoccupied with their own domestic situations; but the rise of Islamist forces, particularly in Egypt, and the growing role of public opinion guarantee that the cause of Palestine, particularly the Jerusalem issue, will remain both resonant and volatile in Arab politics if left unresolved.

Finally, the international community remains focused on the issue even though there is no active negotiating process. And while the common refrain that everyone knows what the solution is trivializes the difficulties involved in producing one, an enormous amount of work has been done on the so-called core issues over the past decade or so. The gaps remain wide, but to some extent the issues have been demystified and solutions exist, at least on paper, to bridge them should the two sides choose to do so.

SECOND, OWNERSHIP: THEIRS AND YOURS

To close the gap between the situation in the region today and where you'd like to take it, the Israelis and the Palestinians need to buy into the need to create a new reality. And to say the least, this isn't totally within your control.

In the history of the world, former Treasury Secretary Larry Summers once quipped, nobody ever washed a rental car. People care only about what they own, and what they thus have a stake in protecting, making sure it works and investing in its success.

This simple homespun wisdom is the core requirement for success in Arab-Israeli peacemaking. Ownership can result from many factors. In the case of successful peacemaking—if history is any guide (and it must be to some extent)—ownership derived from a rare combination of incentives and disincentives—pain and gain, really.

In the first of three American diplomatic successes in Arab-Israeli peacemaking, Henry Kissinger's disengagement diplomacy with Israel, Egypt, and Syria during the mid-1970s, the parties had little choice but to invest in diplomacy because there had been pain (the October 1973 War); there was urgency (Israeli, Syrian, and Egyptian forces were staring one another down over cease-fire lines); and there was some prospect of gain, which appeared in the form of a secretary of state who exploited the situation to create a postwar negotiating process.

In the other two successes—the 1978 Camp David Summit resulting in the 1979 Egyptian-Israeli peace treaty and the 1991 Madrid Peace Conference—the same logic applied. An American president—Jimmy Carter—was able to take advantage of Sadat's heroic diplomacy in his visit to Jerusalem to get Menachem Begin into a historic negotiating process. In the case of George H. W. Bush, it was America's success in the Persian Gulf War that enabled the United States to take advantage of an unsettled region that had strengthened some parties and weakened others (particularly the PLO) and gave Washington the space to create a process of negotiation.

In each case, the United States capitalized on a regional event that knocked the parties off balance, changed their calculations, and offered them some potential gains. Given the risks involved for Arabs and Israelis, they will always be reluctant partners. It takes the combination of either a positive or a negative shock and wise diplomacy from the United States to create the disincentives and incentives that give them a stake. None of this existed in either the endgame diplomacy of the Clinton years 1999–2000 or that of the George W. Bush administration. Indeed, the situation was made even more difficult by the fact that the endgame diplomacy involved much tougher issues and greater risk, and there was insufficient urgency and support to get the parties to take those risks.

The question for you is whether, in the absence of such ownership and urgency, you can help to create it. America can be active in looking for opportunities and circumstances that it can exploit even when the parties are not doing so; but it must also recognize the limitations of that role if one party or the other isn't willing or able to make the decisions required, particularly when it involves endgame diplomacy. A US president cannot force or sanction an Arab partner, let alone an Israeli ally, to move on issues that cut to the core of their political or religious identity or security. Presidents can sharpen choices, provide incentives, cajole with disincentives, and under certain circumstances even create new openings. And a president must always sharpen the point that Middle East peace is not just a personal commitment but a vital national interest as well.

But when critics blast the tired old expression that America can't want peace more than the parties themselves, they do so at their own peril. No matter how much will and skill US presidents possess, they cannot impose peace. Indeed, can it be a coincidence that the three most dramatic breakthroughs in Arab-Israeli diplomacy (Israel-Egypt, Israel-PLO, Israel-Jordan) were all preceded by secret contacts between the two sides about which the United States knew nothing or very little?

We need to be especially clear lest we create an expectation for the kind of role America never played. In fifty years of involvement in this conflict, there's only one example of an American president actually brokering an agreement between Israel and an Arab state that involved the return of significant amounts of territory and led to permanent borders. And unlike today, the circumstances surrounding the Egyptian-Israeli peace process were more propitious, though still difficult.

Menachem Begin, a tough, right-wing, ideological Israeli prime minister, wasn't dragged to Camp David because Carter forced him to attend. He saw in Sadat's breakthrough diplomacy an opportunity for a deal with the Arab world's largest and most important state, and he was moved by the prospect of trading Sinai away so he could consolidate Israeli control over the real prize (the West Bank). Carter, to be sure, was indispensable and was tough and reassuring too. But the deal was cut because Sadat and Begin wanted it, had the political power to deliver it, and got their needs met.

And that's the key missing ingredient today. What does a president do when one or more of the parties isn't that committed to an agreement, or can't pay the price that the other needs? Or what happens when the urgency that is required to increase the odds of success is lacking? As we'll see below, in this kind of environment, there are few options, and the odds of success are long indeed.

THIRD, ORGANIZING YOUR TEAM

Under ordinary circumstances, the bureaucratic ticktock of who gets what job in Washington wouldn't matter. But Arab-Israeli peacemaking is a tough, long-term effort even under the best circumstances. And to an extent, policy and personnel become intertwined. More than that, however, who you identify to manage the effort and how you empower that person become part of the ownership issue. Arabs and Israelis can detect very quickly whether an American president is serious or not and whether there's a team in place that knows what it is doing and that has the president's total confidence. Three considerations bear on the team issue.

First, there's no substitute for the intense engagement of the secretary of state. There's no precedent for any breakthrough without the active role of the nation's chief diplomat. Indeed, the three key successes—the disengagement diplomacy of the 1970s, Egyptian-Israeli diplomacy leading to the 1979 peace treaty, and the Madrid Peace Conference—all came about not through special envoys but through strategies managed by the secretary of state (Henry Kissinger, Cyrus Vance, and James Baker, and in the case of the Camp David Summit, the president). In short, the secretary of state should run this show.

Envoys are necessary, but not sufficient. Getting to an agreement is a full-time endeavor that often requires months of steady engagement. But that involvement—if it's to succeed—has to be validated and legitimized at the highest levels. The notion that a lower-level envoy can set up a negotiation and the secretary of state or president just walk in at the tail end to close is an illusion. The secretary of state must become the repository of the confidences of the parties and must be engaged in the setup too; otherwise there may not be an endgame. A balance must be struck too so that the secretary retains the required distance and detachment vital to not being taken for granted. And to maintain that distance while keeping a full-time connection to the parties, you need a relatively senior envoy reporting directly to the secretary of state to handle the day-to-day coordination.

But nothing substitutes for a team leader who represents you and can make real-time decisions with 24/7 White House access. The perception must be that the secretary of state speaks for you; there can be no daylight between the two of you; otherwise the Arabs and Israelis will play the United States like a finely tuned violin. There's only one office that carries this kind of prestige, and that's the secretary of state; you must allow your chief diplomat to play this role and own the issue.

Second, from the beginning you will need to be involved, stay engaged, and in the end almost certainly play the hands-on role required to reach an agreement. Kissinger took the lead in the interim disengagement diplomacy; Baker managed the Madrid Peace Conference. Richard Nixon, Gerald Ford, and George H. W. Bush played important roles in these successes. But when it came to the big deal—the Egypt-Israel peace agreement—it required Jimmy Carter. That we are now dealing with the most sensitive and politically explosive issues—Jerusalem and Palestinian statehood—will demand your intense involvement, almost certainly in endgame summitry. At the same time, you cannot—as Bill Clinton did—become so accessible and available throughout the process that the Israelis and the Arabs begin to take you for granted. Presidential prestige is critical here. And it demands a certain amount of detachment and discipline to know when and how to intercede.

Third, you need a team that reflects a variety of points of view and that is encouraged to debate the issues in front of you and the secretary of state before you make decisions. The biggest danger on the American side is that the circle becomes too narrow and insulated, that different points of view— from inside and outside the government—aren't entertained, or that debate is chilled and/or short-circuited. You'll need a small team for reasons of discretion. But you need one that's balanced—open to understanding and reflecting the needs and requirements of the parties themselves—and willing to consider and present to you and the secretary of state all options to close the gaps.

FOURTH, HAVE AN ENDGAME—BUT BE FLEXIBLE

"If you don't know where you're going," the old expression by Lewis Carroll goes, "any road will get you there." When it comes to Arab-Israeli peacemaking, there's no question that that notion applies, albeit with some qualifiers. In the current climate, the good news is that the endgame—a two-state solution—is loosely the framework within which Israelis, Palestinians, the Arabs, the international community, and the United States are operating. The bad news is that the current Israeli government and the Palestinian Authority have very different conceptions of what that means and how or even whether to get there.

Notionally, the American objective over the past decade and a half—pursued with varying degrees of enthusiasm and energy—has been to get the two sides into a negotiation that will produce a conflict-ending agreement on the so-called four core issues: borders, Jerusalem, security, and refugees. The current Israeli prime minister has added a fifth (recognition of Israel as the nation-state of the Jewish people).

Such an agreement—if it is possible to achieve—would probably be the least bad option for resolving the conflict. The alternatives—a one-state solution, a confederation with Jordan, Israeli annexation, or continuation of the status quo—all carry risks and complications that are worse. And as a practical matter, none of the key parties to the conflict is actively pursuing any of them as an alternative. Should the two sides be open to a workable alternative, you would want to see where it leads. But this is not likely to occur. Conceivably, there may be alternate ways of getting to two states, but for better or worse, that remains the accepted paradigm.

And that leads to the always attractive but never quite attainable idea of an interim accord that would actually facilitate the endgame but on a more gradual basis. This was the organizing principle of the failed Oslo process. In this regard, we aren't talking about an agreement in principle on the core issues that is implemented over time, but rather an agreement on one or two of the core issues (borders and security have been the most discussed) that could serve as a way station to a permanent settlement. It is critical that you make clear at this stage that you are personally committed and that America is determined to work toward a conflict-ending agreement, if only to keep alive and preserve the option.

FIFTH, MANAGE THE PROCESS TO GET TO YOUR OUTCOME

The last decade or so has given the peace process a very bad name. This is largely because it's been directionless, episodic, and pursued with varying degrees of seriousness by all sides. "Process" is really only another way of describing a problem that can't be resolved today and the need to create a pathway to test whether or not it can be resolved tomorrow, figuratively speaking. Process is also critically important to manage expectations, keep options open, and, in the volatile world of Israeli-Palestinian conflict, seek to prevent or moderate violence. But it's essential that whatever process is created be credible.

There are two main issues before you with regard to process and getting to the endgame: a successful negotiation that resolves all the core issues leading to a two-state solution. First, can the gaps on these big issues be bridged either by the two sides themselves or with American help? And if your assessment is that they can, how can you best go about doing that?

If your judgment is that the gaps can't be bridged, then do you have options for moving toward creating a new situation where they somehow can?

Given the gaps between the current Israeli government and the Palestinian Authority, the answer to the first part of the first question is clearly no. With an expanded coalition, Netanyahu may have the power to achieve an agreement, but he lacks the motivation. Given the divisions within Palestinian ranks, President Mahmoud Abbas may have the motivation, but he lacks the power. Moreover, neither Israelis nor Palestinians will likely initiate any kind of peace plan that is remotely acceptable to the other.

So any effort to bridge gaps—should you choose to pursue an initiative—will have to come from you. We don't know the answer to the question—can an American initiative bridge the gaps between Netanyahu and

Abbas?—because we've never tried. My strong suspicion without completely prejudging the answer is that it will be extremely difficult on most of the core issues. In short, if you tried, there would likely be no agreement reached. The question for you is, even so, what might be gained or lost from the effort? (More on this later.)

With regard to process, you are a president with a peace process that has been moribund for years. You need to avoid the mistakes of the past—a focus on settlements or on pushing for a public negotiating process that's almost certain to reach an unbridgeable impasse quickly.

Above all, don't push immediately to resume negotiations and don't raise expectations that you are ready to reengage. That's what happened before. Give yourself some time to assess and consult. What's the situation in Syria? What's the status of the Iranian nuclear issue? And how is the Egyptian-Israeli relationship faring? Palestinians will try to use their UN statehood initiative to push you immediately after the November election to do something on the peace process or they'll threaten to go to the General Assembly. Don't be pressured. It's the wrong issue and will make any initiative you might consider even tougher.

SIXTH, THE US-ISRAELI RELATIONSHIP

From the American perspective, all players in the Israeli-Palestinian peace process aren't created equal. We can choose to deny this, ignoring forty years of our own behavior, or we can work to take advantage of it. The idea that the United States has consistently been a strictly honest broker adopting positions that are balanced equally between the two sides has always been an illusion even when we succeeded in reaching agreements. Begin wanted his separate peace with Egypt, and Carter relented and dropped linkage to the Palestinian issue (as did Sadat); Baker negotiated terms at Madrid that were super-favorable to Yitzhak Shamir, perhaps Israel's most right-wing prime minister. And Clinton all but sided with Ehud Barak at the second Camp David Summit, urging Yasser Arafat to accept the terms the Israelis (and the president) offered.

Israel occupies a pride of place in America's peace process world for several reasons. First, the United States has maintained special ties with the

Jewish state that exist independently of progress or lack thereof on the peace process. That Israel is one of a handful of democratic countries that emerged in the wake of the Second World War and has maintained its democratic character coincides with the broadest definition of the American national interest—support like-minded societies that share common values. Israel's occupation policies notwithstanding, the vast majority of Americans—not just Jews and Evangelicals—regard Israel as a fellow democracy and worthy of support. Otherwise, the US-Israeli relationship could never have lasted and thrived as long as it has.

Second, Israel has a very strong base of support in the United States, and foreign policy—as any president knows—turns on a sustainable domestic base and political durability. And third, America has long accepted the idea that Israel—despite its formidable military power—is still one country surrounded by many Arab states conceived in and marked by continuous war and conflict. That, combined with the dark past of the Jewish people, has created an acute sensitivity to Israel's security needs and requirements.

That said, America's success as an effective, though not strictly honest, broker depends on maintaining a certain degree of credibility in negotiations, particularly when it comes to the sensitive issues of a conflict-ending agreement between Israel and the Palestinians.

In practical terms, that means that the United States must have the capacity to put forward its own ideas with regard to negotiating a permanent deal. That doesn't mean you ignore the positions of the two sides or seek to compel them to accept American proposals, but it is absolutely critical that bridging proposals not be perceived to have been made in Israel, or in Palestine, for that matter.

In a high-stakes negotiation, it's also critical that you not be perceived to be running American ideas by Israel for approval first. This was a serious problem at the second Camp David Summit. We had a no-surprises policy of intimate coordination that resulted essentially in Prime Minister Barak telling President Clinton what he could offer to the Palestinians and what he couldn't. It's one thing for the Israelis to use us to convey their ideas. But when Israel is given a veto power over our thinking and proposals, we can't function credibly. The no-surprise approach should apply to both sides. The exceptions are issues relating strictly to Israeli security needs where we will need to coordinate very closely.

So, too, in an endgame negotiation, if we are asked by both sides to play a central role, we need to control the negotiating text. There wasn't such a text at Camp David II, and there needed to be. During the Carter-Begin-Sadat Camp David Summit, the text of the eventual framework agreement went through more than twenty drafts; and the US team managed it, taking suggestions from both sides, working out compromises, but never losing control of the draft or letting one party dictate terms.

Finally, it should go without saying that to do a deal on the most sensitive issues, you will need a different kind of relationship than the one the United States currently has with Netanyahu. You will need to create a working bond where confidences are respected and where there is a clear sense that you aren't out to undermine him and vice versa. That doesn't mean you need to be best friends, but you need to convey the fact that you understand both the substantive needs at the table and the political ones. This will also apply to your relationship with the Palestinian leader. And with both, you need to set ground rules—no leaking, no betrayal of confidences, and a degree of honesty in which what you say to one another can be counted upon.

The bottom line with the Israelis is stark and unavoidable. Unless you bring the Israelis around on the importance, advantages, and feasibility of a deal with the Palestinians, you won't even be able to get started.

There is also the matter of creating a bond with the Israeli public. Here it's important emotionally that you convey the fact that you understand the risks and the challenges ahead. Remember, this isn't a negotiation about an interim agreement or the procedures of a peace conference. The issues you may be brokering cut to the core of Israel's physical security and identity in a changing and uncertain region in which these things can't be taken for granted.

There is no way you will be able to avoid tension with the Israelis. And if you're not prepared to risk the headaches and problems this will cause, don't start traveling the negotiator's highway. In any negotiation, brokers/mediators push parties beyond where they may have wanted or thought they needed to go. But it's important that the fight—if it comes to that—be over something worthwhile. That's why the effort to make settlements the key issue was doomed to fail. What is worth fighting about—the so-called productive fight—is whatever advances an agreement and in the end not only makes you look good, but promotes American interests and Israeli and Palestinian interests too. What other issue besides a peace agreement on the core issues is worth the struggle with a close ally and the political fallout it will generate?

SEVENTH, YOU AND THE PALESTINIANS

The history of America's engagement with the Palestinians is very checkered. There's responsibility aplenty on both sides to explain the dysfunction. Dealing with non-state actors is always difficult; and despite their heroic effort to build institutions and negotiate their way out of an occupation, there are real problems on the Palestinian side, including the use of terror, violence, and incitement. America's consistent willingness to take Israel's side in most of the substantive issues pertaining to negotiations and the closeness of the US-Israeli connection also sows suspicion and mistrust. That said, the United States and the Palestinians—under both Arafat and Abbas—have found ways to cooperate, at times quite closely.

Today, the situation you'll encounter is in many ways better and in other ways much worse. Abbas is a well-intentioned moderate man who would like to reach an accord but lacks the power to do so. He and the Western-educated and -oriented prime minister, Salam Fayyad, responsible for so much of the positive PA institution building, are at odds. Fatah is split too.

But the real problem is the division within the Palestinian national movement between Fatah and Hamas. The absence of one gun, one authority, and one negotiating position is—on the Palestinian side—the greatest obstacle standing in the way of a successful agreement. And there is no way right now to envision unity between the two that would facilitate a negotiation. In this regard, some may advise you to open a dialogue with Hamas. Under certain circumstances, as part of a strategy to actually reach an Israeli-Palestinian agreement (and assuming Hamas met the conditions set by the Quartet), that might help; but under almost any other imaginable circumstance, it's a key to an empty room that will undermine Abbas and anger the Israelis.

The idea that you can do a West Bank-first agreement, that is to say reaching a negotiated deal between Abbas and the Israelis in the hopes that Hamas-based Gaza would either sign on or face being marginalized, has so far not proved viable, though admittedly it hasn't been seriously tested. For such an approach to work, the terms would have to be compelling enough on the Palestinian side to counter claims that Abbas had sold out. And while your views on the substance of the negotiations may be closer to those of Abbas's than to those of the Israelis, at least to those of this Israeli prime minister, it is not at all clear that the United States could support the terms for a final deal that Abbas may need and demand.

Until you determine what strategy you want to follow in trying to reach an accord, you need to keep the Palestinians focused on the reality that, however bleak things are, negotiations are still the only way forward. This will not stop them from pursuing their drive for recognition as a state in UN agencies and international organizations.

What the Palestinians want from you now—pressure on Israel over settlements, support for statehood at the UN—you should avoid conceding. Keep your powder dry. Should you go for a deal on the big issues, you'll need all the firepower you can muster. Indeed, it's in your interest to continue to be tough on the UN issue; if you aren't, your capacity to bring the Israelis along later in a negotiation will be further eroded.

Bottom line with the Palestinians is this: They have grudgingly come to accept America's catering to Israel on settlements and at the UN. And there is little you can or should do to correct this impression now. Where you can help them is during the course of a negotiation. Are you willing to stand up for terms on Jerusalem, borders, and refugees that reflect their substantive and political needs too? And will you help to make real—with financial, economic, and political support—the idea of a viable, contiguous, independent Palestinian state?

EIGHTH, NO MORE LONE RANGER

There was a time when America could dominate the pursuit of Arab-Israeli peace and pay for it too. Those days are long gone. The complexity of the issues, the comprehensiveness of the problem, and the uncertainties in the region all demand an approach in which others, particularly the Arab states and the Europeans, play a greater role.

The Quartet, paradoxically created in the George W. Bush administration to rein in the Europeans and the UN, was also used to share the responsibility for managing the problem. In the event that an agreement is reached or even on the way to being achieved, an enormous amount of economic and financial support and technical assistance will be required. The Europeans have long resented this payer-versus-player division of labor in which the United States is the mediator/broker and the others foot the bill. But there is no substitute for the United States in a negotiation, particularly because of its close ties to the Israelis.

Perhaps more important will be the question of Arab state support, as a means of helping support the Palestinians financially, perhaps pressing Hamas, marshaling political support for the concessions the PLO will need to make to reach a deal, and reaching out to the Israelis. The Beirut Summit declaration of 2002 that promised Arab state recognition of Israel in return for a resolution of the Israeli-Palestinian problem can be useful here. At the second Camp David Summit, the Clinton administration's failure to involve key Arab states in its thinking and efforts on a final deal made success even more unlikely.

The problem now is that the uncertainties in the region have made this effort more difficult. The absence of strong leaders willing and able to cover Palestinian concessions, particularly on an issue like Jerusalem, and willing to reach out to the Israelis is a serious challenge. The rise of Islamists in Egypt and Tunisia may well make the Israelis even more withholding and make it harder for you to exert much influence. Strong leaders like Egypt's Mubarak and Jordan's King Hussein are gone, and popular sentiment—opposed to American policies—may make it harder to marshal Arab support. The fall of the Asad regime will introduce greater uncertainty into the 1974 Israeli-Syrian disengagement agreement as well as any chance soon for a possible deal on the Golan Heights.

On the other hand, democratized Arab states supporting peace agreements with Israel would generate more legitimate and enduring support, particularly for an Israeli-Palestinian agreement that included Jerusalem. Think about the implications of a Muslim Brotherhood president and parliament actually legitimizing an Israeli-Palestinian agreement and pressing Hamas to accept it as well. That would provide an unprecedented degree of legitimacy and staying power.

NINTH, A US PLAN?

Barring some regionally induced act of confrontation, a political development (a new Israeli prime minister), or a peace initiative that changes the core calculations of the Israelis and the Palestinians, it is doubtful that anything much will move on its own.

If you want to move the situation forward, let alone imagine an agreement, you will have to act. But let's be clear about what that means. The fantasy scenario—you put a plan on the table and, after some tough negotiating, Benjamin Netanyahu and Mahmoud Abbas sign it in the presence of a dozen heads of Arab states—remains just that.

It is more likely that if you went down that route, the locals would pick the plan to death with reservations; and even if you got the Palestinian side to accept it, you would end up with new Israeli elections and a delay of several months, and you would open the door to any number of uncertainties from terror to some regional crisis mucking it all up. And there is no guarantee that new elections would produce an Israeli coalition government any more willing and able to make peace with the Palestinians than the current one.

What you need is a Palestinian or Arab Anwar Sadat-like figure.

But by now, I trust you've figured out that there are no Hollywood endings on Israeli-Palestinian peace. Four things ensure that: an Israeli prime minister who simply may not have the will or desire to make a deal that Abbas could accept; big gaps on the core issues that will be very hard to bridge; divisions within Palestinian ranks; and the Iranian nuclear issue, likely to erupt into some kind of military crisis in 2013, if not before.

The one option you should avoid at all costs is to push for a resumption of highly visible negotiations unless there is a greater consensus between the parties on process and substance. Without such a consensus, high-visibility negotiations are likely to end in a high-visibility failure. If the two sides were really serious, they would go off quietly and produce a secret framework accord of their own. But you won't be so lucky.

I think you have three options, none of them terribly attractive:

1. Wait for an opportunity instead of trying to create one: Low cost, low return. You might get lucky and the situation won't explode, or something will turn up that changes the calculations of one or more of the parties, and you'll have something to work with. This waiting game will be tough to sustain or defend, particularly given the fact that expectations have been raised so high about how important this issue is to American national interests. The Arab states will complain, American credibility will continue to decline (though how much lower it can go is arguable), and the Palestinians will push their international recognition campaign. Some kind of sustained Israeli-Palestinian violence is likely.

2. Try for a modified agreement on borders and security: The logic behind this approach is based on the notion—much better so far on paper than in practice—that these two issues are less controversial than the so-called identity issues, for example, refugees and Jerusalem, and that the gaps separating Israelis and Palestinians are less severe. So far, so good. But the gaps are still there, and the way to bridge them is better served by a full package where the two sides might trade and make compromises if they had more issues to work with. The other problems with this approach are fears on the Palestinian side that the Israelis won't move on the identity issues, and the concern on the Israeli side that they'll give in on the border issue without any commitment to end the conflict. You would also have to placate the Palestinians on settlements with a comprehensive freeze during the negotiations. And how you would finesse the Hamas issue is altogether unclear. No Israeli government would agree to any withdrawal—even in principle—unless it were certain that the Palestinian Authority would be able to control and silence all the guns.

3. Lay out American parameters for a comprehensive agreement: The idea of the United States putting out its own plan—or at least broad parameters on what it believes constitutes the basis for a settlement—has been kicking around Washington for quite a while. With the exception of American ideas put forward by Bill Clinton in December 2000, nobody has tried such an approach. It would be easy enough to do. There is an entire universe of formulations on the issues that could be presented and that are all very reasonable. The question is whether it would work.

That depends on what the definition of "work" is, in short, what the objective of the exercise is. One thing that would not happen is that Israelis and Palestinians would accept the parameters, enter a negotiation, and, with American help, bridge the gaps and live happily ever after.

More likely, given the gaps between this Israeli government and this Palestinian Authority and the suspicions that divide them, both sides would pose endless questions, reservations, and amendments that would give new meaning to the phrase "nickeled and dimed." There are really only two other ways this could go. If you could pre-wire acceptance of the parameters with one side, most likely the Palestinians, and deliver enough Arab states, you might be able to bring pressure on the Israelis. But this is too clever by half, in large part because it's hard to imagine any US ideas that would draw a clean and useable "yes" from Abbas and the Arabs.

No, if you went down the parameters route, you'd have to do so because you felt the time had come to bring clarity to the negotiating process, sharpen choices, and commit the United States to a set of principles in the hopes that doing so would boost our credibility and somehow, over time, bring the Israelis and the Palestinians around to negotiations and an agreement. The downside of this approach is obvious. No president wants to put out a plan only to have it sit there with no takers. The idea of an effective American role as broker/mediator has to do with the right timing. America acts at the right moment to bridge a gap, fix a problem, or broker an accord. There's a role for the United States as reality therapist and teacher, but it is better played out in speeches than in real-time initiatives. The expectation for America is not that it should talk about what's required to reach an accord, but that it should help produce one.

TENTH, THE BOTTOM LINE

Time isn't an ally of the two-state solution. Whether it's five minutes to midnight or a quarter till, the clock is ticking against a negotiated solution. But another failure isn't an ally of a final settlement, either.

If I were you, I'd be patient for now. Try to keep the Israeli-Egyptian relationship on the rails, focus the Palestinians on state building on the ground, not in the international arena. See if you can preserve Israeli-Palestinian security cooperation, maybe even encourage the Israelis to turn over additional territory in Area B and Area C; and press the Israelis to ease economic restrictions.

At the same time, see if Netanyahu and Abbas are ready to begin quiet discussion via trusted representatives on the core issues. In January 2013, make an assessment of the regional situation and determine how ambitious you want to be. The region has changed. And the challenges standing in the way of a conventional peace process have grown much more complex. At the same time, much detailed work has been done on all the issues. There are no mysteries anymore.

But one thing hasn't changed, and that's how invested the Israelis and Palestinians need to be in order for you and the United States to succeed. You can choose to bet against the house on this one—go for some big-bang peace plan. But unless there's more ownership by the locals, you're going to lose.

Some say you can create that urgency and ownership. Others—and I'll put myself in that camp—say you really can't. Or let's put it this way: there's no precedent on our side for doing it. You still may want to roll the dice, but if you ignore the ownership issue, you do so at your own peril. It's not pretty and really quite tragic. Nobody ever lost money betting against Arab-Israeli peace, and you probably won't either. But keep looking for opportunities to keep the Israelis and the Palestinians focused on the issue and be ready to exploit one yourself should it emerge. The story of Israelis, Palestinians, and the search for a durable two-state solution is far from over.

10

INTEGRATING THE TOP-DOWN WITH THE BOTTOM-UP APPROACH TO ISRAELI-PALESTINIAN PEACE

Robert M. Danin

In 1991, the United States successfully launched the first serious direct Israeli-Palestinian negotiations in Madrid. In the more than twenty years since, Washington has endeavored to facilitate Israeli-Palestinian talks as the way to end the more than century-long conflict over the land between the Jordan River and the Mediterranean. The core approach underlying these efforts has been negotiations based on the principle of land-for-peace, enshrined by United Nations Security Council Resolution 242 in November 1967. Some forty-five years later, that formula, while still paramount, has not produced an Israeli-Palestinian settlement. The problem with the American emphasis on negotiations, and the source of its failure to deliver, is not that it is ill conceived, but rather that it is incomplete.

The US approach toward negotiations based on land-for-peace has tended to assume that the negotiators for the two sides can reconcile their differences in a vacuum. It has frequently failed to take into account the larger political realities in which decision makers operate. While talks are an essential element for resolving the Israeli-Palestinian conflict, other tools of statecraft are required to help instill confidence and build constituencies for a genuine peace. To be sure, leaders must be prepared to make painful concessions for peace. But they will only be able to do so when their peoples are prepared to support them. For Israelis and Palestinians to support such compromises, they must believe that they have a real partner for peace on the other side and that the pain of compromise is worthwhile. Put simply, negotiating success requires that the Israeli and Palestinian people believe that negotiations are desirable, that they can succeed, that they should succeed, and that their leaders should be supported and empowered at the negotiating table.

After twenty years of negotiations, and despite real achievements, such as the 1993 Oslo Accords, most Israelis and Palestinians have lost faith in the prospects for a negotiated settlement, however much they may want one. The Second Intifada, launched after the Camp David negotiations in 2000 ended in failure, resulted in the deaths of thousands of Palestinians and Israelis. Palestinian security forces that had worked closely with their Israeli counterparts turned their weapons on their erstwhile partners. Israel attacked Palestinian Authority (PA) institutions and reoccupied some West Bank territory from which it had earlier withdrawn. Along with human loss came the loss of hope in true reconciliation. Both Israelis and Palestinians felt that they had taken a historic gamble only to be betrayed by one another. Having seen their hopes and trust dashed, they remain complacent in a comfort zone from which they are reluctant to venture out a second time.

NEGOTIATIONS: NECESSARY BUT INSUFFICIENT

Resolving the core issues dividing Israelis and Palestinians requires both to challenge their respective core narratives, self-identities, and collective myths and histories. This is no easy feat. Meanwhile, negotiations between governing elites have dragged on without a precise destination or timeline for producing conclusive results. One key reason for the two sides' failure has more to do with circumstances surrounding the talks than with issues on the negotiating table. Simply put, while those at the top (Israeli, Palestinian, and international leaders) have sequestered themselves to negotiate, those at the bottom (their respective publics) have been divorced from the process. This divergence between negotiating-room discussions at the top and empty results on the ground contributed to past failures. In hindsight, we can see four fundamental reasons for this.

First, negotiators have not built public support for making necessary concessions in advance. Ehud Barak, Ehud Olmert, Yasser Arafat, and Mahmoud Abbas all were constrained at various times from making negotiating concessions since each of them had failed to prepare their publics or create popular support for them. For example, when Israeli and Palestinian leaders locked themselves up at Camp David under the auspices of President Clinton for more than two weeks, both Barak and Arafat lacked the domestic backing required to make key compromises necessary at the moment of truth. At other times, when they were even willing to contemplate fundamental concessions, their negotiating position lacked credibility since they were perceived as politically incapable of delivering public support for a deal. They had not conditioned their publics prior to negotiations for the types of compromises necessary.

Second, and more critically, negotiations have at times been undermined by public disenchantment with the fundamental process in which the parties engaged—a situation that continues today. While a majority of Israelis and Palestinians polled consistently support a negotiated two-state solution, they nonetheless believe that a deal is not possible, that they have no real negotiating partner, or that the other side is unwilling to make necessary concessions for peace. This has sometimes made the mere act of negotiating, or the price of entering such talks, too politically costly for one or both of the parties.

Third, the prolonged nature of the process, continuing in fits and starts for nearly two decades without conclusion, has only exacerbated public disillusionment and rendered a deal more difficult. The Oslo Accords were meant to produce a final settlement by 1999, and the 2003 Roadmap called for a Palestinian state by 2005. These deadlines were missed with impunity. For the Palestinians in particular, negotiations were increasingly seen as conferring legitimacy and buying time for Israel to perpetuate the occupation with its undesired effects on the ground, especially settlement activity.

Fourth, the increased gap between what transpired in negotiating rooms and the deterioration in people's daily lives exacerbated the disenchantment. In the nearly seven years between the Oslo Accords and the 2000 Camp David Summit called to end the conflict, while negotiators met in comfortable hotels and locations around the world, conditions for ordinary Palestinians and Israelis deteriorated rather than improved. Palestinians witnessed increased restrictions and settlement expansion, while Israelis experienced increased violence, terrorism, and reduced personal security. After Camp David's failure and the subsequent Second Intifada, this trend rapidly accelerated, with both Israelis and Palestinians feeling betrayed by the other and entirely disillusioned over the possibility of a negotiated peace.

BROADENING THE APPROACH: THE NEED FOR "BOTTOM-UP" MEASURES

Given the sheer difficulty of the issues involved plus the violence, terrorism, and cynicism shared by both sides following the Second Intifada, it is remarkable that American-led diplomacy succeeded in reconstituting Israeli-Palestinian negotiations at Annapolis in 2007. Against all expectations, Olmert and Mahmoud and their teams were able to sustain serious engagement in talks throughout 2008.

One fundamental reason negotiations were successfully renewed is that policy makers had learned from their past experiences over the course of the peace process and had taken steps to address some of their earlier shortcomings. For example, President Clinton set out a series of "parameters" in December 2000 to give Israelis and Palestinians a greater sense of the shape and destination for their talks. President George W. Bush sharpened the US vision in a speech on June 24, 2002, explicitly and publicly identifying a democratic Palestinian state as a key element for comprehensive peace. Bush asked Secretary of State Colin Powell to develop a comprehensive plan for statehood, working with international partners, to support Palestinian reform and institution building to help realize this vision.

That plan was the Roadmap, released on April 30, 2003, by the Quartet. The Roadmap identified the need for both Israel and the Palestinian Authority to take real and tangible steps to create an improved context that would be conducive to negotiations. It provided clear timelines, target dates, benchmarks, and steps in the political, security, economic, humanitarian, and institution-building fields. It also laid out a sequenced process of actions on the ground leading to possible Palestinian statehood and subsequent negotiations to resolve all outstanding issues. Israel was called upon to freeze all settlement activity, including natural growth, and to withdraw to the lines that existed before the Second Intifada to help address widespread Palestinian concerns. At the same time and in parallel, the Palestinians were called upon to address Israel's core concern and end all violence and terrorism, rebuild and restructure their security services, and confront and dismantle the terrorist infrastructure. Moreover, the Palestinians were to "undertake comprehensive political reform in preparation for statehood."[1] Here was the first serious effort to introduce the "bottom-up" approach into the peace process.

Inherent in this approach was a core trade-off to address the shortcomings of previous negotiations. To support negotiations and demonstrate the utility of the peace process, Palestinian security efforts were now a sine qua non for political progress. At the same time, Israeli actions on the ground were prescribed to help bolster Palestinian confidence in the overall process and instill a belief that cooperation, rather than the armed struggle, would allow the Palestinians to fulfill their national aspirations.

Despite the important corrective that the Roadmap introduced—concrete steps on the ground by both sides to help shape an improved daily context to help negotiations flourish—this document alone was insufficient to overcome the inherent challenges to forging peace. The Roadmap's core flaw as a diplomatic tool was that the steps required by the parties were not self-implementing. The Roadmap was and remains an important pathway toward ending the Israeli-Palestinian conflict, specifying concrete actions by both Israelis and Palestinians to take in parallel to build critical elements for peace. But it possessed neither a mechanism to enforce compliance, nor consequences for failure to do so. It is an important guide and template outlining the types of steps the parties must undertake to realize peace. Most important, it provides a key conceptual contribution: negotiations alone will not resolve the Israeli-Palestinian impasse. Both sides, along with the international community, have to take steps independent of the other to help structure an environment more conducive to peacemaking. However, the Roadmap formed the foundation for an important new phase in Israeli-Palestinian peacemaking.

BREAKTHROUGH FOR THE BOTTOM-UP APPROACH

In June 2007, Hamas, which had won Palestinian legislative elections in early 2006, violently took over Gaza after protracted fighting, defeating and expelling Fatah forces from the Strip. Palestinian Authority President Mahmoud Abbas immediately dismantled the Hamas-led PA government and appointed Salam Fayyad as prime minister and a government of independents in its place. This development would have far-reaching ramifications for the course of Israeli-Palestinian relations. It allowed the launching of two interrelated initiatives necessary for peacemaking: the top-down and the bottom-up approaches.

The first, representing a reconstituted top-down approach, was the Annapolis Peace Conference, convened by the United States on November 27, 2007. The United States seized the opportunity to bring the two parties together, with some forty-nine countries and international organizations in attendance. President Bush read a joint understanding stating that the Israeli and Palestinian leaders had expressed their commitment to end their conflict through negotiations to resolve all outstanding issues. Israelis and Palestinians returned to formal negotiations for the first time in seven years. As part of their effort, the two sides pledged to implement their respective obligations under the Roadmap leading to the attainment of a peace treaty.[2] Negotiations proceeded at the Israeli and Palestinian summit level throughout the course of 2008 with dozens of bilateral negotiating teams working in parallel on the broad range of issues. This represented the revitalization and reconstitution of top-down political negotiations.

Of far more lasting consequence, however, was the first systematic effort at a bottom-up approach led by the new Palestinian government of Prime Minister Fayyad. Its main elements were economic development and security reform. As finance minister under Arafat, Fayyad had won international recognition for introducing transparency and accountability to the Palestinian Authority. He now set off with a comprehensive reform plan to provide basic services and pay civil servant salaries in the West Bank and Gaza while encouraging fiscal discipline, delivering a systematic two-year development plan for good governance, and improving the investment climate.[3]

The effort at self-reliance and transformation represents a fundamentally new Palestinian approach aimed not only at preparing Palestinian institutions for independence, but also transforming Palestinian attitudes in doing so. The goal was not only to prepare Palestine and Palestinians for complete self-governance, but also to use the process of state building to remove the reasons for Israel's continued occupation of territories since 1967, particularly those pertaining to security.[4]

Over time, the international community, including Israel, came to see that the Palestinians had become more effective in governance, economic development, and, most important to Israel, security. In early 2008, Israel adopted steps to loosen its grip in the West Bank to allow Fayyad's government to improve West Bank economic and security conditions. An effort supported by the United States and former British prime minister Tony Blair, the Quartet's newly appointed special representative, aimed to bring about rapid change and to increase PA control on the ground. The PA undertook hundreds of development projects and, over the next year, Israel slowly allowed reconstituted PA forces, trained under the auspices of the US Security Coordinator, Lt. General Keith Dayton, to deploy and retake control of West Bank population areas. At the Quartet's prodding, some key Israeli physical barriers to movement within the West Bank and between it and Israel were eased or removed over the course of 2008 and 2009, precipitating a trade-led economic spurt. Areas in the West Bank, such as Jenin and Nablus, that had been controlled by renegade militias came under the control of unified security forces accountable to civilian authority. Palestinians could now walk the streets of towns that earlier in the decade had been hotbeds of lawlessness and sources of violence. What started as an effort to reform and provide good governance became an approach that sought not only to be transformative for the Palestinian territories, but also for the Palestinian people.

The West Bank economy took off. It averaged annual GDP growth of 9 percent from 2008 to 2010, with closer to 6 percent in 2011.[5] Fayyad initiated a program to complete the process of building state institutions and finalizing the creation of central and local institutions, upgrading delivery of government services, and launching infrastructure projects. Government spending remained within budgetary targets, tax collection rates increased threefold between 2006 and 2010, resulting in higher than anticipated tax revenues, unemployment was cut by a nearly a third, hundreds of schools, thousands of miles of roads, and nearly one thousand miles of new water networks were established. In that 2008–2010 period alone, the PA constructed three new hospitals, rehabilitated fifty healthcare centers, renewed and expanded electricity networks in 221 rural villages, resulting in 99.9 percent of Palestinian households now connected to the public electricity network.[6] To date, eight full PA National Security Forces (NSF) special battalions and two Presidential Guard battalions have been trained in Jordan under the auspices of the US security coordinator, with an additional NSF battalion currently in training.[7] The international economic assistance organizations confirmed that the PA had halved its reliance on foreign aid while slashing its own budget deficit.

By 2011, a number of the technical organs monitoring Palestinian institutional reform and development determined that the PA was ready for statehood, to the extent possible while Israel still occupies most West Bank territory and key points of leverage. Norway's foreign minister, Jonas Store, who also chairs the Ad Hoc Liaison Committee (AHLC), the key PA donor support group consisting of the World Bank, the International Monetary Fund (IMF), the UN, the Quartet, the PA, Israel, and a number of other donor countries, declared that the Palestinian institutions had "achieved a level above the threshold for a functioning state in key sectors as revenue and expenditure management, economic development, service delivery and security and justice. In this respect, Palestine has achieved more than many states that are full UN members, and has passed a tougher economic stress test than many EU member states."[8]

To say that the Palestinian Authority has made significant achievements and is prepared to assume the reins of power as an independent state is not to imply that there is not room for significant improvements in many areas of governance and economic development. A number of practical steps can and should be taken, even within the existing context, to further improve Palestinian institutions. The PA should press ahead to improve public sector efficiency, reduce reliance on foreign assistance, institute more comprehensive pension reform, and increase financial transparency where there has been some recent recidivism. In addition, the PA should do more to create an enabling business environment to attract investment, including expanding land registration in the West Bank, reforming existing laws governing businesses, and building the PA's capacity to regulate the economy. More can be done to tighten the legal, institutional, and attitudinal approaches toward corruption. Surveys suggest that the Palestinian public have little faith in their government's willingness to prosecute corruption cases or enforce rulings, making Palestinians reluctant to report corrupt activities.[9] Other steps to improve conditions would include Israel's promoting further access and movement within the West Bank, allowing trade, development, and reconstruction in Gaza, improving living conditions in East Jerusalem, improving the rule of law covering the judicial and security sectors, and allowing Palestinian economic access and development in Area C, the 60 percent of the West Bank under full Israeli control.[10]

Still, the bottom line today is that the Palestinian Authority has pretty much realized its potential within the existing constraints that accompany the fact that, while it administers virtually all the Palestinian population of the West Bank, Israel still retains control of 60 percent of contiguous West Bank territory. Palestinians are not allowed to build in most of the Israeli-controlled areas, and in the remaining parts it is nearly impossible for Palestinians to obtain permission to build or repair infrastructure. For the Palestinians to be able to progress to a new level in their state-building project, some larger fundamental political issues—both internal to Palestinian politics and also pertaining to the peace process—need to be addressed.

On the ground, sustainable economic growth and an improved fiscal status require unleashing the private sector's potential. As the World Bank notes, this in turn requires Israel to lift restrictions on access to land, water, raw materials, and export markets. As long as nearly 60 percent of the West Bank remains off-limits to Palestinian development, opportunities will remain limited and growth will be minimal at best.[11]

POLITICS REVISITED

Real achievements on the ground have now outpaced the stalled Israeli-Palestinian political process. The bottom-up approach has successfully produced robust, well-functioning institutions and serious and sustained Israeli-Palestinian security coordination. All this has undoubtedly kept a tenuous Israeli-Palestinian reality on the ground from descending into violence, though it still could unravel at any time. But the top-down approach—negotiations to resolve the final-status issues—is stalled and lags behind in efforts to resolve the conflict.

A snapshot of the current situation may lead some to conclude that the status quo, while suboptimal, is not so terrible, particularly given the broader violence, unrest, and uncertainty sweeping the Middle East. The chaos and violence that characterized the West Bank a decade ago have been replaced by an expanding economy, a government that has met many international benchmarks of success, and Palestinian lives improved both materially and in the realm of personal security. Meanwhile, Israelis, particularly those living west of the security barrier, see little urgency to resolve the conflict with the Palestinians since the two sides are effectively separated from one another, and Israelis have seen very little violence emerge from the West Bank. Only those Israeli communities located in the south near Gaza feel an acute security threat from the frequent barrage of mortars and rockets that regularly sends Israelis into bunkers for shelter.

However, a more dynamic analysis suggests that the trend-lines are working to undermine this tranquility. The possibilities for a two-state solution are diminishing over time, given demographic changes, population growth, continued settlement activities, and increased popular skepticism about the possibility and even desirability of two independent states, Israel and Palestine, living side by side in peace and security.

More critically, the progress and successes of the last half-decade's bottom-up approach, described in this chapter, are not self-sustaining. The irony of today's situation is that whereas earlier top-down political progress had been stymied by the absence of a serious bottom-up effort, the opposite is true today: the last few years' bottom-up successes cannot be sustained in a political vacuum. Without the prospects for further momentum, foreign assistance dries up, as does a sense of hope and the vision of an endgame. Palestinians and outside investors will only underwrite the state-building venture to the extent that they see a real Palestinian state emerging from that effort. Otherwise, they fear that they are mistakenly helping to alleviate the burden of Israel's prolonged occupation. One key reason that wealthy Arab donors and private businessmen have become increasingly reluctant to invest in Palestine is that they don't believe their investment will pay off.

Internal Palestinian political paralysis thwarts further movement toward the development of fully functioning democratic institutions. The 2007 division of the West Bank under the Palestinian Authority from Gaza under Hamas has led to the breakdown of real Palestinian politics. The Hamas-Fatah split has thwarted the process of holding new elections for the presidency, the parliament, or even local councils, eviscerating the vibrancy of Palestinian institutions. Inactive since 2006, the Palestinian Legislative Council (PLC) no longer serves as an institutional check on the executive authority of the PA. Prior to 2006, the PLC had been engaged in active accountability efforts, providing oversight to executive conduct. The absence of checks and balances not only harms the prospects for good governance, but further diminishes the economic climate for those who seek solid institutions in which to invest.

One step to help mend the West Bank–Gaza split would be to encourage legitimate Palestinian businesses in Gaza to thrive and interact with the West Bank. Such actions would help weaken Hamas's standing, if not its control, in Gaza. For now, the economic sequestration of Gaza strengthens Hamas, as it controls a booming underground economy and tunnel trade with Egypt that only harms established business interests that would just as soon be done with Hamas. Weakening Hamas's economic monopoly in Gaza through legitimate trade with the West Bank would be one important step toward reestablishing broken links between the two bifurcated segments of Palestine.

Israel, as the occupying power in the West Bank, also has a critical role to play. It retains final say as to what the PA can and cannot do. For Palestinians to support the bottom-up approach, Israel must convince them that the occupation will end and that there is a real prospect for an independent Palestinian state soon. The more that Palestinians feel that they are taking real control over their lives, the more credible will be the peace process and the more Palestinians will be prepared to support political compromises in final-status negotiations. It is in this context that the Roadmap obligation of a settlement freeze takes on such saliency: it is the most potent barometer that Palestinians use to judge Israeli intentions vis-à-vis the West Bank. The more that settlements expand to take more West

Bank land (while at the same time preventing Palestinians from developing their land), the less Palestinians believe that Israel is either willing or able to allow a Palestinian state to emerge as part of a credible two-state solution.

A NEW CONCEPTUAL APPROACH

In recent years, efforts to improve conditions on the ground have far outpaced the political process. While negotiations have effectively not advanced since 2008, considerable progress has been made in the Palestinian quest to build durable institutions for a peaceful and democratic Palestinian state. These efforts have provided dramatically improved prosperity and security on the ground for Palestinians and, by extension, Israel. Paradoxically, the effort to prepare Palestinian territories for statehood was set back dramatically by the Palestinian political move to seek UN Security Council recognition, drawing badly needed attention away from cooperation on the ground and toward diplomatic confrontation. The irony and challenge for the United States in pursuing Middle East peace is that whereas the fundamental flaw in previous such efforts was US and Israeli-Palestinian inattention to developments on the ground and outside the negotiation room, today the situation is the reverse: inattention to the political track threatens to undermine the dramatic on-the-ground improvements of the last few years that have provided stability, prosperity, and security for both Palestinians and Israelis. This achievement provides a foundation on which Israeli-Palestinian negotiations stand a better chance for success.

Today, however, the West Bank faces a precarious future with a slowdown in growth and a widespread sense of uncertainty. The IMF and the World Bank estimate that there is a high risk that growth will diminish further due to fiscal retrenchment, declining aid and resulting liquidity difficulties, and a lack of further Israeli easement on movement and access restrictions. Israel continues to adopt additional limited measures to allow Palestinian development to proceed, and has also allowed the Palestinian security forces to expand their reach, authorizing, for example, an additional seven police stations to be built in that part of the West Bank that falls under joint Israeli and Palestinian control (Area B).

For the United States to conduct a truly effective strategy, a new, more comprehensive, and integrated approach is necessary, fully integrating the bottom-up approach with the top-down. This is not simply a function of adding more elements to the diplomatic to-do list. It means a conceptual shift integrating negotiations, economic development, and attention to security concerns into one coherent integrated whole. Throughout the past two decades, American leaders of all stripes have gravitated toward the political track while relegating the security and economic components to subordinates or third parties. This has reflected a false division of labor and an inability to see the pieces as an organic whole. This segmented approach has mistakenly signaled the parties that the real priority is negotiations and that the economic and security aspects are merely supporting elements. This constrains progress in some fundamental ways.

First, this focus on negotiations leads public opinion, both in the region and worldwide, to measure progress solely in terms of political progress, failing to see fundamental changes taking place on the ground. This is critical because negotiations, by their private and confidential nature, are successful only at their end when an agreement is produced. They mainly provide inspiration and hope once they are concluded. High-level attention to on-the-ground developments allows the parties to highlight ongoing progress and the fruits of efforts to build peace.

Second, treating the on-the-ground measures as divorced from the final-status political issues obfuscates some key reasons inhibiting progress on the ground. While outsiders tend to look at so-called confidence-building measures or other on-the-ground steps as separate from negotiations, the parties themselves see them as integrally linked in two basic ways. In a negotiating environment where the parties look askance at unilateral concessions, both Israelis and Palestinians often seek outside compensation for any compromises. While American officials may see the various streams of activity as related but not integrated, the parties themselves see them as vitally integrated.

The parties are often reluctant to make seemingly innocuous gestures out of concern for their implications for an overall final-status agreement. Thus, allowing Palestinians to dig a well or pave a road in a certain location will be viewed by Israeli officials through the prism of the precedential nature of these acts and their implications for a final-status agreement. Integrating the bottom-up with the top-down would allow peace brokers to draw from and trade across a much broader menu of items. It would recognize that the parties see these interconnections and would allow savvy diplomats to draw from a much broader set of options in proffering trade-offs and proposals.

While no one American official can do it all, the top leadership must convey the sense that the bottom-up approach is as important as the top-down. Otherwise, Israelis and Palestinians might draw mistaken conclusions about what the United States views as the real priorities and the areas where they must focus their energy. A singular focus on the political track by top American officials leads Israeli and Palestinian leaders to pay less attention to the economic and security spheres. Nonetheless, since so many of these bottom-up issues are viewed as linked by the parties to a final settlement, it is often the case that movement can come through the intervention of the highest Israeli and Palestinian leaders. If they know that authorizing such measures will be recognized as important by the United States, they will be more motivated to take such steps.[12]

The United States provides the most assistance of any country to the Palestinian Authority. From fiscal year 2008 to the present, US bilateral assistance to the Palestinians has averaged $600 million, including some $200 million in annual direct budgetary assistance, $100 million in non-lethal West Bank security assistance, and some $300 million dedicated to non-governmental project assistance.[13]

Yet the United States does not always put its mouth where its money is. The PA frequently faces financing gaps resulting in delays in paying wages to 150,000 Palestinian earners in the West Bank and Gaza. This is mainly because some key donor countries, particularly in the Gulf, routinely fulfill their pledges to the PA only in part and after considerable delay.[14] This might be otherwise were the United States to provide top-level political visibility to its economic support efforts. For example, senior officials visiting the region should regularly visit program sites and areas where the PA is making a difference. Confining themselves to bilateral meetings with political leaders reinforces the message that the top-down is what counts and that the bottom-up is secondary.

A sustained effort that provides equal political weight to the top-down and the bottom-up stands a greater chance of reaping the benefits that have been sown over the past few years. Today's reality—one that provides enhanced security for Israelis and improved living standards for Palestinians—alone will not produce peace, nor will it continue indefinitely. But it provides a solid basis to support serious and intensive negotiations. Pursued in coordination and as part of a unified American policy, the top-down and bottom-up approaches stand the best chance of realizing the goal that has eluded US leaders for decades—a comprehensive Israeli-Palestinian peace. Failure to build upon the more recent hard-earned progress risks forfeiting what had seemed unthinkable just a decade ago—an effective Palestinian Authority combating terrorism and delivering decent government—back when Israelis and Palestinians were mired in deadly conflict. The only way to avoid sliding backward is by pushing forward.

NOTES

1. See "A Performance-Based Roadmap to a Permanent Two-State Solution to the Israeli-Palestinian Conflict" in the appendix.
2. "Joint Understanding Read by President Bush at Annapolis Conference," November 27, 2007, Memorial Hall, United States Naval Academy, Annapolis, Maryland, http://georgewbush-whitehouse.archives.gov/news/releases/2007/11/20071127.html.
3. Palestinian National Authority, *Building a Palestinian State: Towards peace and prosperity,* December 17, 2007, http://unispal.un.org/pdfs/PRDPFinal.pdf.
4. For a description of the revolutionary and transformative approach adopted by Salam Fayyad, see Robert M. Danin, "A Third Way to Palestine: Fayyadism and Its Discontents," Foreign Affairs, Volume 90, No. 1, January/February 2011, 94-109.
5. International Monetary Fund, *Recent Experience and Prospects of the Economy of the West Bank and Gaza,* March 21, 2012, 5. http://www.imf.org/external/country/WBG/RR/2012/032112.pdf.
6. For a full summary of the PA's achievements, see Palestinian National Authority, *National Development Plan 2011-13: Establishing the State, Building Our Future.* April 2011. http://www.mopad.pna.ps/en/attachments/article/5/EstablishingtheStateBuildingourFutureNDP202011-13.pdf.
7. Jim Zanotti, *U.S. Foreign Aid to the Palestinians,* Congressional Research Service, June 15, 2012, 15. http://www.fas.org/sgp/crs/mideast/RS22967.pdf
8. Jonas Gahr Store, "Ready for Statehood," *International Herald Tribune,* September 23, 2011, http://www.nytimes.com/2011/09/23/opinion/23iht-edstore23.html.
9. The World Bank, "Improving Governance and Reducing Corruption, 2011," May 18, 2011 https://openknowledge.worldbank.org/bitstream/handle/10986/2814/617010ESW0WHIT0portWBGEngMay1802011.pdf?sequence=1.
10. "Summary of Office of the Quartet Representative Development Agenda to Support Palestinian Economic Sustainability and Institution-Building," March 21, 2012. http://www.tonyblairoffice.org/page/-/quartet/documents/OQR%20AHLC%20Report%20March%2021%202012.pdf.
11. The World Bank, "Stagnation or Revival? Palestinian Economic Prospects," March 21, 2012. http://siteresources.worldbank.org/INTWESTBANKGAZA/Resources/WorldBankAHLCreportMarch2012.pdf.

12. Asked once by a Quartet official why Israel refused to authorize more Palestinian requests steps that would provide economic benefits to the Palestinians, one senior Israeli official conceded that it was because the American leadership doesn't ask. Why should Israel give the Palestinians something of consequence if it won't be acknowledged by the Americans, he asked.

13. Zanotti, p. 1.

14. International Monetary Fund, *Recent Experience and Prospects of the Economy of the West Bank and Gaza: Staff Report Prepared for the Meeting of the Ad Hoc Liaison Committee,* March 31, 2012.

11

THE SECURITY CONUNDRUM

P. J. Dermer and Steven White

"Insanity: doing the same thing over and over again and expecting different results."

—attributed to Albert Einstein

This chapter provides an analysis of the complicated security context on the ground and how US efforts to solve it play into the broader picture of forging peace between Israel and a future Palestinian state. It assesses how the parties view the world they live in—including the relevance of the ongoing regional upheaval and the Arab uprisings. Next is a synopsis of the key final-status security-related issues as last discussed at the negotiation table and an evaluation of the parties' fundamental security prisms and requirements. The chapter then draws on the authors' experience to assess how the parties' requirements *could* be approached and what lessons can be learned from past— even those that largely failed—US and international attempts to build security capacity. We conclude with an inside look at the most successful endeavor to date—the work of the United States Security Coordinator (USSC)—during the second term of the George W. Bush administration, which resulted in nascent Palestinian security sector reform and, more importantly, in fostering a renewed modicum of trust and confidence in the security domain between Israel and Palestine. The chapter concludes with prescriptions for a viable pathway to a long-term security solution that builds on the lessons learned from previous efforts—consistent with the military principle of "reinforcing success."

Both the Israelis and the Palestinians have critical security requirements that are interconnected, do not exist in a vacuum, and require dedicated American and international attention. Ultimately, a sensible American security strategy will dictate that the requirements of one party cannot be accepted as legitimate to the exclusion of those of the other.[1]

SECURITY VIEWS OF THE PARTIES

Israeli Perspective

Prior to the eruption of the Arab uprisings in 2011, Israel prioritized its security focus on two main fronts: externally and existentially toward Iran and internally toward the Palestinian terror dilemma. The situation on Israel's borders with its treaty partners, Jordan and Egypt, was stable; the threats posed by Hezbollah in the north and Hamas in Gaza were contained; and the security issues on the border with Syria were unchanged from the disengagement agreement reached in 1974.

Security challenges faced by Israel have always been dynamic. Key historic Israeli security concerns focused on attacks against its population via non-conventional weapons and conventionally armed surface-to-surface missiles and attacks from armed opponents across its borders. These attacks could be asymmetrical—such as Hamas's armed raids and rocket assaults, Hezbollah's aggression in 2006, and the more recent cross-border infiltration from the Sinai Peninsula in 2012. Or the assaults could be conventional; for example, the War of Attrition waged by Egypt during the 1969–1970 period or the large-scale Arab army air/land movements like those in 1948, 1967, and 1973. The objectives of these conventional attacks included imposing a strategic defeat on Israel, recovering lost territories, or, as in the Syrian-Egyptian attack in October 1973, creating conditions to gain political advantages in negotiations.[2]

In the wake of the regional upheavals, Israel again faces uncertainty and a realization that conventional regional political stability may be a thing of the past. The emergence and growing power of political Islam—for example, the Muslim Brotherhood's assumption of power in Egypt—is of particular concern for Israel. Even Israel's most reliable security neighbor, Jordan, is now seen as being at risk—with the stability of the Hashemite Kingdom being slowly chipped away by internal and external threats. Meanwhile, Iran looms large—both in its drive to nuclearization and as a subversive participant in ongoing regional events, particularly along Israel's borders. The Iranian threat is branded as an existential one by Israel's leadership.

Conversely, given Israel's intensive anti-terror efforts in the Second Intifada, Palestine is seen as a manageable security issue despite the continued hostile, on-again, off-again actions of Hamas in Gaza and some terrorist elements in the West Bank. Israel thus relegates Palestine to a reduced-security priority compared to the bigger issues elsewhere in the region. While many Israelis would agree that the security status quo with Palestine is not a placeholder for real peace and therefore unsustainable for a long period of time, they believe it is the least of their problems for the foreseeable future.

The fundamental mission of the Israeli security establishment is to ensure the safety and security of Israel's citizens wherever they may be. Part of this security challenge is self-generated: the need to protect the 350,000-plus settlers who live across the Green Line in the Palestinian territories. The security and safety of these settlers, many of whom are armed and radical and do not recognize the rule of law in the territories, remain the responsibility of Israel. For Israel, then, its security mission extends literally beyond its borders—to protect its citizens who are living in territory that is not internationally recognized as belonging to Israel.

Palestinian Perspective

Palestinian security interests are, not surprisingly, less traditional. Their requirements focus on creating the conditions for independent statehood, forging national identity, protection of people under occupation, border protection and internal defense, civil policing, and counterterrorism.[3] The Arab upheaval has had little real effect on the Palestinian strategic security calculus. For Palestinians, the Israeli occupation is the primary strategic concern. Palestinians do not enjoy sovereignty in any of the territory designated by the Oslo Accords—Areas A, B, or C. For Palestinians, the everyday reality is occupation and the continued expansion of Israeli settlements—those authorized by the Israeli government and those set up without government approval.

While indigenous Palestinian access and movement throughout the West Bank has improved over the last few years as a result of nascent security progress, the overarching restrictions and their human, economic, and social dimensions remain. The Israeli Defense Forces (IDF) continue nightly incursions into Palestinian villages and cities in Area A, where Oslo designated the Palestinians as responsible for security. The result is a dual reality: Israeli support for Palestinian economic and institutional advancement, but almost total Israeli control over these undertakings on the ground. Palestinian Authority (PA) security forces cannot act to protect their own citizens without complying with Israeli dictates and tolerating the sometimes oppressive IDF presence. Any unilateral PA action is undertaken at the security persons' own risk. Moreover, Israeli settlers pose severe security problems for Palestinians as some increasingly take the law into their own hands.[4]

A second Palestinian security challenge is the continuing internal ideological-political struggle between Fatah and Hamas, including conflict between their militias. This struggle is played out in a family- and clan-dominated society that sometimes trumps national ideology, as was seen in the internal Palestinian dynamics in Jenin in May–June 2012.[5]

In recent years there have been marked positive improvements in interactions between Israel and Palestine. Israeli and Palestinian officials attribute the improved security environment to several factors, including Israeli and Palestinian forces once again beginning to work together. The cooperation, while notable, is embryonic, with the parties asserting it to be in their own respective national security interests. Of note, the evolving renewal of Israeli-Palestinian security cooperation has had to bridge the inherent psychological and emotional traumas of myriad unsuccessful international efforts and

systemic conflict, most notably the Second Intifada. Renewed security cooperation on the ground has contained the possibility of renewed large-scale
violence for the foreseeable future. That said, in the absence of peace, the
current security calm on the ground cannot be assessed as permanent.

FINAL-STATUS ISSUES

Although serious movement toward final-status negotiations has been at
a standstill for several years, in previous talks the parties narrowed differences on the security framework for a peace agreement. Key issues under
discussion included the definition of final borders, shared and independent
early warning capabilities, delineation of civilian and military airspace
use, allocation of the electromagnetic spectrum, status of residual IDF
deployment and/or future access in the Jordan Valley, commercial crossing procedures between Israel and Palestine, the composition of Palestinian
armaments and force structures, maritime declarations, and establishment
of West Bank-Gaza linkage(s). Table 11.1 summarizes the parties' positions
to date.

While the full history of the security negotiations is beyond the scope
of this chapter, the fact is that an agreed security structure is within reach of
agreement between the parties.[6]

That said, it is important to highlight the philosophical or conceptual
positions that underlie the parties' approaches to negotiations on security.
Israel maintains two overriding assumptions. First, Israel seeks a limited,
phased withdrawal of its forces from the West Bank, according to an Israeli
timetable and based on an Israeli assessment of Palestinian security/gover-
nance performance. Second, Israel seeks a physical presence or latent/virtual
direct role in each security subcategory, unwilling to turn over complete control outside of its own purview.[7]

For their part, Palestinians have two overriding concerns as well, predicated on their need to achieve full sovereignty. First, Palestinians insist on no
residual Israeli forces in the state of Palestine and no unilateral Israeli intru-
sion—virtual or otherwise—into any part of Palestinian territory. Second,
Palestinians want an international monitoring force or other third party
organization to safeguard their sovereignty from overzealous Israeli actions.

Security Issues in the Negotiations*

Israel	Palestine
Palestine to be a de-militarized or non-militarized state.	Rejects terminology of de-militarized or non-militarized status.
Weapons and technology restrictions and limits on Palestinian armaments, and restrictions on size and structure of Palestinian Security Forces.	Doctrine of "defensive security"—accepts limitations on procurement and deployment of certain types of weapons.
Complete absence of Palestinian strategic defensive or operational offensive capability.**	
Residual Israeli military/security presence—real or virtual—in the Jordan Valley and along the Jordan River.	Opposes any Israeli security-related presence in Palestine.
Israeli early warning presence in Palestine.	Full sovereignty and control of all Palestinian territory.
Pre-positioned Israeli logistical sites in Palestine.	
Goal is strategically "defensible" borders, ruling out a return to the June 4, 1967, lines.	Final border demarcation by agreement, not dictated by Israel's assessment of its security needs.
Palestinian border defense limited to small arms.	Control over border crossings and borders.
Israeli security responsibility over the land corridor linking the West Bank and Gaza.	Control over Gaza-West Bank land corridor.
Israeli control or influence over the electromagnetic spectrum and air space. Israeli control of Gaza's maritime area.	Full control over Palestinian air space and electromagnetic spectrum.
Monitoring and verification system in place for each sub-category.	Third-party monitoring force.

*See Geoffrey Aronson and P. J. Dermer, "U.S. Policy in a Time of Transition," Stimson Institute, May 2012. https://www.dropbox.com/s/mszz5ujh4gd46g9/Pickering%20Report.pdf, for more details of the Israeli and Palestinian positions and American views.

**For example, land-based missiles, heavy artillery, modern fighters, battleships, and the like.

Thus, both parties see the need for monitoring and verification, but differ conceptually on almost every other aspect of the framework for security.

STRATEGIC CONTEXT: MISMATCHED AUTHORITIES AND COMPETING REQUIREMENTS

Israeli security forces continue to deploy at will throughout Palestinian territory and along Israel's borders. In the West Bank, this means that Palestinian forces are precluded from arming or deploying in a manner consistent with developing a national security doctrine or in the defense of an internationally defined and agreed-upon (albeit transitional) homeland. Palestinian activities, force structure, and the development of doctrine are, by tacit agreement with the United States and Israel, currently subordinated to Israeli interests. In the recent renewal of US participation in the security sphere via the activities of the United States Security Coordinator, every move concerning PA security developments has had to be approved by Israel. Current operations thus present a unique paradox: on the one hand, Israel demands that Palestinians provide the long-term security Israel seeks, while on the other hand, Israeli actions hinder Palestinian abilities to develop this security capacity in a manner that will satisfy their stated needs.

For their part, Palestinians have not yet restructured their own security concept to address the problems created by Yasser Arafat's tight-gripped management of Palestinian politics. Although newly trained and equipped security forces have deployed in Palestinian cities over the last several years, there remain redundant security services and intrinsic rivalries that compete for primacy, retarding unity of national focus and effort. Even taking into account the difficult political and operational realities that Palestinians confront vis-à-vis Israeli activities in the territories, the Palestinian Authority still has much to do to get its own house in order for the transition to statehood.

A core problem, therefore, is that the security requirements of the two parties are of a totally different nature: Israel's security prism is the quest by an established state for an ever-increasing sense of security from Palestinian (and other regional) threats; while Palestine's security outlook is the quest of a non-state actor for greater political, security, and sovereign control and the chance to develop its own national security doctrine in preparation for statehood.

Despite these apparent contradictions, our experience on the ground indicates that the requirements of the parties are not mutually exclusive, but in fact could be symbiotic. Absolute security for either Israel or Palestine is unattainable, and the quest for such an objective is itself destabilizing. To be lasting and effective, the long-term security parameters for Israel and a Palestinian state must be mutual and reciprocal. Israeli security demands need to be seen in context with Palestinian sovereignty requirements and vice versa. At a minimum, the United States will need to make it very clear that the security demands of both parties are not absolute, but rather need to be balanced against the requirements of the other.

A LOOK BACK AT SECURITY FACILITATION EFFORTS

"We're lost, but we're making good time" —attributed to Yogi Berra

To build mutuality into the resolution of the security conundrum, trust and confidence need to be established between the parties, and this will require hard work and careful preparation. Past US policy efforts have tended to play out as a mismatch between pronouncements and desires masquerading as strategy and between the tactics adopted on the ground. As such, attempts to advance the parties' security interests have consistently fallen short, with one exception. Building a better American strategy will require improving our assumptions and methodologies, integrating elements that have worked, and assimilating lessons learned about what did not work.

Faulty Assumptions

Our experience teaches that two long-held strategic assumptions are flawed. First, advancement in the security realm is not the panacea for what ails Israelis and Palestinians. A viable strategy to achieve a two-state solution requires a "whole-of-government" approach—that is, a full-scale, policy-driven effort inclusive of the political, economic, social, and security fronts. Without tangible security progress enabled by an atmosphere of trust enjoyed by both parties, there is no foundation on which to build a comprehensive and durable political solution. While mutual security is vital for Israel and Palestine to live in peace, it is not sufficient by itself. Security is a living, evolutionary process, not something that can be measured according to strict metrics or quantitatively. Its human aspect contains psychological/subjective elements important to both Israelis and Palestinians that cannot be fulfilled with mechanical fixes or ever larger numbers of security forces on either side.

The second fundamental flaw has been an almost exclusive American focus on the security needs of Israel. The United States is committed to maintaining Israel's "qualitative military edge" (QME) for its conventional military strength against regional threats, existential or otherwise. This is important to assure Israel that it can provide for its security while taking necessary risks associated with the peace process. But US commitments and actions have often gone well beyond this; for example, not pushing back against Israel's claims to the West Bank or Israeli occupation practices that undermine Palestinian confidence in the peace process. Palestinians are realistic in understanding the special United States-Israel relationship, but they believe that the United States has its own needs and that it should take their interests and requirements into account as well.

It is important to review past security efforts by the United States and others and to indicate why they came up short.

CIA in the Lead

In the wake of the groundbreaking Oslo Accords in 1993, the Clinton administration tasked the CIA with managing security cooperation and facilitation between the parties. This meant that the interaction between the parties was worked primarily behind the scenes. The CIA administered the large-scale purchase of administrative and operational equipment to support uniformed and armed Palestinian security personnel in various roles. The agency also fostered a modicum of bilateral cooperative efforts on the ground, notably through District Coordination Offices (DCOs) in the West Bank and Gaza.

This tool was inadequate to the task for a variety of reasons. The CIA tended to focus on building capacity in Palestinian intelligence services, and in the complex security environment of Palestine this led to the development of shadowy authorities in competition with public entities. Palestinian security partners were drawn primarily from the diaspora, those who entered the territories in 1994 after living abroad for decades. Many Palestinians living in the West Bank and Gaza did not welcome this, seeing it as separating the security services from the people. Security negotiations were held out of the public view and attended by a very small group of carefully chosen senior Palestinian interlocutors, detached from and distrusted by local leadership.

The negotiations and indeed the entire security structure established by the CIA collapsed in September 2000 after the outbreak of the Second Intifada. This effort suffered from the absence of an open and whole-of-government approach. Too many security services were permitted to operate without oversight and dedicated function, which is contrary to building a nascent democratic state.

Special Envoy Missions

During the Second Intifada, the United States appointed a number of special envoys who focused largely on security. George Mitchell was asked to head an international committee to look into the causes of the Intifada. CIA Director George Tenet was tasked with developing a security plan. Retired United States Central Commander General Anthony Zinni was appointed to build on Tenet's efforts. Assistant Secretary of State John Wolf was assigned to monitor the performance of the parties in fulfilling their Roadmap obligations. The Mitchell report and the Tenet plan fell victim to escalating Intifada violence. Their post-Oslo assumptions and security structures fell apart as violence spiraled. None of their recommendations, or those of Zinni, had operational consequences, as one or both parties endlessly quibbled with details or simply rejected the ideas.

The special envoy tool is a seductive one that looks for quick results at a high level with a short-term investment in time and effort. However, it is routinely unsuccessful. By its very nature, the special envoy mission is short term and sporadic, while the nature of the Palestinian-Israeli problem is persistent, requiring total commitment, in part through a continuous presence on the ground. The idea that the special envoy is the direct representative of the president is important, but experience shows that unless the special envoy is prepared to live in the region day in and day out, the parties can either wait him or her out for "wheels up" to the next envoy or continue their quarreling and lack of cooperation without consequence.

When the missions depart the region, so does their influence. This was the case even with the professionally led and staffed mission of former Supreme Allied Commander Europe (SACEUR) James Jones. His mission's charter was to work with Israelis and Palestinians on a full range of security issues, including engaging with key regional countries. The expected deliverable was a new US government plan for security assistance to the Palestinian Authority and for security cooperation with the Israelis and Palestinians. For over a year, Jones and his small team worked with the parties and international interlocutors to draft a working document to try to reconcile Israeli and Palestinian security needs. However, even this promising mission lacked follow-through and genuine empowerment, and when Jones was selected to be national security advisor to President Obama, the mission ended. The lack of continuous presence on the ground by most special envoys was seen by the parties as a lack of seriousness and commitment on the part of the United States.

Presidential Summitry

Like the idea of a special envoy, the concept that the president, if only he is determined enough, can use the prestige of his office at a summit meeting of the Israelis and Palestinians to hammer out a solution is an alluring one that has not paid recent dividends. The extremely complex and visceral nature of the Israeli-Palestinian conflict demands a deliberate, patient, and consistent US approach over a long period of time. While the support and episodic involvement of the president are important, they are meaningless unless the fundamental security issues have been worked out by the two sides beforehand and a modicum of trust and confidence have been established. Otherwise, the president squanders his precious political capital and prestige in a fruitless cause. The groundwork must be carefully laid before the presidential "tool" should be used, and that groundwork inevitably requires painstaking and sustained security preparation.

The Quartet

Early in the George W. Bush administration, the United States joined with the European Union, the United Nations, and Russia to form the Quartet in an effort to present a unified international front to the parties. The Office of the Quartet Representative (OQR) was established as a team of international diplomats and development experts to support the Quartet Special Envoy (QSE) on non-security developmental issues in the West Bank and Gaza. Former World Bank Chairman James Wolfensohn was the first QSE; the post has been held since 2007 by former British Prime Minister Tony Blair. This tool has promise. The OQR operates at a very high international level, includes key players from outside the region, and has a senior representative who has a permanent staff presence in Jerusalem.

Thus far, however, the OQR has not performed up to its potential. First, the QSE has never been empowered by the Quartet to spearhead the developmental process. He lacks resources and has to rely on persuasion, a tough task in this environment. Moreover, he has been absent for extended periods of time. Finally, his focus has been on non-security issues, *without* a strong working connection to the security coordinator.

UN and Third-Party Mechanisms

There are more UN and international third-party organizations in Israel, the occupied territories, and surrounding areas than in any other part of the world. The alphabet-soup list of mechanisms includes UNTSO, UNDOF, UNIFIL, MFO, EUBAMM, USSC, TIPH, UNOCHA, UNRWA, UNDP, OQR, and dozens of NGOs. Some of these have existed for decades, others have come and gone. The majority of these efforts share the same characteristic: they are free-standing endeavors that are not attached to or integrated with any coherent, overarching, strategic vision. Almost all have been unsuccessful in making a contribution toward lasting peace, particularly in the security conundrum. From the Israeli perspective, most are unwelcome but a necessary political pill to swallow. From a Palestinian perspective, the missions are perceived as a counterweight to Israeli desires and activity, and Palestinians are loath to let them go. This tool may prove useful after Israel and Palestine have established a level of security cooperation between themselves, but not before.

American Diplomats on the Ground

The United States is represented in this area by two independent diplomatic missions—the American embassy in Tel Aviv, normally headed by an experienced foreign service officer, that interacts almost exclusively with the Israeli government; and the consulate general in Jerusalem, headed by a more junior chief of mission, that works almost exclusively with the Palestinian Authority. Historically, there are probably good reasons for such a division of labor and divided effort, but the result has been a largely dysfunctional US diplomatic approach in what should be a unified national effort. There have been moments when the two diplomatic missions have worked together, but more often, there has been tension between them, and their work has operated at cross purposes. Too often, the two missions fight "turf" battles over responsibility for different issues, failing to work together to facilitate US national interests. A most egregious example involves severe restrictions—sometimes including a veto—imposed by the consulate over travel by the embassy's defense attachés in the West Bank. Whereas personal security considerations are argued as the prime reason for the consulate's assertion of control, in most instances this relates to the fact that the attachés report to the ambassador in Tel Aviv and not to the consul general in Jerusalem.

This diplomatic tool—hampered by inter-mission rivalry and lack of unified purpose—needs reform. There is too much expertise and regional experience among American diplomats to be wasted. Diplomacy needs to operate under a whole-of-government approach.

In sum, traditional models of choice—based on intermittent engagement by Washington, high-profile but largely absent, poorly prepared presidential summitry, or diplomatic mismanagement in the field—have not worked. It is important, therefore, to build on this experience and exploit the one model that has worked, namely, the Office of the US Security Coordinator (USSC).

WHAT HAS WORKED—THE EXCEPTION TO THE TREND

"You can send George Mitchell back and forth to the Middle East as much as you like, but expanding what [former USSC Keith] Dayton is doing in the security realm to [foster] other sectors of Palestinian governance and society is really the only viable model for progress. What we've learned from the peace process is that there are no Nobel Prizes at the end of this road. We have to build a foundation for progress street by street, and city by city."—Michael Oren[8]

Office of the US Security Coordinator (USSC)

The final tool in the kit is the USSC, which has been successful largely due to its structure and mission: a continuous presence on the ground, the ability to work with the security entities of both sides and a host of international and regional partners, and a focus on building security cooperation from the ground up. The authors of this chapter worked for or with the USSC, are intimately familiar with its structure, functioning, and tests of endurance, and believe the mission offers insights and prescriptions for future policy endeavors. It is important to point out that the USSC is but one tool, albeit a fundamentally important one, in the prospective whole-of-government approach and peacemaker's tool kit. It should not be seen as a stand-alone venture.

The USSC's charter was developed overtly and in consultation with the parties. At its inception, it enjoyed the full support of both the president and the secretary of state; two secretaries of state later recognized the USSC as the success story of America's forays into Middle East peacemaking.[9] The USSC was originally conceived as part of an overarching strategy to energize negotiations on final-status issues. Then-American ambassador Daniel Kurtzer noted that, at the time of its inception, "The USSC was designed to get someone in the room who could work both sides of the street [equally] and as but one part of an over-arching policy/strategy move."[10] The real value then was the deployment of energetic, risk-taking American military officers on the ground who were committed to working through the byzantine security conundrum with Israelis, Palestinians, and international actors. Its leadership and staff complement, many with recent experience in Iraq and Afghanistan, are deployed full time.

While the USSC mission is sometimes viewed as a limited tactical "train and equip," in reality this was never the main point. The primary results achieved were in the strategic realm. First, the USSC was able to play a positive role in reinvigorated security cooperation between senior Palestinian and Israeli security leadership. With a senior American interlocutor ever present on the ground, local buy-in was eventually achieved with a small circle of senior Palestinian and Israeli security officials who worked together in a manner unseen since the Second Intifada. The USSC became the visible evidence of America's sustained commitment.

With local buy-in achieved, opportunities opened to facilitate success in other bottom-up institution-building efforts, while simultaneously furthering top-down issues related to final-status negotiations. The USSC parlayed the trust and confidence it had built with Israel's security establishment to lobby on behalf of the Quartet's "access and movement" objectives; Europe's Palestinian civil police initiatives; and European Union, British, and Canadian border and economic issues. Moreover, Israeli and Palestinian security officials proved willing to surpass even the Oslo period level of security cooperation. As Secretary of State Condoleezza Rice noted, "It became harder for Israelis to claim the Palestinians weren't fighting terror . . . and there was no partner for peace."[11] Disappointingly, neither the USSC's tactical gains nor its strategic openings have been exploited to date. The current mission has been relieved of its strategic duties and relegated to a traditional "train and equip" function with virtually no public profile.[12]

How then to bridge the gap from the current situation to a path of success? What is the best tool?

The first order of business is to build upon the trust and cooperation painstakingly achieved on the ground. The one tool that has had success in this complicated enterprise and that is still active is the USSC. It has established a modicum of cooperation and trust in parallel with meaningful and measurable actions on the ground. The USSC should be empowered and supported in a way that enables it to execute its part of a whole-of-government approach.[13]

The USSC should not be asked to solve political, economic, and social issues. There is much work to be done by other agents of the American government and the international community. Rather, the US security team can provide active leadership to mitigate the security conundrum, including reducing the prospects of conflict and encouraging confidence-building measures. In this process, the USSC can play the important role of enabling the parties to take the next hard steps both in the realm of security and in parallel institution-building efforts.

SHOWING RESOLVE—A REFRESHED STRATEGIC FRAMEWORK

A clear vision, a viable set of policy goals, a strong security mechanism, and the right personnel constitute the best combination for a refreshed American strategic framework. Next steps should include the following concepts.

First, the new administration should try to bridge the conceptual tension between Israel's legitimate security requirements and Palestinian sovereignty. While US support for Israel's long-term security remains important, the United States must also recognize Palestine's right to have a competent national security force to deal with internal challenges and defend its borders against external challenges.

Second, the president should empower the USSC to lead the security effort—noting publicly that the USSC is his personal representative on the ground. Only if the parties view the US security interlocutor as fully invested by the White House can the security foundations for a lasting peace be achieved. In concert, the USSC should be given chain of command responsibility over *all* US security-related agencies involved in training, equipping, and mentoring the Palestinian Authority. Entrenched and debilitating bureaucratic stovepipes on the ground must be removed. An authoritative single address for security will defuse Israeli and Palestinian confusion with regard to the authorities and seeming contradictions between US entities and their activities. This will also enhance its international authority as the security lead with other international actors.

Third, the USSC should work under the Department of Defense, not the State Department, so as to emphasize the paramount security role it plays.

Fourth, the USSC must be led by an active duty ground forces (US Army or Marine Corps) general officer with experience in similar mission sets.

Fifth, the USSC should resume its role as an active strategic interlocutor. "Train and equip" should remain a part of the mission, but the central focus should be to lead willing allies and sometimes-reluctant Israeli and Palestinian security partners to advance larger political/security goals.

Finally, the administration should accept that in the absence of a political agreement that includes boundaries, the removal of settlers, and security guarantees to Palestinians, it would be unwise to initiate a process to transfer full security responsibility to Palestinians—it will not work and could jeopardize the prospects of reaching an eventual agreement.

OPERATIONAL CONSIDERATIONS—FREEDOM OF MANEUVER

First, a normalized environment for security and its rule of law component do not equal a zero rate of incidents or zero threats. No country enjoys a 100 percent security guarantee en route to greater political progress. Rather, the goal should be an authority that can provide sufficient rule of law and an overall security capacity to enable civil society to function within international norms and room for the tenets of democracy to begin to take hold.

Second, reliance on benchmarks/metrics to measure success in the security sphere is an antiquated, failed concept. Progress in this conundrum is anything but step-by-step or linear. Both sides have responsibilities and actions to take towards peace, and these need to be done simultaneously and semi-independently of what the other side does.

Third, confidence-building measures (CBMs) tend to act as inhibitors, rather than as facilitators, of potential success. Confidence building surely is required by both sides for domestic buy-in and in order to take additional steps. But this should be encouraged and managed as part of the overall political process, not dictated as stand-alone, tit-for-tat demands.

Fourth, timelines do not work. Things move as fast as they are able to move on the ground in support of political self-interests or otherwise. Timelines are artificial and tend to focus the parties on the clock rather than on their behaviors.

CONCLUSION

The Palestinian-Israeli security conundrum has dominated American policy in the Middle East for more than a generation and remains a key component of lasting regional security. Resolution of the Israeli-Palestinian conflict represents a giant gain for American interests. It is time to put these American interests in synch with reality.

We have offered a strategic model for dealing with security as part of the larger vision for a two-state solution. We have offered practical methodologies which have been proven in the complex landscape of Israel and Palestine. We have shown what tools have not worked and why, and we have highlighted the success story of the USSC, and why it should be built upon as a gateway to a reinvigorated effort.

The alternative models—unilateral Israeli security responsibility, long-term occupation, Palestinian violence, unilateral Israeli withdrawals, and the status quo—don't work. Israeli and Palestinian goals are best served when the parties treat each other as security and political partners. The two peoples can live side by side on the basis of agreed principles, a strong security framework, and accountability. The United States can provide the leadership to move toward achievement of these goals.

The United States must show firmness with both parties in pursuit of American national interests, refraining from policies that unduly favor one party over the other. Israel and Palestine both have legitimate security concerns and requirements, and these should not be viewed as mutually exclusive or antagonistic. America's commitment to Israel's qualitative military edge is not challenged by an equal commitment to Palestinian sovereignty and the resolution of the security conundrum.

Israel and Palestine need the United States to lead them through the maze they have created for themselves. Only American political leadership can give the parties the support and cover they need to work toward longer-term mutual benefits that will also advance American strategic interests. An American president willing to lead this process with patience and sustained determination can advance the cause of peace.

NOTES

1. This chapter focuses on the complicated security conundrum in the West Bank; the situation in Gaza requires separate analysis.
2. For a more in-depth discussion of the security environment, see Geoffrey Aronson and P. J. Dermer, "U.S. Policy in a Time of Transition," Stimson Institute, May 2012, where the parties' views are put in context and possible future US positions on security architecture are laid out. https://www.dropbox.com/s/mszz5ujh4gd46g9/Pickering%20Report.pdf.
3. Ibid., 21.
4. The Israeli settler community is not just a problem for Palestinians. Some within that community do not recognize the authority or rule of law of Israel.
5. In the wake of the assassination of Qaddura Musa, the governor of Jenin, in May 2012, the Palestinian Authority launched a security crackdown, arresting scores of suspects including members of its own Palestinian security services and residents of surrounding refugee camps. Those arrested were accused of perpetrating illegal activities and weapons trafficking, which

the PA viewed as threats to public order. To date no definitive explanation for this crackdown exists beyond speculation that either the PA acted to thwart Palestinian clan activities directed against the authority or former and current security officials were involved in political intrigues against the PA.

6. Aronson and Dermer.

7. Israelis envision cameras, radios, and electronic or other sensors that they view as unobtrusive and therefore viable. Palestinians regard this as intrusive, regardless of the technology.

8. Quoted in James Kitfield, "United They Fall; Divided They Stand," *National Journal*, March 28, 2009.

9. Lt. General Keith Dayton meeting with Secretary Clinton, September 2010, Washington D.C. See also Condoleezza Rice, *No Higher Honor: A Memoir of My Years in Washington* (New York: Crown, 2011), 573-575. Rice wrote: "When the press talks about the peace process, it focuses on borders, security, Jerusalem, refugees, water rights—matters that must be resolved to end the conflict. But there are other complex problems concerning the daily lives of the Palestinians and security for the Israeli people . . . Fortunately, both the Israelis and Palestinians trusted the Americans to help them achieve these goals. And the IDF trusted the U.S. military in particular . . . The painstaking work rarely made headlines, but it made a difference . . . and would pay off as we looked to foster negotiations on the final status issues."

10. Interview with Ambassador Daniel Kurtzer, April 26, 2012, Washington, D.C.

11. Rice, *No Higher Honor*, 573-575.

12. In a meeting with Lt. General Keith Dayton in July 2009, former IDF Chief of Staff LTG Amnon Lipkin Shahak stated that "the USSC has bought time, time for the politicians, yours, mine and the Palestinians to do the diplomatic work necessary to forward the peace process, and they have wasted it." The truth and relevance of that statement are more applicable today than they were in 2009.

13. There is additional value in having an empowered security presence on the ground. It provides a mechanism for constant contact to prevent backsliding in times of political turmoil (for example, Arab unrest or regional elections), and it makes it easier to ramp up again once the turmoil is over.

12

AMERICAN POLICY, STRATEGY, AND TACTICS

Daniel C. Kurtzer

The United States has invested heavily in Middle East peacemaking for decades. While the strategic goal has been to achieve a peace settlement, the United States has tended to focus on the essentially tactical objective of bringing about face-to-face negotiations between the parties. With some exceptions—for example, the Clinton Parameters in 2000 and the George W. Bush letter to Ariel Sharon in 2004—administrations have eschewed articulating positions on the substantive outcome the United States seeks. Because of the serious problems confronting the region and the peace process today, described below and throughout this volume, it is time for the United States to adopt a new policy, a new strategy, and new tactics.

WHY TILT AT MIDDLE EAST WINDMILLS?

This essay argues for the development of a new, comprehensive American policy and a sustained strategy for advancing the Israeli-Palestinian peace process. It advocates for American creativity, flexibility, and initiative in crafting the tactics required to engage the parties and help them approach the required mutual concessions. This argument does not rest on either the inevitability or even the likelihood of early success, nor on the readiness of the parties to overcome legitimate concerns and powerful internal opposition to confront the tough decisions required to make peace. Indeed, there are strong reasons to avoid working on the peace process at all.

However, doing nothing or continuing down the same path that the United States has traveled before—simply trying to get to negotiations—not only will not succeed, it will deepen the challenges the United States faces in the Middle East and it will exacerbate the very conflict that the United States has tried to resolve over many decades. There are hard realities in the Middle East and the Israeli-Palestinian conflict that some try to ignore or argue away. It is time to confront those realities and develop a reasonable but also bold policy and diplomatic strategy worthy of American values and interests. Developing a sound policy, a sophisticated strategy, and appropriate tactics to advance the peace process is not tilting at windmills. It is doing what the United States has shown itself capable of doing in the past to advance prospects for peace.

The idea of a two-state solution—the cornerstone of American policy in the region—is now on life support, and its chances of surviving cannot improve without active diplomacy. Not only are governments losing interest, but more importantly, public opinion is losing confidence that such an outcome is achievable. The issues in the peace process are complex, and American policy needs to address this complexity, whether or not there is a promise of immediate success.

Current upheavals in the region argue for investing in Israeli-Palestinian conflict resolution. Hunkering down or managing the status quo is not a policy when it assures the United States less leverage and less support for our policies elsewhere in the region. With growing skepticism about and opposition to American policy in the Middle East, a serious effort to advance peace can have a transformative effect on our standing and credibility.

There is no magic formula for success, whether it involves intense American diplomacy or conflict management. Periods of engagement have often ended in frustration, violence, and war. Trying to manage the con-flict—for example, by focusing solely on improving the situation on the ground—is not only a recipe for inaction; it is actually far more dangerous than it appears.

Status quos are not static. They either improve or they worsen. The status quo in the West Bank appears to be improving, evidenced by eco-nomic activity in Palestinian cities, the relative absence of terrorism, and several important signs of Israeli-Palestinian cooperation, for example, in security and in economic affairs. This is, however, a misleading picture. Israeli settlement activity has accelerated in recent years, and the Israeli government's active support and funding of settlement infrastructure have skyrocketed. As more settlers move into the occupied territories, the area of the prospective Palestinian state is shrinking, becoming less contigu-ous and less viable. To believe that Palestinians will accept a state limited to their main population centers—so-called Areas A and B in the West Bank—is delusionary. Calm on the surface masks growing frustration and anger below. Any spark can ignite a conflagration that will consume the status quo.

More fundamentally, the Israeli-Palestinian conflict drains energy from the parties and from the United States to deal with more pressing issues in the region, in particular, Iran's nuclear ambitions. Yitzhak Rabin recognized this in 1992, when he reportedly told then-President George H. W. Bush that Israel required comprehensive peace with all its neighbors in order to free its energies to prepare for the emerging threat from Iran, which Rabin assessed would be evident within ten years. In 2002, Saudi King Abdullah and other Arab leaders also recognized this reality when they adopted the Arab Peace Initiative, a cosmic change in the position of Arabs toward Israel and the conflict. Arabs no longer insisted on dealing with the "problem" of 1948, that is, the very existence of the State of Israel, but rather promised Israel peace, security, and recognition if the 1967 occupation of Arab territories and the persistence of the Palestinian issue could be resolved. Iran was as much on the minds of Abdullah and other Arab leaders in 2002 as it was on Rabin's in 1992.

So, while some argue that it is a waste of time for the United States to invest in the peace process, the opposite is really true. Such an investment will pay dividends if it moves the conflict toward resolution and allows the region to act in concert to deny Iran its power ambitions. Doing nothing, or doing too little, is a prescription for trouble.

OUTMODED ASSUMPTIONS

In crafting the policy, strategy, and tactics the United States should pursue, it is important to discard outmoded assumptions about peacemaking. First, the peace process is not simply about getting to negotiations. Rather, the goal is a conflict-ending, claims-ending, fair, and just peace agreement between Israel and the Palestinians. Negotiations—that is, fixation on process—must not become the consuming objective. The United States must formulate a policy that treats the central issues in dispute: territory, borders, security, Jerusalem, refugees, the nature of peace, religion, ideology, and narratives.

Second, not every idea for resolving this conflict has been created equal. Arguments in favor of one state, three states, long-term interim arrangements, trusteeship, armistice, cantonization, Jordan-is-Palestine, and the like are misleading, dangerous, and wrong. There is no serious, viable alternative to the partition into two sovereign states of the territory that Palestinians and Israelis claim as their exclusive homeland. Partition will not respond to the full aspirations or the entire national/religious/historical narratives of the parties. But partition provides for a historic decision in which both sides will be able to enjoy independence and exercise sovereignty in part of their national patrimony.

Third, the United States must stop viewing the conflict-resolution process as an American monopoly. Israelis and many Arabs still regard the United States as the essential third party. However, the Middle East is in the midst of a radical transformation, and new power configurations require a new way to marshal regional and international efforts on behalf of peace. Palestinians need the support that other actors could provide, and Israel needs the recognition that international interaction could ensure.

Fourth, it's time to end the silly debate in the United States over "linkage." Resolving the Arab-Israeli conflict will not in itself transform the region; but, so too, democratic transformations in the region will not necessarily lead to resolution of the Arab-Israeli conflict. America's diverse and complex interests demand that we invest in both policy goals simultaneously. Thinking or trying to act sequentially misses the point.

CONTOURS OF AMERICAN POLICY: SEVEN CRITICAL ELEMENTS

The United States needs to think strategically and employ wise tactics. Stand-alone tactics, such as confidence-building measures, do not succeed, for they require the parties to pay a heavy domestic political price with no discernible political or substantive payoff. As part of a broader strategy, however, smart tactics can help the parties understand trade-offs and benefits. The first order of business is to construct a cohesive American policy.

1. Create the physical template—borders—of Israel and Palestine. It is illogical that sixty-five years after the UN partition resolution, there is still no agreed border that demarcates the State of Israel and the future state of Palestine. This must be a core component of American policy: to realize the goal of secure, recognized, and defensible borders. President Obama got it right in May 2011 when he urged that negotiations produce borders that are based on the 1967 lines with mutually agreed swaps. Israelis and Palestinians need to know where their respective states begin and end.

2. Address Israeli and Palestinian fundamental security requirements. The United States should lead the effort to define and address the security requirements of the two peoples. In 2008, President George W. Bush asked General James Jones—later to become Obama's national security advisor—to undertake a comprehensive security assessment. Jones's study was never published, but the work he started should be refined and completed. In parallel, the on-the-ground work of the United States Security Coordinator (USSC)—tasked with interacting daily with both sides, training and equipping the Palestinian Security Force, and rebuilding security cooperation and coordination—should be intensified.

These security requirements and the means to address them are complex, as detailed in chapter 11 in this volume. But a security system, composed of many different elements and a heavy dose of American commitments and involvement and a variety of security tools and practices, can work. The United States has always said it understands that the parties need to believe that their security will improve under conditions of a peace agreement; now is the time to demonstrate that with American leadership.

A critical part of this will be the degree to which Israel believes the United States will continue to provide it with the wherewithal to defend itself and the security assurances needed to operate in a hostile regional environment. Israel's security needs will expand dramatically in the context of an agreement with the Palestinians, and the United States should thus be prepared to address Israel's legitimate needs. An Israel that feels secure regarding its own capabilities and the constancy of American commitments will likely be more willing to take the serious risks that peace will entail.

3. Adopt an American view of the parameters on the core issues. Negotiations require terms of reference to start and to succeed, but Israel and the Palestinian Liberation Organization (PLO) cannot agree on any terms of reference. The irony is that the two sides have narrowed gaps substantially on the core issues in dispute since the Taba negotiations in 2001. None of this progress has been memorialized in an agreed record, but the progress achieved cannot be doubted.

Before deciding whether or how to resume negotiations in a manner that has a chance to succeed, the United States needs to decide for itself its own views on the shape of a final settlement, that is, the parameters for resolving the core issues. Without this, American policy lacks focus and is ineffectual, limited to carrying messages or proposing discrete fixes to negotiating impasses. Just as the parties need to have a comprehensive view of all the issues in the negotiations in order to be able to weigh concessions against possible gains, so too the United States needs an internal policy on the shape of a settlement. Let no one doubt the significance of this tool should the United States decide to employ the parameters as draft terms of reference for negotiations: President Clinton constructed such parameters in 2000, shared them with the parties, then withdrew them when the parties refused to commit to negotiate on the basis of those parameters—but then they went off and negotiated at Taba essentially on the basis of Clinton's parameters. It is critical for the United States to develop a policy on substance, even if the decision on what to do with the parameters is not taken until later.

The most persuasive reason for the United States to develop its own views on the core issues was articulated by Lewis Carroll: "If you don't know where you are going, any road will get you there." Not every road will get the parties to the desired two-state solution. On each core issue, there are possible outcomes that fall outside the minimum requirements of one of the parties and that thus endanger a successful outcome. For the United States to be able to act wisely and creatively to help the parties, it has to know where it is going and what road can best take the parties to an agreed outcome. A proposed model of American parameters can be found in the appendix.

4. Ensure Palestinian institutional and economic capacity. As detailed in chapter 10 of this volume, Palestinians have made great strides in creating the institutional and economic structures to sustain independent statehood. The United States and many others have assisted these efforts, but it is time to kick this process into higher gear. The creation of a successful, economically viable, and democratic state of Palestine will serve two critical American interests: it will resolve the Palestinian-Israeli conflict, and it will promote democracy in the Middle East. The United States must invest more resources in this effort.

5. Change Israeli and Palestinian behaviors. In 2003, the United States and the other members of the international Quartet (the European Union, Russia, and the United Nations) developed the Roadmap, which required mutually reinforcing actions by Israelis and Palestinians to change bad behaviors—stop settlement activity; permit greater Palestinian mobility; uproot terrorist infrastructure; create accountable institutions; stop incitement. These goals are already part of American policy; as elements in a broader strategy, the United States needs to do more to try to achieve them.

The United States should establish a robust system of monitoring Roadmap performance, hold the parties accountable—publicly—for their actions, and exact consequences for failure to abide by commitments or to change behaviors. The objective is not to be punitive, but to get serious. The parties basically agreed that these are the behaviors that need to change; the United States is the only party with the weight to follow through. To be sure, Roadmap implementation cannot be expected independently of other actions; it makes sense only as part of an integrated American policy.

6. Involve the region in building the infrastructure of peace. In the 1990s, Arabs and Israelis met constantly in a range of multilateral meetings and public-private economic summits. These interactions gave real-life meaning to the more rarefied atmosphere surrounding diplomatic negotiations. They helped build personal and professional relationships between Arabs and Israelis and strengthened the public's support for the peace process.

Indeed, over the past decades, a cottage industry of people-to-people, non-governmental organizations (NGOs), and so-called Track II activities has proliferated. Today, Palestinians and Israelis know each better than almost any other two peoples in the world. The US government helped create many of these opportunities, but over the years, American administrations have paid less attention and devoted fewer resources to maintain these activities to foster Arab-Israeli interaction.

As Marwan Muasher writes in chapter 2 of this volume, in 2002 the Arab Peace Initiative was adopted at the Arab Summit in Beirut, but thus far, it has had no practical effect—either as a safety net to support the Palestinians or as an inducement for the Israelis to take hard decisions for peace. In the meantime, the region's problems have worsened: there is a severe shortage of water; arable land is under pressure from growing populations; most countries are food importers; health problems abound across political boundaries; and environmental degradation continues. There is no justification for this situation to continue when regional dialogue and mechanisms for action can be created.

The United States should seek ways to capitalize on the earlier examples of Arab-Israeli interactions: lend support to the Arab Peace Initiative, exploit the contacts that already exist, and broaden the base of public support and activities tied into building a culture of peace. Even modest resources and time devoted to NGO, Track II, and people-to-people activities will pay large dividends.

Doing this will not be easy. Arab governments are very skeptical and suspicious about American (and Israeli) motives, concerned that these processes will substitute for a serious effort to resolve the underlying conflict. Because of this, any American effort to encourage Arab-Israeli interaction will need to be tied closely to progress on the Palestinian-Israeli track. Each element of this integrated policy framework needs to be undertaken in conjunction with the others so that all parties see the larger picture in which they are being asked to move forward. Arab-Israeli cooperation is one important component of this larger policy framework.

7. Don't ignore religious, ideological, and historical narratives. Under the best circumstances and the smartest American policy, peace will be challenged by mutually exclusive Israeli and Palestinian religious, ideological, and historical narratives. Diplomats traditionally shy away from these issues, for they are not amenable to quick fixes, and they speak to the deepest psychological and emotional instincts of the two peoples. However, as much as policy makers would prefer to ignore these issues, they need to be considered if the goal is a conflict-ending, claims-ending agreement. Robert Malley and Gershom Gorenberg have noted earlier in this volume the central role of segments of Palestinian and Israeli society whose views about peace will be critical if an agreement is to be reached.

Today, there are some modest non-governmental activities focused on fostering internal dialogue within the two communities, involving those who don't play a direct role in peace talks—especially settlers and refugees. As a matter of policy, the United States needs to pay attention without interfering in these NGO-led efforts. American funding can help these activities expand.

DEVELOPING SMART STRATEGY AND TACTICS

With this kind of strong, integrated policy, the United States will be better placed to consider the right strategy and tactics for advancing the peace process. Tactical choices are quite important, but the United States should approach tactics with flexibility and avoid confusing tactics with policy.

Do smart diplomacy. Aaron Miller and others in this volume have offered valuable lessons on the conduct of smart diplomacy. There are many useful guides for what worked and what did not work in the past.[1] A first order of business, as the integrated policy is adopted, is to stand back, assimilate the tactical lessons of the past, and empower our diplomats to act creatively, flexibly, and boldly.

Negotiations. Negotiations will be critical but only when constructed carefully, on the basis of strong terms of reference. Asking the parties to negotiate agreed terms of reference is unlikely to produce results. The United States will thus need to consider when and how to break the logjam. The best alternative at that time might be to offer the US parameters as the terms of reference for the negotiations.

In doing so, the United States would describe its approach as positioning the parties as though at the wide end of a funnel. We would direct the parties to, so to speak, the light at the end of the funnel, by helping them navigate the choices required to narrow differences and bridge gaps. The parties would remain the central actors in negotiations, but the United States would not be an absent party when it comes to fixing problems and achieving results.

Public diplomacy. The United States already invests heavily in public diplomacy. With a good product—that is, strong and determined policy—savvy public diplomacy can focus on bringing the Israeli and Palestinian publics to support the peace effort. From the president and the secretary of state on down, American officials should talk directly to the people in the region about the requirements of peace and all the good that will flow from a peaceful settlement.

Think outside traditional boxes. At a time when American officials are reaching out to Islamists in the Middle East, it no longer makes sense to maintain inflexible conditions for engagement with Hamas. To be clear, Hamas needs to renounce terrorism and accept Israel's right to exist as an independent state before the United States enters a formal dialogue. But American and international conditions have been cast in stone so impenetrable that it has been impossible to assess whether, as Robert Malley suggests, change may be under way within Hamas.

One way to test this is to rethink our approach to Palestinian unity and reconciliation. Since 2006, the United States has assigned more value to the choices confronting Hamas than to the continued commitment of the PLO and the Palestinian Authority (PA) to the peace process. If our objective is to strengthen PLO and PA decision makers, and if they believe that a unity accord with Hamas will help them, then we ought to be supportive, provided PLO and PA policy does not change to accommodate Hamas's wishes. The focus of American policy needs to be on what the PLO and the PA do, not on what Hamas says or thinks. The great irony is that American and Israeli efforts to isolate Hamas in Gaza have weakened the PA financially and politically, while strengthening Hamas's financial and institutional control. It makes no sense to continue in this direction.

The United States should also reconsider its position with regard to Palestinian diplomatic recognition. There are substantial benefits to be had for both Palestine and Israel in a carefully crafted process of formal diplomatic recognition.[2]

REALISTIC SHORT-TERM OUTCOMES

Rebuild American influence, power, and prestige. The position of the United States in the Middle East is in crisis and is worsening over time. All of our traditional Arab allies are either in the midst of transitions to regimes that are likely to be far less supportive of our interests or are under pressure from populations that see alliance with the United States as part of the problem, not part of the solution to their country's shortcomings. Events since the onset of the Arab upheavals in January 2011 have demonstrated that the United States has significantly reduced leverage and few assets to bring to bear in dealing with these emerging political constellations. Our assistance does not buy us much anymore, and there appears to be little price to pay for ignoring American advice or preferences. The one issue that can change this—indeed, that can transform American standing overnight—is strong American leadership in Arab-Israeli peacemaking.

A robust American role in the peace process is not a magic bullet, but it is the closest thing to a discrete policy that can have dramatic, transformative impact on developments elsewhere. Every American-led or American-assisted breakthrough in the past has changed the regional dynamics. As a result of the Madrid process, for example, American influence skyrocketed, and tangible gains were registered for the United States and Israel: Syrian Jews were permitted to emigrate; Israel's diplomatic recognition and relations expanded, including those with Turkey, India, and China; trade and commercial relations were established with several Arab countries; official contacts with most Arab states were launched in the context of formal multilateral negotiations. In other words, American diplomatic leadership achieved substantial results, even though the peace process itself ultimately faltered. Imagine the important and tangible gains possible if progress is achieved in a US-led Israeli-Palestinian peace process.

The point is that what the United States does or fails to do in the peace process has an outsized impact on US standing in the region. We benefit when we act confidently and boldly; we are weakened when we don't.

Provide tangible security and other benefits to Israelis and Palestinians. The United States spends an extraordinary amount of money, time, and political capital to help Israel achieve the security and well-being that it deserves, and to help Palestinians cope with the challenges of occupation while building the capacity for independent statehood. There is no other country as generous in this regard, and no other country as committed to these goals. Congress and the American people have been supportive of these costs, even at times of economic stringency at home. In other words, we do it because it is the right thing to do.

A peace process—even a peace agreement—offers no certainty that the security or well-being of Israelis or Palestinians will improve immediately. Indeed, the opposite could occur in the short term, as opponents of peace mobilize or engage in violence to try to block negotiations or implementation of an accord. However, the durability of existing negotiated peace agreements argues that security and well-being are deeply enhanced by the peace process. However painful the immediate human and material costs of implementing treaties, the long-term result is an environment less susceptible to the threat of war. Unilateral withdrawals and unilateral actions don't work, for there is no shared responsibility; signed agreements do work, and their net result is enhanced security and well-being for Israelis and Arabs.

Rescue and possibly advance the prospects of the two-state solution. The two-state solution is not self-implementing, and the longer the idea does not move forward, the more likely it is to lose ground and become more problematic to implement. The publics in Israel and Palestine are increasingly skeptical of the idea, Palestinian violence is destroying the Israelis' belief in peace, and Israeli settlement activity is making it more difficult daily to imagine the evacuation of tens of thousands of settlers in the context of an agreement. As this book points out, we are in a race against time to rescue and implement the two-state solution.

It will be very hard to construct, conduct, and sustain a determined and comprehensive peace strategy, even harder to imagine positive results. But doing nothing is the easiest pathway to a deepening crisis for American interests in the Middle East. The United States can do hard diplomacy, and in this case, it must.

The components of a comprehensive, robust, and sustainable American policy and strategy—that is, the analysis and policy recommendations in this chapter and this book—thus represent the best chance for a transformative change in the Middle East and in America's standing in the region. The time is now for confident American leadership to advance the prospects of Israeli-Palestinian peace.

NOTES

1. Daniel C. Kurtzer and Scott B. Lasensky, *Negotiating Arab-Israeli Peace: American Leadership in the Middle East* (Washington, D.C.: United States Institute of Peace Press, 2008) contains ten critical lessons from American experience since the Madrid conference. See also Daniel Kurtzer, William Quandt, Scott Lasensky, Steven Spiegel, and Shibley Telhami, *The Peace Puzzle: America's Quest for Arab-Israeli Peace* (Ithaca, NY: Cornell University Press, forthcoming) for a detailed analysis of negotiations during the past two decades and lessons learned.
2. See, for example, Daniel Kurtzer, "A 'Win-Win' for Palestine and Israel *Is* Possible," *HuffPost World*, August 17, 2011, which suggested tangible ways that both Israel and Palestine could benefit from a well-constructed UN diplomatic scenario.   http://www.huffingtonpost.com/daniel-kurtzer/a-winwin-for-palestine-an_b_928199.html.

APPENDIX

PARAMETERS: POSSIBLE TERMS OF REFERENCE FOR ISRAELI-PALESTINIAN NEGOTIATIONS

In chapter 12, an argument was advanced that, as part of a cohesive American policy and strategy for advancing Palestinian-Israeli peace prospects, the United States should craft substantive parameters for internal use and consider using them as the terms of reference for negotiations. Following is a model of parameters:

    I.   **Goal of the Negotiations**
    II.   **Territory and Borders**
    III.   **Security**
    IV.   **Israeli Settlements and Refugees**
    V.   **West Bank and Gaza "Safe Passage"**
    VI.   **Places of Historical and Religious Significance**
    VII.   **Jerusalem**
    VIII.   **Water**
    IX.   **Implementation**

I. GOAL OF THE NEGOTIATIONS

The Palestine Liberation Organization and the State of Israel ("the Parties") seek a just, lasting, and comprehensive peace, consistent with the United Nations Charter, that will fulfill UN Security Council Resolutions 242 and 338 and constitute the end of the Israeli-Palestinian conflict and all claims related to it. As a result of negotiations, the State of Palestine and the State of Israel will live side by side in peace and security. Israel will recognize Palestine as the national home of the Palestinian people and all its citizens; and Palestine will recognize Israel as the national home of the Jewish people and all its citizens. Each State will affirm the importance of maintaining and strengthening peace based on freedom, equality, justice, respect for human rights, and respect for human dignity. Each state will work to eliminate incitement against the other state, as well as efforts to delegitimize it. The Parties agree to the full and orderly implementation of the terms of the agreement, in accordance with agreed means, methods, sequencing, timelines, and provisions.

II. TERRITORY AND BORDERS

In fulfillment of UN Security Council Resolution 242, Israel will withdraw from territories occupied in the 1967 war. The Parties will negotiate the withdrawal and the border of the two States based on the June 4, 1967, line. The final border will reflect minor, reciprocal, and agreed-upon boundary modifications, including 1:1 land swaps, reciprocal in terms of both quantity and quality. The outcome of negotiations will be a secure, recognized, and defensible border that ensures the territorial integrity, contiguity, and viability of both States.

III. SECURITY

The agreement will base Israeli-Palestinian security relations on mutual trust and advancement of joint interests and cooperation. The agreement will stipulate that each State will refrain from the threat or use of force or weapons, conventional, non-conventional, or of any other kind, against each other, or of other actions or activities that adversely affect the security of the citizens, residents, territorial integrity, or political independence of the other. The two States will also refrain from organizing, instigating, inciting, assisting, or participating in acts or threats of belligerency, hostility, subversion, or violence against the other Party. The Parties shall also agree to take necessary and effective measures to ensure that acts or threats of belligerency, hostility, subversion, or violence against the other Party do not originate from, and are not committed within, through, or over their territory (hereinafter "territory" includes the airspace and territorial waters).

The agreement will provide that all disputes between the two States will be settled by peaceful means, including but not limited to negotiations, mediation, and/or arbitration. The agreement will also provide for a liaison system to facilitate implementation of the security provisions.

The agreement will stipulate that the two States will not join or assist any alliance, the objectives of which include launching aggression or other acts of military hostility against the other State. The agreement will prohibit each State from allowing the entry, stationing, and operating on its territory, or through it, of military forces, personnel, or matériel of a third party, in circumstances that may adversely prejudice the security of the other Party. The two States will agree to take necessary and effective measures and will cooperate in preventing and combating terrorism, subversion, and violence of all kinds or any other act of violence emanating from their territory, and to prevent and disband the formation of any force, militia, or group aiming to incite or carry out violence against the other. The Parties will agree to take necessary and effective measures to prevent the entry, presence, and operation in their territory of any group or organization that threatens the security of the other State by the use of, or incitement to the use of, violent means.

The State of Palestine will develop and maintain adequate internal security forces and will limit arms and equipment to levels and types to maintain internal security and enforce the rule of law within its borders. No armed forces, arms, other implements of war, or dual-use material may enter, be stationed, transit, or be deployed in the State of Palestine except as agreed by the Parties. International monitors will observe, monitor, and report on implementation of these provisions. The monitors will have enforcement authorities as agreed.

The agreement will provide for a timetable for implementation of security arrangements that will, inter alia, include early-warning and related facilities; and international observers, monitors, and forces as required to oversee and ensure implementation of the security provision of the agreement.

The State of Palestine will be responsible for security at its borders and points of entry. Palestinian border security and control over international passages, including future land, sea, and airports, and entry into the State of Palestine will be monitored by an international body, which will work in close cooperation and coordination with the Parties and neighboring states.

The Parties will reach agreement on control over the airspace, maritime areas, and electromagnetic spectrum. Each State shall recognize the right of vessels of the other State to innocent passage through its territorial waters in accordance with the rules of international law.

IV. ISRAELI SETTLEMENTS AND REFUGEES

In accordance with an agreed implementation timeline, all Israeli settlers and all Israeli civilians will be evacuated from the territory of the State of Palestine. In accordance with the laws of the State of Palestine, individual Israeli citizens may apply for residency and citizenship in the State of Palestine. The Parties will reach agreement on the disposition of all fixed assets and infrastructure within Israeli settlements, with the goal being the transfer of such assets and infrastructure in good condition to the State of Palestine in return for fair and reasonable compensation.

In fulfillment of UN General Assembly Resolution 194, and in view of the suffering experienced by the Palestinian refugees, Palestinian refugees will have the right of return to the State of Palestine, consistent with the absorptive capacity and laws of that State. Those refugees who choose not to exercise their right to return to the State of Palestine or who are prevented from returning by the State of Palestine will be assisted to resettle in their countries of current residence or in other countries willing to receive them, while respecting the sovereign rights of those states. The State of Israel will offer a program of family reunification, including citizenship, for a limited number of refugees.

An international fund will be established to help defray the costs of compensation and resettlement of Palestinian refugees and Jewish refugees from Arab countries.

V. WEST BANK AND GAZA "SAFE PASSAGE"

The Parties will agree on the size, modalities, and administration of a "safe passage" corridor that links the West Bank and Gaza. The corridor should be of sufficient size to accommodate a four-lane highway, a rail link and underground pipelines, cables, and utility lines. The State of Israel will have sovereignty, but not administrative authority, over the corridor and will exercise control over external security. The corridor will have sufficient access points to ensure effective emergency response, and it will be transected by an agreed number and location of crossings to ensure effective communication for Israel for all purposes. The State of Palestine will administer the corridor, bear responsibility for maintenance and upkeep, exercise control over security within the corridor, and monitor the people and goods transiting the corridor to assure effective security and law enforcement. The passage will operate continuously.

VI. PLACES OF HISTORICAL AND RELIGIOUS SIGNIFICANCE

Each State will provide freedom of access for visitors and worshippers to all places of religious and historical significance within their territory. The Parties will agree on a list of such places in the two States. The two States will agree to protect and respect all sites of religious, historic, and cultural significance. Each State will ensure adequate protection for freedom of access and worship. International monitors will oversee implementation of these provisions to all the sites so listed.

VII. JERUSALEM

The agreement will provide that Jerusalem is a site of sacred, religious, historic, and cultural importance and will provide for the geographic limits of the city. The Parties will agree to act in accordance with the dignity and sanctity of the city.

The agreement will provide that Jerusalem will become the capital of the two States—Al-Quds as the capital of Palestine, and Yerushalayim as the capital of Israel. The city should be undivided and free of permanent barriers and other physical obstructions that impede daily life. The Parties will develop an agreed plan for the control of entry into and exit from the city and for its security.

The Parties will agree to establish a negotiating process and timeframe to determine their boundary and to provide that:

- Outside the walls of the Old City, the Parties will define their boundary on the basis of demography, that is, predominantly Jewish neighborhoods will be included in the State of Israel, and predominantly Arab neighborhoods will be included in the State of Palestine.
- With regard to the Old City, pending an agreement between the Parties on the boundary, they will establish by agreement a special regime to administer the Old City under an international administrator appointed by them.

VIII. WATER

The Parties will agree on a fair and equitable distribution of water, including but not limited to underground aquifers, desalinated water, and water from the Jordan River system. The agreement shall provide for cooperation in managing existing and searching for new sources of water supply, including development of existing and new water resources, increasing the water availability, including cooperation on a regional basis as appropriate, and minimizing wastage of water resources. The Parties shall also agree to cooperate to prevent contamination of water resources, and to assist in the alleviation of water shortages. An international fund will be established to assist with desalination and other water-supply development and delivery infrastructure to satisfy the needs of Israel, Palestine, and other riparian states of the Jordan River system.

IX. IMPLEMENTATION

The Parties, with the assistance of the Quartet and other international organizations as appropriate, will establish an international mechanism to monitor and facilitate implementation of the agreement, and ensure full compliance with all its terms.

THE ARAB PEACE INITIATIVE, BEIRUT, 2002

The Council of the League of Arab States at the Summit Level, at its 14th Ordinary Session,

- Reaffirms the resolution taken in June 1996 at the Cairo extraordinary Arab summit that a just and comprehensive peace in the Middle East is the strategic option of the Arab countries, to be achieved in accordance with international legality, and which would require a comparable commitment on the part of the Israeli government.
- Having listened to the statement made by his royal highness Prince Abdullah Bin Abdulaziz, the crown prince of the Kingdom of Saudi Arabia in which his highness presented his initiative, calling for full Israeli withdrawal from all the Arab territories occupied since June 1967, in implementation of Security Council Resolutions 242 and 338, reaffirmed by the Madrid Conference of 1991 and the land for peace principle, and Israel's acceptance of an independent Palestinian state, with East Jerusalem as its capital, in return for the establishment of normal relations in the context of a comprehensive peace with Israel.

Emanating from the conviction of the Arab countries that a military solution to the conflict will not achieve peace or provide security for the parties, the council:

1. Requests Israel to reconsider its policies and declare that a just peace is its strategic option as well.

2. Further calls upon Israel to affirm:
   a. Full Israeli withdrawal from all the territories occupied since 1967, including the Syrian Golan Heights to the lines of June 4, 1967, as well as the remaining occupied Lebanese territories in the south of Lebanon.
   b. Achievement of a just solution to the Palestinian refugee problem to be agreed upon in accordance with U.N. General Assembly Resolution 194.
   c. The acceptance of the establishment of a Sovereign Independent Palestinian State on the Palestinian territories occupied since June 4, 1967 in the West Bank and Gaza Strip, with East Jerusalem as its capital.
3. Consequently, the Arab countries affirm the following:
   a. Consider the Arab-Israeli conflict ended, and enter into a peace agreement with Israel, and provide security for all the states of the region.
   b. Establish normal relations with Israel in the context of this comprehensive peace.
4. Assures the rejection of all forms of Palestinian patriation which conflict with the special circumstances of the Arab host countries.
5. Calls upon the government of Israel and all Israelis to accept this initiative in order to safeguard the prospects for peace and stop the further shedding of blood, enabling the Arab Countries and Israel to live in peace and good neighborliness and provide future generations with security, stability, and prosperity.
6. Invites the international community and all countries and organizations to support this initiative.
7. Requests the chairman of the summit to form a special committee composed of some of its concerned member states and the secretary general of the League of Arab States to pursue the necessary contacts to gain support for this initiative at all levels, particularly from the United Nations, the security council, the United States of America, the Russian Federation, the Muslim States, and the European Union.

http://www.jordanembassyus.org/arab_initiative.htm.

A PERFORMANCE-BASED ROADMAP TO A PERMANENT TWO-STATE SOLUTION TO THE ISRAELI-PALESTINIAN CONFLICT (APRIL 30, 2003)

The following is a performance-based and goal-driven roadmap, with clear phases, timelines, target dates, and benchmarks aiming at progress through reciprocal steps by the two parties in the political, security, economic, humanitarian, and institution-building fields, under the auspices of the Quartet [the United States, European Union, United Nations, and Russia]. The destination is a final and comprehensive settlement of the Israel-Palestinian conflict by 2005, as presented in President Bush's speech of 24 June, and welcomed by the EU, Russia and the UN in the 16 July and 17 September Quartet Ministerial statements.

A two-state solution to the Israeli-Palestinian conflict will only be achieved through an end to violence and terrorism, when the Palestinian people have a leadership acting decisively against terror and willing and able to build a practicing democracy based on tolerance and liberty, and through Israel's readiness to do what is necessary for a democratic Palestinian state to be established, and a clear, unambiguous acceptance by both parties of the goal of a negotiated settlement as described below. The Quartet will assist and facilitate implementation of the plan, starting in Phase I, including direct discussions between the parties as required. The plan establishes a realistic timeline for implementation. However, as a performance-based plan, progress will require and depend upon the good faith efforts of the parties, and their compliance with each of the obligations outlined below. Should the parties perform their obligations rapidly, progress within and through the phases may come sooner than indicated in the plan. Non-compliance with obligations will impede progress.

A settlement, negotiated between the parties, will result in the emergence of an independent, democratic, and viable Palestinian state living side by side in peace and security with Israel and its other neighbors.

The settlement will resolve the Israel-Palestinian conflict, and end the occupation that began in 1967, based on the foundations of the Madrid Conference, the principle of land for peace, UNSCRs 242, 338 and 1397, agreements previously reached by the parties, and the initiative of Saudi Crown Prince Abdullah—endorsed by the Beirut Arab League Summit—calling for acceptance of Israel as a neighbor living in peace and security, in the context of a comprehensive settlement. This initiative is a vital element of international efforts to promote a comprehensive peace on all tracks, including the Syrian-Israeli and Lebanese-Israeli tracks.

The Quartet will meet regularly at senior levels to evaluate the parties' performance on implementation of the plan. In each phase, the parties are expected to perform their obligations in parallel, unless otherwise indicated.

PHASE I: ENDING TERROR AND VIOLENCE, NORMALIZING PALESTINIAN LIFE, AND BUILDING PALESTINIAN INSTITUTIONS—PRESENT TO MAY 2003

In Phase I, the Palestinians immediately undertake an unconditional cessation of violence according to the steps outlined below; such action should be accompanied by supportive measures undertaken by Israel. Palestinians and Israelis resume security cooperation based on the Tenet work plan to end violence, terrorism, and incitement through restructured and effective Palestinian security services.

Palestinians undertake comprehensive political reform in preparation for statehood, including drafting a Palestinian constitution, and free, fair and open elections upon the basis of those measures. Israel takes all necessary steps to help normalize Palestinian life. Israel withdraws from Palestinian areas occupied from September 28, 2000, and the two sides restore the status quo that existed at that time, as security performance and cooperation progress. Israel also freezes all settlement activity, consistent with the Mitchell report.

At the outset of Phase I:

- Palestinian leadership issues unequivocal statement reiterating Israel's right to exist in peace and security and calling for an immediate and unconditional ceasefire to end armed activity and all acts of violence against Israelis anywhere. All official Palestinian institutions end incitement against Israel.
- Israeli leadership issues unequivocal statement affirming its commitment to the two-state vision of an independent, viable, sovereign Palestinian state living in peace and security alongside Israel, as expressed by President Bush, and calling for an immediate end to violence against Palestinians everywhere. All official Israeli institutions end incitement against Palestinians.

Security

- Palestinians declare an unequivocal end to violence and terrorism and undertake visible efforts on the ground to arrest, disrupt, and restrain individuals and groups conducting and planning violent attacks on Israelis anywhere.
- Rebuilt and refocused Palestinian Authority security apparatus begins sustained, targeted, and effective operations aimed at confronting all those engaged in terror and dismantlement of terrorist capabilities and infrastructure. This includes commencing confiscation of illegal weapons and consolidation of security authority, free of association with terror and corruption.
- Rebuilt and refocused Palestinian Authority security apparatus begins sustained, targeted, and effective operations aimed at confronting all those engaged in terror and dismantlement of terrorist capabilities and infrastructure. This includes commencing confiscation of illegal

weapons and consolidation of security authority, free of association with terror and corruption.

- GOI [Government of Israel] takes no actions undermining trust, including deportations, attacks on civilians; confiscation and/or demolition of Palestinian homes and property, as a punitive measure or to facilitate Israeli construction; destruction of Palestinian institutions and infrastructure; and other measures specified in the Tenet work plan.

- Relying on existing mechanisms and on-the-ground resources, Quartet representatives begin informal monitoring and consult with the parties on establishment of a formal monitoring mechanism and its implementation.

- Implementation, as previously agreed, of U.S. rebuilding, training and resumed security cooperation plan in collaboration with outside oversight board (U.S.-Egypt-Jordan). Quartet support for efforts to achieve a lasting, comprehensive cease-fire.

  - All Palestinian security organizations are consolidated into three services reporting to an empowered Interior Minister.

  - Restructured/retrained Palestinian security forces and IDF [Israel Defense Forces] counterparts progressively resume security cooperation and other undertakings in implementation of the Tenet work plan, including regular senior-level meetings, with the participation of U.S. security officials.

- Arab states cut off public and private funding and all other forms of support for groups supporting and engaging in violence and terror.

- All donors providing budgetary support for the Palestinians channel these funds through the Palestinian Ministry of Finance's Single Treasury Account.

- As comprehensive security performance moves forward, IDF withdraws progressively from areas occupied since September 28, 2000 and the two sides restore the status quo that existed prior to September 28, 2000. Palestinian security forces redeploy to areas vacated by IDF.

Palestinian Institution-Building

- Immediate action on credible process to produce draft constitution for Palestinian statehood. As rapidly as possible, constitutional committee circulates draft Palestinian constitution, based on strong parliamentary democracy and cabinet with empowered prime minister, for public comment/debate. Constitutional committee proposes draft document for submission after elections for approval by appropriate Palestinian institutions.

- Appointment of interim prime minister or cabinet with empowered executive authority/decision-making body.

- GOI fully facilitates travel of Palestinian officials for PLC [Palestinian Legislative Council] and Cabinet sessions, internationally supervised security retraining, electoral and other reform activity, and other supportive measures related to the reform efforts.

- Continued appointment of Palestinian ministers empowered to undertake fundamental reform. Completion of further steps to achieve genuine separation of powers, including any necessary Palestinian legal reforms for this purpose.

- Establishment of independent Palestinian election commission. PLC reviews and revises election law.

- Palestinian performance on judicial, administrative, and economic benchmarks, as established by the International Task Force on Palestinian Reform.

- As early as possible, and based upon the above measures and in the context of open debate and transparent candidate selection/electoral campaign based on a free, multi-party process, Palestinians hold free, open, and fair elections.

- GOI facilitates Task Force election assistance, registration of voters, movement of candidates and voting officials. Support for NGOs involved in the election process.

- GOI reopens Palestinian Chamber of Commerce and other closed Palestinian institutions in East Jerusalem based on a commitment that these institutions operate strictly in accordance with prior agreements between the parties.

Humanitarian Response

- Israel takes measures to improve the humanitarian situation. Israel and Palestinians implement in full all recommendations of the Bertini report[1] to improve humanitarian conditions, lifting curfews and easing restrictions on movement of persons and goods, and allowing full, safe, and unfettered access of international and humanitarian personnel.
- AHLC [Ad Hoc Liaison Committee] reviews the humanitarian situation and prospects for economic development in the West Bank and Gaza and launches a major donor assistance effort, including to the reform effort.
- GOI and PA continue revenue clearance process and transfer of funds, including arrears, in accordance with agreed, transparent monitoring mechanism.

Civil Society

- Continued donor support, including increased funding through PVOs [private voluntary organizations]/NGOs [non-governmental organizations], for people to people programs, private sector development and civil society initiatives.

Settlements

- GOI immediately dismantles settlement outposts erected since March 2001.
- Consistent with the Mitchell Report, GOI freezes all settlement activity (including natural growth of settlements).

PHASE II: TRANSITION—JUNE 2003–DECEMBER 2003

In the second phase, efforts are focused on the option of creating an independent Palestinian state with provisional borders and attributes of sovereignty, based on the new constitution, as a way station to a permanent status settlement. As has been noted, this goal can be achieved when the Palestinian people have a leadership acting decisively against terror, willing and able to build a practicing democracy based on tolerance and liberty. With such a leadership, reformed civil institutions and security structures, the Palestinians will have the active support of the Quartet and the broader international community in establishing an independent, viable state.

Progress into Phase II will be based upon the consensus judgment of the Quartet of whether conditions are appropriate to proceed, taking into account performance of both parties. Furthering and sustaining efforts to normalize Palestinian lives and build Palestinian institutions, Phase II starts after Palestinian elections and ends with possible creation of an independent Palestinian state with provisional borders in 2003. Its primary goals are continued comprehensive security performance and effective security cooperation, continued normalization of Palestinian life and institution-building, further building on and sustaining of the goals outlined in Phase I, ratification of a democratic Palestinian constitution, formal establishment of office of prime minister, consolidation of political reform, and the creation of a Palestinian state with provisional borders.

- **International Conference:** Convened by the Quartet, in consultation with the parties, immediately after the successful conclusion of Palestinian elections, to support Palestinian economic recovery and launch a process, leading to establishment of an independent Palestinian state with provisional borders.
  - Such a meeting would be inclusive, based on the goal of a comprehensive Middle East peace (including between Israel and Syria, and Israel and Lebanon), and based on the principles described in the preamble to this document.
  - Arab states restore pre-intifada links to Israel (trade offices, etc.).
  - Revival of multilateral engagement on issues including regional water resources, environment, economic development, refugees, and arms control issues.
- New constitution for democratic, independent Palestinian state is finalized and approved by appropriate Palestinian institutions. Further elections, if required, should follow approval of the new constitution.

- Empowered reform cabinet with office of prime minister formally established, consistent with draft constitution.
- Continued comprehensive security performance, including effective security cooperation on the bases laid out in Phase I.
- Creation of an independent Palestinian state with provisional borders through a process of Israeli-Palestinian engagement, launched by the international conference. As part of this process, implementation of prior agreements, to enhance maximum territorial contiguity, including further action on settlements in conjunction with establishment of a Palestinian state with provisional borders.
- Enhanced international role in monitoring transition, with the active, sustained, and operational support of the Quartet.
- Quartet members promote international recognition of Palestinian state, including possible UN membership.

PHASE III: PERMANENT STATUS AGREEMENT AND END OF THE ISRAELI-PALESTINIAN CONFLICT—2004–2005

Progress into Phase III, based on consensus judgment of Quartet, and taking into account actions of both parties and Quartet monitoring. Phase III objectives are consolidation of reform and stabilization of Palestinian institutions, sustained, effective Palestinian security performance, and Israeli-Palestinian negotiations aimed at a permanent status agreement in 2005.

- **Second International Conference:** Convened by Quartet, in consultation with the parties, at beginning of 2004 to endorse agreement reached on an independent Palestinian state with provisional borders and formally to launch a process with the active, sustained, and operational support of the Quartet, leading to a final, permanent status resolution in 2005, including on borders, Jerusalem, refugees, settlements; and, to support progress toward a comprehensive Middle East settlement between Israel and Lebanon and Israel and Syria, to be achieved as soon as possible.
- Continued comprehensive, effective progress on the reform agenda laid out by the Task Force in preparation for final status agreement.

- Continued sustained and effective security performance, and sustained, effective security cooperation on the bases laid out in Phase I.
- International efforts to facilitate reform and stabilize Palestinian institutions and the Palestinian economy, in preparation for final status agreement.
- Parties reach final and comprehensive permanent status agreement that ends the Israel-Palestinian conflict in 2005, through a settlement negotiated between the parties based on UNSCR 242, 338, and 1397, that ends the occupation that began in 1967, and includes an agreed, just, fair, and realistic solution to the refugee issue, and a negotiated resolution on the status of Jerusalem that takes into account the political and religious concerns of both sides, and protects the religious interests of Jews, Christians, and Muslims worldwide, and fulfills the vision of two states, Israel and sovereign, independent, democratic and viable Palestine, living side-by-side in peace and security.
- Arab state acceptance of full normal relations with Israel and security for all the states of the region in the context of a comprehensive Arab-Israeli peace.

Source: Bureau of Public Affairs, U.S. Department of State. http://www.state.gov/r/pa/prs/ps/2003/20062.htm.

Accessed at: http://www.usip.org/files/file/resources/collections/peace_agreements/roadmap_04302003.pdf.

NOTE

1. Catherine Bertini, Personal Humanitarian Envoy of the UN Secretary-General, Mission Report, August 11-19, 2002, http://domino.un.org/bertini_rpt.htm.

ACKNOWLEDGMENTS

The editor and the contributors wish to thank a number of people who were instrumental in seeing this very fast-moving book project through to a successful conclusion, indeed, almost miraculously translating an idea in mid-July into a book in November. Farideh Koohi-Kamali, Sara Doskow, and Alan Bradshaw, as well as a host of other professionals at Palgrave Macmillan, such as copyeditor Georgia Maas, made this happen. Numerous colleagues at Princeton University's Woodrow Wilson School of Public and International Affairs played vital roles, especially Debbie Nexon, Elisabeth Donahue, Robert Lecke, and Ticiana Jardim Marini, whose creative design graces the cover of this volume. Tamar Ariel made a substantive contribution to this effort and did the yeoman work of organizing the index. We also want to thank Lili Zemon, Sandy Hatcher, Laura Huber, Joe Barnes, and John Williams. The generosity of S. Daniel Abraham and his foresight in providing program support to Princeton helped underwrite some of the costs of the book.

The editor, P. J. Dermer, and Steven White thank Lieutenant General Keith Dayton for his critical contribution to our understanding of security issues. Robert Malley thanks the International Crisis Group team in Israel-Palestine—Rob Blecher, Nathan Thrall, Ofer Zalzberg, Azmi Keshawi, and Suheir Freitekh. Gershom Gorenberg thanks Dr. Rafi Ventura and Chanan Cohen of the Guttman Center at the Israel Democracy Institute for providing historical polling data from the Center's rich database.

NOTES ON CONTRIBUTORS

Samih Al-Abid served as minister of public work and housing in the Palestinian Authority, as an adviser to the Palestinian Investment Fund, and as the general director of an independent development company aiming to strengthen the local economy and generate investment. He currently heads the Palestinian Housing Council. During final-status negotiations with Israel, he headed the committee on borders and territory and was a key participant in the negotiations in the Camp David, Taba, and Annapolis processes. Al-Abid earned a PhD in regional development planning and an MA in urban design.

Yossi Alpher is a consultant and writer on Israel-related strategic issues, and is coeditor of the bitterlemons.net family of Internet publications. Alpher served in the Israel Defense Forces as an intelligence officer, followed by service in the Mossad. From 1981 to 1995 he was associated with the Jaffee Center for Strategic Studies at Tel Aviv University, ultimately serving as its director. During the Camp David Summit, he served as special adviser to the prime minister of Israel, concentrating on the Israeli-Palestinian peace process.

James A. Baker III served in senior government positions under three US presidents. He was the nation's sixty-first secretary of state under President George H. W. Bush. He was the sixty-seventh secretary of the treasury under President Ronald Reagan, and he served as White House chief of staff to President Reagan during his first term. Mr. Baker's record of public service began in 1975 as undersecretary of commerce to President Gerald Ford. It concluded in January 1993 with his service as White House chief of staff and senior counselor to President Bush. Mr. Baker graduated from Princeton

University in 1952, and received his JD with honors from the University of Texas School of Law at Austin. Mr. Baker received the Presidential Medal of Freedom in 1991 and has been the recipient of numerous other awards and honorary academic degrees. He is presently a senior partner in the law firm of Baker Botts, and is honorary chairman of the James A. Baker III Institute for Public Policy at Rice University.

Samuel Berger served as national security adviser to President Bill Clinton from 1997 to 2001. In that capacity, he drove policy advancing the peace process in the Middle East. Mr. Berger also served as deputy national security adviser during President Clinton's first term; as director of national security for the 1992 Clinton-Gore transition; and as senior foreign policy adviser to Governor Clinton during the 1992 presidential campaign. He currently serves as chair of Albright Stonebridge Group, a global strategy firm.

Robert M. Danin is the Eni Enrico Mattei Senior Fellow for Middle East and Africa Studies at the Council on Foreign Relations. He headed the Jerusalem mission of the Quartet representative, Tony Blair, from April 2008 until August 2010. A former career State Department official with over twenty years of Middle East experience, Danin served as deputy assistant secretary of state for Near Eastern affairs and at the National Security Council as director for Israeli-Palestinian affairs and the Levant. He earlier served as a Middle East specialist on the secretary of state's Policy Planning Staff and as a senior State Department Middle East analyst. Danin earned a doctorate in the international relations of the Middle East from St. Antony's College, Oxford University.

P. J. Dermer (Colonel, retired) is one of the US Army's foremost Middle East regional experts. His career spanned over thirty years of experience, including military and civilian arenas in Washington and overseas. He has extensive coalition-building experience working with international counterparts to advance the Middle East peace process, as well as rebuilding Iraq's critical national security institutions. In his post-military career, he has used his skills to foster private business enterprise development, including development of several entrepreneurial start-up ventures. Countries and areas of expertise include Israel, Lebanon, Syria, Egypt, Iraq, North Africa, and the Persian Gulf.

Avi Gil served as the director-general of Israel's Ministry of Foreign Affairs from 2001 to 2002. He was closely involved in Israel's policy-making and peace efforts, including the negotiations that led to the Oslo Accords and the peace treaty with Jordan. Ambassador Gil is a senior fellow at the Jewish People Policy Institute and a senior strategic adviser at the S. Daniel Abraham Center for Middle East Peace.

Gershom Gorenberg is the author of *The Accidental Empire: Israel and the Birth of the Settlements, 1967-1977* and *The Unmaking of Israel*, which examines the impact of occupation and settlement on Israeli democracy and society. As a journalist he has covered Israeli politics for over twenty-five years. In 2010 he was a visiting professor at Columbia University. He lives in Jerusalem.

Samir Hileleh joined PADICO Holding as chief executive officer in 2008. Prior to that, he was the managing director of the Portland Trust in Palestine, served as the cabinet secretary general of the Palestinian government (2005–2006) and as the assistant undersecretary for the ministry of economy and trade (1994–1997). He is an active member in the Palestine Trade Center, the Palestine Economic Policy Research Institute (MAS), the International Chamber of Commerce in Palestine, and the Palestine International Business Forum. He is president of Birzeit University Alumni Association and a member of the board of trustees of the Friends Schools in Ramallah.

Ghassan Khatib is vice president for advancement and lecturer on cultural studies at Birzeit University, where he previously served as vice president for community outreach. He has served as director of the Palestinian Government Media Center and as minister of labor (2002) and minister of planning (2005–2006). He founded and directed the Jerusalem Media and Communication Center. He was a member of the Palestinian delegation to the Madrid Middle East Peace Conference and the bilateral negotiations in Washington. Khatib cofounded and codirected bitterlemons.org, a Palestinian-Israeli Internet-based political magazine. Khatib holds a PhD in Middle East politics from the University of Durham. He is the author of *Palestinian Politics and the Middle East Peace Process: Consensus and Competition in the Palestinian Negotiation Team*.

Daniel C. Kurtzer is the S. Daniel Abraham Professor of Middle East Policy Studies at Princeton University's Woodrow Wilson School of Public and International Affairs. During a twenty-nine-year career in the foreign service, he served as the United States ambassador to Egypt and to Israel. He is the coauthor of *Negotiating Arab-Israeli Peace: American Leadership in the Middle East* (United States Institute of Peace Press, 2008) and *The Peace Puzzle: America's Quest for Arab-Israeli Peace* (Cornell University Press, 2013). He received his PhD from Columbia University.

Robert Malley is director of the International Crisis Group's Middle East and North Africa program. In that capacity, he directs teams of analysts in Israel, Iraq, Syria, Egypt, Lebanon, Tunisia, Libya, Morocco, and the Gulf. Until January 2001, Mr. Malley was special assistant to President Clinton for Arab-Israeli affairs and director for Near East and South Asian affairs at the National Security Council. He served as a law clerk to Supreme Court Justice Byron R. White in 1991–1992. He is a graduate of Yale University, Harvard Law School, and Oxford University, where he was a Rhodes Scholar. He is the author of *The Call from Algeria: Third Worldism, Revolution and the Turn to Islam*.

Aaron David Miller is currently a distinguished scholar at the Woodrow Wilson International Center for Scholars in Washington, D.C., where he is finishing a new book—*Can America Have Another Great President?* For two decades, he served in the Department of State as an analyst, negotiator, and adviser on Middle Eastern issues to Republican and Democratic secretaries of state. He has written four books, including *The Much Too Promised Land: America's Elusive Search for Arab-Israeli Peace* (Bantam Books, 2008). His articles have appeared in the *Washington Post*, the *New York Times*, and the *Los Angeles Times*; his column "Reality Check" appears weekly in *Foreign Policy* magazine. He is a frequent commentator on CNN, Fox News, MSNBC, and NPR.

Marwan Muasher is vice president for studies at the Carnegie Endowment. He served as foreign minister (2002–2004) and deputy prime minister (2004–2005) of Jordan, and as Jordan's ambassador to the United States and to Israel. Between 2007 and 2010, he was senior vice president of external affairs at the

World Bank. He is the author of *The Arab Center: The Promise of Moderation* (Yale University Press, 2008).

William B. Quandt is the Edward R. Stettinius Professor of Politics at the University of Virginia. From 1972 to 1974 and from 1977 to 1979, he served on the staff of the National Security Council and participated in the peace talks that led to the Egyptian-Israeli peace treaty. He is the author of *Peace Process: American Diplomacy and the Arab-Israeli Conflict since 1967*, 3rd ed. (Brookings Institution Press, 2005).

Steven White is an independent Middle East consultant, currently writing the history of the United States Security Coordinator (USSC) Mission. As a Marine Corps Reserve Major, he served as the senior Middle East adviser to three US security coordinators and as the mission's liaison to the government of Israel, the UN, Office of the Quartet Representative, and the British diplomatic missions in Jerusalem and Tel Aviv. He was educated at the Military College of South Carolina, The Citadel, and was one of the first co-recipients of the Anna Sobol Levy Graduate Fellowships to the Hebrew University of Jerusalem (1990–1991).

INDEX